BEAUTIFUL LOSERS

BEAUTIFUL LOSERS

Essays on the Failure of American Conservatism

Samuel Francis

University of Missouri Press
Columbia

Library of Congress Cataloging-in-Publication Data

Francis, Samuel T.
    Beautiful losers : essays on the failure of American conservatism
  / Samuel Francis.
      p. cm.
    Includes index.
    ISBN 0-8262-0976-9 (pkb.)
    1. Conservatism—United States—History.   2. United States—
Politics and government—20th century.   I. Title.
JA84.U5F73 1993
320.5'2'0973—dc20   93-15848
                                                            CIP

♾ ™ This paper meets the requirements of the American National Standard
for Permanence of Paper for Printed Library Materials, Z39.48, 1984.

Designer: Rhonda Miller
Typesetter: Connell-Zeko Type & Graphics
Printer and Binder: Thomson-Shore, Inc.
Typeface: Garamond

To My Mother

Contents

Acknowledgments

"Foreign Policy and the South," in Fifteen Southerners, *Why the South Will Survive,* edited by Clyde Wilson (Athens: University of Georgia Press, 1981), 91–104.

"Henry Clay and the Statecraft of Circumstance," *Continuity* 15 (Fall-Winter 1991): 45–68.

"Message from MARs: The Social Politics of the New Right," in Robert W. Whitaker, ed., *The New Right Papers* (New York: St. Martin's Press, 1982), 64–83. Reprinted with permission, copyright © 1982 by St. Martin's Press.

"Prophet of the Heartland," *The World & I* 1, no. 2 (Feb. 1986): 662–69.

"The Harmless Persuasion," review of Irving Kristol, *Reflections of a Neoconservative: Looking Back, Looking Ahead, Modern Age* 29 (Winter 1985): 76–79.

"Neoconservatism and the Managerial Revolution," *The World & I* 1, no. 9 (Sept. 1986): 547–63.

"The Case of George Will," review of George Will, *Statecraft as Soulcraft: What Government Does, Modern Age* 30 (Spring 1986): 141–47.

"The Other Side of Modernism: James Burnham and His Legacy," *The World & I* 2, no. 10 (Oct. 1987): 675–82.

"The Evil That Men Don't Do: Joe McCarthy and the American Right," *Chronicles* 10 (Sept. 1986): 16–21.

"The Cult of Dr. King," *Chronicles* 12 (May 1988): 25–29.

"Who's In Charge Here?" *Chronicles* 12 (Mar. 1988): 12–15.

"Imperial Conservatives?" *National Review* (Aug. 4, 1989):37–38.

"Inhospitable Neos," *National Review* (Apr. 7, 1989):43–46.

"As We Go Marching," review of Gregory A. Fossedal, *The Democratic Imperative: Exporting the American Revolution,* in *Chronicles* 13 (Sept. 1989): 29–33.

"Rouge on a Corpse's Lips," review of Whittaker Chambers, *Ghosts on the Roof: Selected Journalism of Whittaker Chambers, 1931–1959,* ed. Terry Teachout, in *Chronicles* 14 (Apr. 1990): 27–30.

"The Secret of the Twentieth Century," review of Kevin Phillips, *The Politics of Rich and Poor: Wealth and the American Electorate in the Reagan Aftermath, Chronicles* 14 (Nov. 1990): 31–34.

"Equality as a Political Weapon," *Essays in Political Economy* (Auburn, Alabama: The Ludwig Von Mises Institute), No. 10 (July 1991), a lecture delivered at a Conference on Equality and the Free Society, sponsored by the Ludwig Von Mises Institute, in Princeton, N.J., April 13, 1991.

"Beautiful Losers: The Failure of American Conservatism," *Chronicles* 15 (May 1991): 14–17.

BEAUTIFUL LOSERS

Introduction
Ideas and No Consequences

Probably the most difficult part of compiling a collection of essays written over a period of some twelve years is not the actual composition of them so much as it is the effort to explain to the reader why you wrote certain things in the first place, what you meant by them, and why you think they should be preserved. Of course, the easy way out is to claim you didn't mean what you said at all, that you wrote it when you were too young to know any better, and that only a ruthless integrity compels you again to push it beneath the reader's weary eye. Unfortunately, that dog won't hunt for me, since I wrote the earliest of the pieces collected here when I was well into my third decade. Whatever foolish things I said or wrote by that age can find little defense now as the fruit of juvenile excess.

As far as concerns what I really meant then as opposed to what I would like to mean now, there is actually not much of a problem, since for the most part I continue to subscribe to the perspective from which most of these pieces were written, and I find that I have little to retract or explain. Perhaps this is proof that my juvenile excesses still prevail after all, that I simply never grew up. Nevertheless, some of the events, personalities, and books that served as the predicates of several of these essays have proved evanescent, and the passage of time, if not the maturation of the author, demands a certain amount of explanation and clarification.

The general theme of these articles and review essays is the transformation of American conservatism and, more generally, of American political culture in the 1980s, and even those that are historical in nature, such as the articles on Henry Clay and Joseph McCarthy, were intended in part as commentaries on subjects beyond their immediate topics. They do not offer an explicit exposition or definition of conservatism but rather seek to locate the relationship of the American Right to the social and political forces that prevailed in that decade and seem to be prevailing now. In the later essays in particular, I make use of James Burnham's theory of the managerial revolution in an adapted form to explain what I believe has been the result of the transformation of American conservatism, namely, its virtual extinction both as a serious body of social and political thought and as a serious vehicle of political expression.

The presuppositions of these pieces are perhaps somewhat different from those of most of the writing produced by conservative intellectuals since World War II. Those writers tended to approach political theory in a way that might be called formalistic and normative—that is, they sought to offer morally right and philosophically true prescriptions for public affairs—and they did so in terms of philosophy, theology, and ethics, with a good deal of attention to imaginative literature. Eric Voegelin, Leo Strauss, Richard Weaver, and most of their disciples are examples of this approach to conservative thought at the highest levels of academic theory; Ludwig von Mises and F. A. Hayek are similar examples in economic theory, and, among many others, *National Review*'s Frank S. Meyer was representative of it in conservative journalism.

My conclusion that conservatism has transformed itself into virtual extinction will surprise and perhaps even anger those who favor the formalistic and normative approach, which does not easily stoop to considerations of social change and historical fluctuation and is reluctant to admit that some things, even ideas, fail. Regarding political events as the earthly manifestations of timeless abstractions, the intellectual mainstream of the "Old Right" from the end of World War II developed a highly sophisticated body of ideas and a highly articulate body of spokesmen to express them. Perhaps because they were too uxoriously wedded to Weaver's principle that "Ideas Have Consequences," most of the conservative intellectuals who subscribed to this body of thought always seemed to assume that it was only a matter of time before their own beliefs would creep up on the ideas of the Left, slit their throats in the dark, and stage an intellectual and cultural coup d'état, after which truth would reign. I have never thought so, in part because I have less faith in the power of intellectual abstractions than most of my conservative colleagues. The historian Lewis Namier remarked that "new ideas are not nearly as potent as broken habits," and Burnham, describing Vilfredo Pareto's view of human rationality, wrote that "rational, deliberate, conscious belief does not, then, in general at any rate, determine what is going to happen to society; social man is not, as he has been defined for so many centuries, a primarily 'rational animal.'"[1] In the tradition of Namier (who briefly studied under Pareto) and Burnham, I place more emphasis on the concrete forces of elites, organization, and psychic and social forces such as class and regional and ethnic identity than on formal intellectual abstractions and their "logical" extrapolations as the determining forces of history. Ideas do have consequences, but some ideas have more consequences than others, and which consequences ensue from which ideas is settled not simply because the ideas serve human reason through their logical implications but also because some ideas serve human interests and emotions through their attachment to drives for political, economic, and social power, while other ideas do not.

However sophisticated and well expressed conservative intellectualism may have been in the years after World War II, its virtues did not assure it victory, mainly because there existed in American society and political culture no significant set of interests to which its ideas could attach themselves. Hence, post–World War II conservatism in its political efforts generally ignored the philosophical contributions of its highbrow exponents and fell back on the more mundane considerations of low taxes and small budgets, anticommunism and law and order; and the preoccupation of the Old Right mind in that era with an abstract and abstruse intellectualism helped ensure its eventual irrelevance. For the most part, any suggestion that the savants of the Right ought to have attended to the concrete social, regional, and ethnic dimensions of the human and American conditions rather than to their purely philosophical aspects was greeted with accusations of "determinism," though why it is less deterministic to say that ideas, rather than nonintellectual forces, are the major causal agents in human affairs has never been clear to me.

The truth is that, for all their talk about social "roots," conservative intellectuals in the postwar era were often rootless men themselves, and the philosophical mystifications in which they envel-

---

1. James Burnham, *The Machiavellians: Defenders of Freedom* (New York: John Day Company, 1943), 180.

oped themselves were frequently the only garments that fit them. Alienated from the prevailing intellectual and political currents as well as from traditional social forms that were ceasing to exist or cohere, the conservative intelligentsia was able to find explanations for and solutions to the civilizational crisis it perceived only in the most esoteric theory, and the "practical" applications of such theory often took the form of some species of romanticism or archaism— a pretentious medievalism, accompanied by antimodernist posturings and colored with a highly politicized religiosity; an attraction to archaic social and political forms such as the antebellum South, the *ancien régime* of eighteenth-century Europe, or the era of nineteenth-century laissez-faire; and a distaste for and often an ignorance of American history that derived from a mirror-image agreement with the Left-liberal understanding of America as an "experiment" dedicated to an egalitarian and progressivist proposition. If the intellectuals of the Right did not adhere to some form of archaism, they tended, like Whittaker Chambers, simply to withdraw from the world in despair and acknowledgment of defeat.

In contrast, the approach that I take in these essays seeks to avoid archaism and to identify what is and what is not politically and socially possible, given the predominant and largely irreversible vectors of history, for a serious movement of the Right on a political and cultural level. The archetype of this approach is James Burnham himself and the "neo-Machiavellian" school of political analysis that he developed and applied (mainly to foreign affairs in the latter part of his career), and the essay on Burnham included in this collection is an exposition of some of the philosophical underpinnings of that approach. One charge to which this approach is open is that it surrenders too much, that, just as Leo Strauss accused Machiavelli of "lowering the sights" of political man by concentrating on how human beings really behave at the expense of how they ought to behave, so an approach that concentrates on the socially and politically possible lowers the sights of the morally right and philosophically true artillery of conservatism away from the big game and takes potshots only at such harmless fauna as lie within range. The answer to the charge is the same for me as for Machiavelli: those who make the charge and favor the alternative formalistic and normative approach have yet to show that their preferred targets can be hit by aiming higher, and the results of their fusillades so far are not particularly encouraging.

The first essay presented here, "Foreign Policy and the South," in some ways represents an effort to move beyond the postwar Right's proclivity to abstraction and to suggest ways in which the concrete regional and cultural identity of the American South, rather than the abstract anticommunism of the Right or the equally abstract Wilsonian millenarianism of the Left, might contribute to American understanding of the nation's role in world affairs. The essay was written in 1979 as a contribution to Clyde Wilson's symposium, *Why the South Will Survive,* a fiftieth-anniversary sequel to the southern Agrarians' manifesto *I'll Take My Stand.* The most obvious flaw of the piece as it reads today is that most of the discussion of foreign policy is quite dated and even recondite. It is difficult to recall today— in the wake of the "second Cold War" under President Reagan, the subsequent collapse of the Soviet Union, the disintegration of communism in Eastern Europe, the Persian Gulf War of 1991, and the globalist euphoria of the 1990s—the malaise and near paralysis that afflicted American foreign policy in the late 1970s. The principal immediate cause of that malaise, which led to a number of international embarrassments for the United States, was the apathy about world affairs that followed the fall of Vietnam. As the essay argues, however, the more deeply seated reason for the malaise was less the loss of the war itself than the deflation of the ideological rationale for waging war there in the first place, and that rationale was the aforementioned millenarianism that dates from and had generally predominated in U.S. foreign policy since the time of Woodrow Wilson.

Today, however, despite the essay's allusions to ephemeral policy issues and agendas and its preoccupation with such problems as "appeasement" and "isolationism," other concerns raised in it appear still relevant. The defining idea of Wilsonian millenarianism is what the essay called "the belief that America was capable of teaching the world how to become like America, that the rest of the world did indeed aspire to be like America, and that the ultimate justification of American power was the practical fulfillment of this capacity—through American wealth, through American example, and, at the last, through American arms." Since the time when that passage was written, with President Bush's "New World Order," the almost universally approved agendas of "exporting democracy," even by military force, and adapting our national political and economic institutions to a "global economy" and a "borderless world," millenarianism has been resurrected. If, in their earlier incarnations, millenarian ideals took the American "City on a Hill" as the model to which the rest of the world was commanded to conform, today it is an even more elusive "global community" that is supposed to be the blueprint for the reconstruction of the whole planet, though there can be little doubt that the "American experiment" continues to glimmer as the prototype of the global cosmopolis in the mind's eye of many of its architects. In short, most of the calls for and prophecies of a "New World Order," a "global economy," or "global democracy" proceed from the same universalist and abstract premises of millenarianism that animated its older, Wilsonian and Cold War versions.

Like vaudeville, then, millenarianism in the late 1970s was not dead but only sleeping, and in the last decade, with the help of conservatives themselves, it has woken up and resumed its self-appointed role as the dominant ideological framework of American foreign policy. It was the Right of the 1980s that first seriously proposed official policy projects for exporting democracy and intoned the imperative of spreading the democratic gospel to the heathen, and President Reagan himself constantly made use of the Puritan millenarian "City on a Hill" image to describe his own vision of what America should be and do, not only in the world but also at home. The original rationale for conservative support for a Wilsonian foreign policy was that the anticommunist goals of the Right seemed to demand the assertion of some "positive" principle, and despite all the principles that conservative literati had enunciated and expounded for thirty years, the best the Reaganite Right could concoct was Wilsonianism. Well before Mr. Reagan had left office, however, the anticommunist origins of conservative democratism had been largely forgotten and in any case, with the collapse of Soviet communism, were soon irrelevant, and conservative apologists for global democracy such as Gregory Fossedal found Thomas Paine and H. G. Wells more useful for their dubious purposes than Voegelin and Weaver. Conservatives in the 1980s thus came to recapitulate the same millenarian premises that historically have been the property of the Left, and their adoption of millenarian metaphors, slogans, and actual policies is one of the major indications of the effective death of a serious conservatism in that period.

Since much of the democratism that the post-Reagan Right now affects is based on abstractions, its exponents show little inclination to count the practical results of spreading democracy or to weigh the virtues of democracy against its vices. In the review of Fossedal's *The Democratic Imperative,* written in the summer of 1989, I noted that "the genuine democratization of the Soviet Union and Eastern Europe . . . would almost certainly transform world power relationships and perhaps lead to the disintegration of the USSR and even to protracted warfare in Europe, Western Asia, and the Far East." I cannot claim that that prediction has literally been fulfilled, but it has come too close to fulfillment for comfort. The former totalitarian regimes of the Soviet Union and Eastern Europe have not perhaps become "genuine democracies," but certainly the iron grip they kept on the leashes of subnational, religious, racial, and ethnic conflicts has been sufficiently loosened so that the subject peoples have enjoyed an opportunity to leap at each others' throats. That development, of course, does not imply that the end of communist power in Eastern Europe was not worth the price but only that democracy does carry a price tag that needs to be considered before nondemocratic societies buy it or the United States sells it.

Today the only opposition to the globalism that both Right and Left preach is that of the "new nationalists" and so-called neoisolationists, mostly drawn from the remnants of the Old Right, who dissented from the war against Iraq and are generally skeptical of a continuing or expanded American global role in the absence of a clearly visible threat to American national security. This kind of "isolationism," however, is conceptually distinct from the sort that prevailed on the Left in the 1970s, when the prospects of millenarian meddling were dim and millenarian spirits were low. Indeed, the isolationism of the 1970s was no less millenarian than Wilsonian globalism in its assumption that the American City on the Hill might suffer a certain amount of urban decay if its government actually did anything in pursuit of the national interest or took concrete measures against American enemies. The isolationism of the Left in the 1970s couched itself in a typically millenarian and utopian refusal to deal with the world as it is, and it is hardly surprising that twenty years later its exponents easily persuaded themselves to promote a "global community" that exists only in their imaginations as what they would like the world to be.

The globalist millenarianism of the 1980s and 1990s has yet to meet its Vietnam, but sooner or later its utopian illusions will crack up on the same kind of reef. Yet the resurrection of millenarianism as the main conceptual framework for our foreign policy, with enthusiastic endorsement even from the Right, suggests that the remedy proposed in "Foreign Policy and the South"—namely, the salutary cultural traditions of the South itself—may not be so therapeutic after all. The embarrassing truth is that Woodrow Wilson, Lyndon Johnson, and Jimmy Carter were all southerners, and their performance in foreign policy is among the least happy of their legacies and achievements. The South, as it historically flourished, could indeed have provided a brake on the runaway train of millenarian foreign policy, but in this century the region has generated national political leadership that has only accelerated it, and with the homogenization of the South that economic, political, and cultural centralization promises, the section seems unlikely to provide any significant alternative or opposition to the revival of millenarianism in either domestic or foreign forms in the future.

If the insinuations of optimism in "Foreign Policy and the South" were not well founded, neither were they entirely justified in the essay "Message from MARs: The Social Politics of the New Right," written early in 1981 for Robert W. Whitaker's *The New Right Papers,* an interesting collection of then-young Rightists that attracted a fair amount of hostile attention from liberal reviewers but was largely ignored by the Right itself. The New Right movement as it existed in 1981 had some claim to optimism, however, with the landslide election of Reagan and the Republican seizure of the U.S. Senate for the first time since the 1950s. The New Right materially assisted both Reagan's election and the victories of several of the Republicans in the Senate that year, but in the event neither the president and the senators nor the movement itself was able to fulfill the promise of a genuinely radical effort to redirect the political and cultural currents of the nation. As the essay indicates, the New Right movement represented a hope that a new political identity was emerging that would be composed of something besides academics, journalists, and professional youth leaders, an identity that could actually speak to and for the Middle American core of American society. Within a couple of years, however, the New Right as it existed in 1981 had virtually disappeared, and by the later part of the decade, the phrase "New Right" itself had become obsolete.

Nevertheless, the argument of the essay that the New Right was more than simply a political movement and constituted the political expression of an underlying social and cultural force that sociologist Donald I. Warren had called "Middle American Radicals" (MARs) remains, I think, valid. Not only was it valid in 1981, but it continues to be valid today as well, and the continuing importance of Middle American discontent in American politics became evident in the Right-leaning candidacies of David Duke, Patrick J. Buchanan, and Ross Perot in 1992 and in the nomination by the Democrats that year of a ticket that explicitly appealed to Middle American interests and values and invoked antiestablishment and anti-incumbent themes.

The essential reason for the failure of the New Right, I believe, was that its leadership quickly moved to divorce it from genuinely popular discontents voiced by groups that did represent significant social interests and concentrated instead on formal political, policy-making, and electoral conflicts with which most of its Middle American constituency had no concerns. By doing so, the New Right was sucked into a process of bargaining and power-mongering with Washington-based elites and eventually was absorbed by them without significantly influencing them. The movement thus became isolated from its popular base and found itself easily distracted and deflected by the largely trivial concessions it gained in the bargaining process. Moreover, while Old Right conservatives were often preoccupied with an abstract and rootless intellectualism, the New Right was openly contemptuous of any kind of intellectualism, with the result that it arrived in Washington with only a vague notion of what it wanted to do and how to do it and thus was all the more easily swallowed up by the political establishment it confronted. The assimilation and emasculation of the New Right by the incumbent political elites in the early 1980s meant that the popular social and political movement that it had led was effectively decapitated. The decapitation perhaps destroyed the movement, but the emerging Middle American social force on which the movement rested continued to exist in a dormant stage until the early part of this decade, and its revival as a new Middle American Radical movement in the 1990s is likely to be the major political development of the next ten years.

While "Message from MARs" can claim to have foreseen the emergence of a Middle American Radical movement, some of the tactics the essay endorsed or recommended for the movement may not have been appropriate. The essay's endorsement of a "new nationalism" is perhaps even more relevant today than in 1981, but since most of the external forces then perceived as hostile to U.S. national interests and security have now vanished, it is likely that a new Middle American nationalism in foreign policy today would emphasize less expansionism and activism abroad and more opposition to a globalist foreign policy that jeopardizes Middle American economic and cultural interests. Economic nationalism and the struggle to preserve national sovereignty and cultural identity are likely to be more important issues for Middle American nationalists than fighting communists, anti-American plug-uglies from the Third World, and international terrorists.

The essay also explicitly envisions a far more powerful presidency as the "spearhead" of an emerging Middle American counterelite than Old Right conservatives generally supported. In the course of the Reagan-Bush presidencies, however, the American Right, in part due to the influence of neoconservative theorists and in part for partisan political reasons, effectively abandoned its earlier, Taftian skepticism about an "imperial presidency" and championed virtual supremacy for the executive branch over Congress in foreign policy. In two subsequent articles, "Who's In Charge Here?" and "Imperial Conservatives?" I questioned both the constitutional and political theory behind neoconservative support for executive supremacy as well as the practical value for the Right of the new "presidentialist" position. In some respects, those later articles represent a retreat from or a contradiction of my earlier support for a powerful presidency in "Message from MARs." What reconciles them, however, is that while my earlier support for a strong executive was predicated on the assumption that the presidency would represent MAR interests, would work aggressively on behalf of such interests, and, using a "Caesarist" tactic, would challenge the entrenched elite that predominated in the intermediary institutions, my later criticism of the apologists for an imperial presidency was based on the view that these apologists entertained no such purposes. Whereas my main reason for supporting executive power in 1981 was to challenge and resist the dominance of incumbent elites, their main reason for supporting executive supremacy was simply to protect the national security apparatus of the Cold War state from congressional intervention and thereby to preserve intact the machinery of managerial globalism. The pretensions of the Reagan-Bush administrations to executive supremacy were not authentic but counterfeit Middle American posturing. An authentic Middle American Radical view of the presidency would be supportive of a strong executive if the executive served MAR interests, but it would oppose an "imperial" presidency" if the executive merely continues, as it did under Reagan and Bush, to express the interests of the incumbent managerial and bureaucratic elites in the executive branch.

"Message from MARs" offered a critique of the Old Right and urged that a New Right pursue a radically different direction from the one its predecessors had followed since World War II. Old Right conservatism, especially in its classical liberal and libertarian forms, was essentially the political formula or ideology of the American bourgeois elite and reflected bourgeois values and interests—small government, local autonomy and states' rights, an isolationist or national interest–based foreign policy, and a social ethic that emphasized individualism restrained and informed by bourgeois social and cultural norms drawn from the Protestant ethic. The limited political success of the Old Right in the aftermath of the Great Depression, the New Deal, and World War II was due largely to its inability to attach itself to any significant social and political force after the managerial elite described by Burnham had displaced the bourgeois elite as the dominant force in American society. The new managerial elite, lodged in the large corporations and unions, the national bureaucratic state, and the bureaucratized educational, media, and

cultural organizations, possessed radically different and antibourgeois interests and found in liberalism a useful formula for their
expression and rationalization.

In the late 1960s and 1970s, however, it became evident that liberalism was not adequately performing its social and political function of supporting managerial interests, and the appearance of neoconservatism as an ideological category distinct from both the Old
and New Rights in that period can be seen as an attempt to adapt
and reformulate liberalism for a more effective support of managerial institutions and hegemony. That view of neoconservatism is
implicit in my review of Irving Kristol's *Reflections of a Neoconservative,* which is perhaps one of the earliest installments in what
became a protracted and bitter controversy within the Right in the
late 1980s. While Kristol and the neoconservatives in general exhibit the virtue of avoiding the hyperintellectualism of the Old Right,
they also exhibit the vice of failing to mount a serious and radical
critique of modern liberalism, and, in fact, they are largely exponents of a variation of liberalism. Thus, Kristol is well aware of the
cultural crisis produced by the managerial revolution (which he calls
the "corporate revolution") but his corrective for the crisis is mainly
to urge the revival and importation of bourgeois morality into managerial policies and institutions—not, as the Old Right advocated,
to dismantle the managerial power structure in the state. The attraction Kristol expressed for bourgeois morality seemed to rest largely
on his perception that it renounces the "heroic" and "transcendent"
and settles for the practical virtues of the Protestant ethic. What he
failed to see is that precisely because bourgeois morality is content
with the homely virtues and avoids heroic and transcendent ideals,
it is incapable of creating or resolving cultural crises that demand
heroism and the transcendence of self-interest. It was the virtue of
at least some thinkers of the Old Right that they did understand that
flaw of bourgeois society, but for the most part the Old Right critique of bourgeois society and morality failed to appeal either to the
remnant of the bourgeois elite itself, which preferred to rehearse its
political formula of classical liberalism, or to any other social force,
and Old Right intellectualism therefore remained an elegant but isolated and politically irrelevant body of ideas.

Yet, as I also suggested in the Kristol review, the quarrel between the Old Right and neoconservatives arose not so much from intellectual and philosophical conflicts as from social, ethnic, political, and professional differences between them, and the philosophical differences were, in fact, expressions of these social divisions. This was a view that I developed further in the long article on "Neoconservatism and the Managerial Revolution," also reprinted below. Neoconservatives undertook the defense of the very structures that the Old Right had sought to dismantle and in fact resisted every effort to develop a radical New Right populism that could construct a mass political and cultural base for a challenge to the managerial apparatus. The understanding of neoconservatism as a new version of managerial ideology has been borne out by later developments since the essay was written in 1986. Thus, what Fred Barnes of the *New Republic* has approvingly called "Big Government conservatism" is essentially identical to neoconservatism, and neoconservative opposition to Old Right and bourgeois "Small Government conservatism" has become evident in recent years in neoconservative resistance to attempts to abolish the National Endowment for the Arts; neoconservative support for expanded federal roles in education, health care, housing, and welfare policies; and neoconservative endorsement of a democratic globalist foreign policy. All these policy preferences reflect the function neoconservatism performs in adapting managerial liberalism to serve as the ideological defense for and a legitimizing formula of the political and cultural apparatus of the managerial elite. Similarly, neoconservative support of an "imperial presidency," coupled with support for congressional term limits and hostility to Congress, should be seen not merely as positions reflecting the partisan interests of a Republican presidency against a Democratic-controlled Congress but also as perfectly consistent with and reflective of the interests of the managerial elite in the bureaucracy of the executive branch.

The conflict between the Old Right or "paleoconservatives" (as they clumsily began to call themselves) and the neoconservatives became increasingly bitter in the course of the decade, and philosophical differences had less to do with the anger displayed in the controversy than with harsh personal attacks on the integrity and bona fides of the contestants. One of the first battles between the two sides was a struggle in 1981 over the nomination to the chairmanship of the National Endowment for the Humanities under President Reagan, the paleoconservative candidate being the late M. E. Bradford of the University of Dallas and the neoconservative being William Bennett. The bitterness felt by many Old Rightists at Bennett's finally winning the nomination was due not so much to losing the post for their own candidate as to what they regarded (accurately, in my view) as a neoconservative smear campaign against Bradford that insinuated he was, among other things, a Nazi sympathizer rather than an unreconstructed southern conservative who publicly and repeatedly had criticized Abraham Lincoln. Unwilling to contend against his expressed views in public, some neoconservative supporters of Bennett (though not Bennett himself) launched a sub-rosa attack on Bradford's character, even as they professed admiration for him in public. Similar neoconservative attacks on conservative columnists Joseph Sobran in 1986 and Patrick Buchanan in 1990 and on the Rockford Institute's unapologetically Old Right magazine *Chronicles* in 1989 also fed the anger of the Old Right at their supposed political allies. On top of these feuds, many Old Right organizations complained privately that neoconservative-controlled foundations were deliberately starving them of funds while lavishly endowing neoconservative figures and groups. Clearly, there was more to the disagreements between the two factions of the Right than mere ideas.

It was in the context of this controversy that I wrote a response to Ernest Van den Haag's defense of neoconservatism in *National Review*. Van den Haag, who had been a noted conservative writer since the 1950s, was perhaps an unlikely ally of the neoconservatives, who began to claim a conservative label only in the late 1960s or 1970s. The exchange, which was properly confined to the intellectual and political differences between the two groups, of course resolved nothing, and the whole conflict soon escalated to even more vitriolic rock-tossing and mud-slinging than before. On the whole, the Old Right generally had the brains, but the neocons had the money, and by the end of the Reagan Administration they had become the dominant faction on the American Right, with the Old Right effectively withdrawing into a newly formed group called the John Randolph Club and rallying around the presidential candidacy of Buchanan. These results did little to disabuse me of my skepticism toward the influence of ideas on political and social reality.[2]

While the mainstream of Old Right thought continued to dwell on philosophical esoterica, the three Old Right conservatives considered in these essays—Burnham, Willmoore Kendall, and Whittaker Chambers—actually departed from the mainstream in formulating ideas by which a popularly based Right could mount effective challenges to managerialism and its liberal formulas. The thrust of Kendall's thought was toward what today would be called a populist strategy, and Burnham, though he seems in the 1950s to have advocated cooperation with what he regarded as the historically irreversible managerial revolution, followed a similar path from the late 1960s and 1970s. Chambers never showed any sympathy for the new managerial regime and recognized in it a domesticated form of communism that was less violent, but no less revolutionary, than its Soviet cousin. Unlike Burnham and Kendall, however, Chambers's response to the revolution was one of intensely personal religious withdrawal. Yet throughout Chambers's work, from his earliest essays and short stories, written in his communist period, through his last letters and articles, he dwelled on the material and psychic suffering of the common man, what he called in *Witness* "the plain men and women of the nation." Despite their differences, these three Old Rightists are perhaps the only major theorists of the first generation of the Old Right who made any significant contribution to the development of a body of ideas and a practical strategy that could bring the Right out of its philosophical clouds and political archaism and point toward a realistic and popularly based challenge to managerial power.

Just as much of the discussion of American foreign policy in "Foreign Policy and the South" is now dated, so the anticommunism that frames the piece on Joe McCarthy is now mostly irrelevant. Nevertheless, I have included the essay in part because it offers a necessary corrective to a good many misconceptions about what McCarthy said, tried to do, and actually did and, more importantly, because it

2. Lest there be any question as to where the author's sympathies lie in the Old Right-neoconservative conflict, it should be noted that he is a contributing editor of *Chronicles* and a charter member of the John Randolph Club.

views McCarthy as the first significant political figure of the post–World War II Right who actually sought to build a mass antiestablishment movement as opposed to an elite cadre of intellectuals. The main argument of the essay is that McCarthy's "anticommunism" derived from his early but distorted perception of the revolutionary and essentially anti-American proclivities of the managerial elite. Lacking a more accurate conceptual framework for his instinctual understanding of the elite and its apparatus of power, McCarthy relied on the charge of "communism" as a label by which to challenge the legitimacy of the elite. Hence, his constant invocation of populist and antiestablishment imagery in his rhetoric, and hence his actual success in mobilizing for a time a mass movement that perceived the revolutionary imperatives that lay at the heart of the American power structure in the postwar era. McCarthy's appeal to small businessmen, union members, and northern ethnics thus foreshadows the more explicit antimanagerial and antiestablishment appeals later expressed by George Wallace, the New Right, and the Middle American revolt of 1992, and the continuing strength of this populism of the Right suggests that its national political role is far from over.

But even if it has a future, the Right will not be riding in a conservative vehicle, at least not one that would be recognizable to most of those who have regarded themselves as conservatives since World War II. That vehicle has pretty much ended up on the junk heap of history, and in retrospect it is hard to see where else it could have landed. The meaning of the world-historical change that Burnham called the managerial revolution is that what the Old Right, in any of its philosophical or political forms, represented and championed is defunct. The Old Right demanded a smaller scale of government, both in terms of the money the state took from its citizens and in terms of the size and scope of the state, but the Reagan-Bush era presided over and in several ways contributed to what was the largest expansion of the federal government since the Great Society. The Old Right sought a foreign policy that would defeat or destroy communism and reflect the interests of the United States as a sovereign and independent nation-state, but, while Soviet communism is even more defunct than the Old Right, the latter can hardly claim to have administered the death blow. In place of a national interest–based foreign policy, what both major parties now endorse is a universalist and millenarian globalism that acknowledges the role of the United Nations as an international arbiter and prepares the nation and the world for evolution into the transnational order of a borderless and bureaucratically managed "global economy." The Old Right sought to conserve a culture that respected social tradition as well as individual and social differentiation, but the 1980s saw the triumphal emergence of "multiculturalism," the cult of "political correctness" (foreshadowed and legitimized, as I argue in "The Cult of Dr. King" reprinted here, by the national holiday established in King's honor), and the aggressive delegitimization of ancient moral, sexual, and social norms. The defeat of the Old Right and its causes would not perhaps be so dispiriting were it not that the Right of the 1980s itself often supported, declined to oppose, or agreed to compromise with these forces of revolution.

If the Old Right stood for anything, it stood for the conservation of the "Old Republic" that flourished in the United States between the American War for Independence and the Great Depression and the civilizational antecedents of the American republic in the history and thought of Europe, and it is precisely that political construct that the managerial revolution overthrew and rendered all but impossible to restore. The Old Republic cannot be restored today because few Americans even remember it, let alone want it back, and even a realistic description of it would frighten and alienate most citizens. The essence of a republic, articulated by almost every theorist of republicanism from Cicero to Montesquieu, is the independence of the citizens who compose it and their commitment to a sustained active participation in its public affairs, the *res publica*. The very nature of the managerial revolution and the regime that developed from it promotes not independence, but dependency and not civic participation, but civic passivity. Today, almost the whole of American society encourages dependency and passivity— in the economy, through the continuing absorption of independent farms and businesses by multinational corporations, through ever more minute regulation by the state and through the dragooning of mass work forces in office and factory and mass consumption through advertising and public relations; in the culture, through the regimented and centralized manufacture and manipulation of thought, taste, opinion, and emotion itself by the mass media and educational organizations; and in the state, through its management of more and more dimensions of private and social existence under the color of "therapy" that does not cure, "voluntary service" that is really mandatory, and periodic "wars," against poverty, illiteracy, drugs, or other fashionable monsters, that no one ever wins. The result is an economy that does not work, a democracy that does not vote, families without fathers, classes without property, a government that passes more and more laws, a people that is more and more lawless, and a culture that neither thinks nor feels except when and what it is told or tricked to think and feel.

To be sure, there are many Americans who resent and fear these trends, and sometimes they flex enough political muscle to gain a few more tax breaks, a handful of increased federal entitlements, or a tenuous and temporary relief from strangulation by the managerial octopus. Their discontents and fears, if properly mobilized, may revive an American Right and may eventually succeed in achieving some of its projects. But almost no one wants a republic or even knows what a republic is, and there can be no possibility of a republic in the United States again until Americans are willing to assume the burdens of civic responsibility and independence that republican life demands. The American Right—Old or New, Paleo or Neo— failed to persuade Americans to take up those burdens, as their ancestors took them up in Williamsburg and Boston, at Fort Sumter and Gettysburg, and those who identified with its cause are only a few of the Americans who will eventually pay the price of that failure. No matter how beautiful its ideas and theories, no matter how compelling a chart of the currents of history's river it drew, American conservatism was not enough to channel those currents into other courses. It is as a chronicle and an explanation of these beautiful losers in our history that these essays may serve.

Foreign Policy and the South

Nearly all observers agree that American foreign policy is undergoing a crisis, a period of indecision and lack of direction in the formulation and execution of our relations with the world. The consensus on the aimlessness of American international relations appears to be universal. From both the Right and the Left we are given advice on how to deal with other nations. It is America's business, say conservatives, to resist Soviet expansion and "adventurism"—in Africa, the Middle East, Central and Southeast Asia, and Latin America—and, we are warned, our withdrawal from the world will only create a power vacuum into which Moscow and its surrogates will quickly move. From the Left comes the admonition that America has been involved too much and in the wrong way with the world; that our investments, military bases, foreign aid programs, and diplomatic functions have been covert forms of conquest and exploitation as well as causes in themselves of economic, political, and cultural destruction. Only a drastic re-design of our international policy (and of our internal arrangements)—we are told—can realize a more just and peaceful world order.

Yet, regardless of this advice, the drift continues, and the world observes, with a mixture perhaps of anxiety and a certain amount of discreet satisfaction, the lack of coherence and leadership from the wealthiest and most powerful state in history, the avenger of tyrants, the champion of the oppressed. Perhaps as remarkable as the incoherence of American foreign policy is the lack of concern of our own citizens. Public discussion of the central problems of foreign affairs—SALT II, the instability of U.S. allies, the meaning and observance of human rights, the Mideast conflict, African and Latin American policy, the North-South dialogue—produces little reaction in a populace understandably obsessed with exorbitant taxation, uncontrollable inflation, and the uncertain availability of routine resources. America's proper role in the world has been a topic of intense debate for at least twelve years, but the discussion has taken place in learned journals, on editorial pages, within academic

19

or professional conferences, and in other largely unread or unattended locations. Probably never before in our history has America stood at so important a crossroads in foreign policy as it does at the present time; probably never before has there been such fundamental and far-reaching debate on what we should do in the world; and rarely, if ever, has there been such apathy about what we will do.

It is not impossible that the demonstrable indifference of most Americans to the issues of foreign policy is related to the current crisis in our foreign relations. Any society governed by deliberative institutions must conduct its foreign affairs with the support and interest of its members, and if the body of citizens is indifferent to the world, there is little reason for the agencies responsible for foreign policy to follow a coherent course. American society—at the present time as well as historically—has been reluctant to come to grips with the world as it is, or at least with the world as most human beings outside America have perceived it. Our apathy and drift today are the result of that most peculiar institution, American democratic orthodoxy. Alexis de Tocqueville noted and predicted the roots of our unsuitability for high designs in the world:

> Foreign politics demand scarcely any of those qualities which are peculiar to a democracy . . . a democracy can only with great difficulty regulate the details of an important undertaking, persevere in a fixed design, and work out its execution in spite of serious obstacles. It cannot combine its measures with secrecy or await their consequences with patience. These are qualities which more especially belong to an individual or an aristocracy; and they are precisely the qualities by which a nation, like an individual, attains a dominant position.[1]

Most students of American foreign policy would probably agree that the immediate cause of our present discontents was the experience of Vietnam, and it is to the Vietnam War that Tocqueville's insights are most applicable. The United States in Vietnam did indeed experience considerable difficulty in "persevering in a fixed design," and our inability to use secrecy effectively became notorious. A large portion of our journalism on foreign affairs, even at its best, has dealt with cover-ups and conspiracies rather than with the

---

1. Alexis de Tocqueville, *Democracy in America,* ed. Phillips Bradley, 2 vols. (New York: Alfred A. Knopf, 1945), 1:243–44.

substance of our policies. Nor were we able to await the consequences of those policies with patience. Perhaps the ultimate and most universal source of aversion to the Vietnam War was the apparent interminability of the conflict—an objection strange to Europeans, who have named their wars for the number of years they lasted, and stranger still to Asians, who have given up measuring war's duration. The discovery by millions of young soldiers that armed conflict is not as brief, clean, easy, or fun as a John Wayne film elicited more shock than one would have anticipated in high school- and college-educated men of eighteen to twenty-six years of age.

There appears to be, in other words, a naïveté or childlike innocence endemic to the American character, a habitual expectation of quick solutions and happy endings, a mentality that is alien to the Old World and its derivative cultures. The belief in the natural innocence of America is a necessary prop for, the logical foundation of, modern democracy, which is unimaginable in a society that takes seriously the idea of original sin or its analogues in ancient and recent thought. The philosophical basis of contemporary American democracy is the Pelagian heresy of the natural goodness of man, and man is most obviously good where democracy has been the most "developed." In the United States, according to this formula, man started anew and brought forth a new order of the ages to which the hagridden evils of the Old World were alien. When Americans have thought about the Old World, East or West, it has been with a mixed feeling of contempt for its unredeemed and solicitude for its continued burdens. In foreign policy, the Pelagian orthodoxy of American democracy received its most nearly complete formulation in the policies of Woodrow Wilson and his millenarian vision of the Old World redesigned in accordance with American legends, prepossessions, and illusions. Yet the "fixed design" of the Wilsonian adventure dissolved when Americans discovered that the Old World did not share the axioms of the design; that its implications had certain unforeseen and undesirable consequences; and that the whole proceeding required more blood, sweat, and tears than it was worth—when, that is, the unpalatable realities of the world as it is stung the callow taste buds of American innocence.

The indecisiveness of American foreign policy, the apathy of our citizens toward the world, and the decay of American power and of foreign respect for America itself are, of course, complicated and have many causes—not the least of which are the rise of rival economies in Europe and Asia since the end of World War II, the withdrawal of the European empires in the 1960s, the development of nationalist and racialist ideologies in the new nations, and the growth of the countervailing power of the Soviet Union. But the international decadence of the United States would not have occurred in the precipitous and often humiliating way that it has without the psychic experience of the Vietnam War and the implosion of the premises of American foreign policy to which that experience led. The psychic consequences of Vietnam, it should be clear, were far more devastating to the United States than the material ones. As cynics have pointed out, the number of American lives lost in Indochina throughout the whole of the war was nearly identical to the number lost on highways each year, and the total financial cost was comparable to the annual budget of some departments of the federal government. It is through the intellectual and moral history of America that Vietnam will enter our folklore; unlike every other war in our history, it has many martyrs and few heroes.

What Americans experienced in Vietnam was not military defeat, but something more serious: the inability to accomplish a set purpose. Prior to the 1970s the premise on which American foreign policy had been conducted since at least the time of Woodrow Wilson was the belief that America was capable of teaching the world how to become like America, that the rest of the world did indeed aspire to be like America, and that the ultimate justification of American power was the practical fulfillment of this capacity—through American wealth, through American example, and, at the last, through American arms. It was in terms of this belief in the historic destiny of American power that President Wilson expressed his ambition to make the world safe for democracy. To a large extent, this belief also animated the benevolent internationalism of the 1950s and the Peace Corps of the 1960s. The Marshall Plan, the Alliance for Progress, and other U.S.–sponsored programs for the modernization (i.e., the Americanization) of undeveloped nations revealed the same underlying assumption. Were not these lands inhabited by "huddled masses yearning to breathe free," and did not freedom consist in either their actual passage to America or, if this were not possible, in the passage of America to the huddled masses in the form of American money, American products, and American troops?

Historically, this belief in the unique capacities and peculiar destiny of America had its origins in the Puritan Yankee establishment of the Northeast, and it is no accident that this same establishment has preserved its most entrenched position in the Department of State. In no other branch of government has it been as dominant, and in no other aspect of policy formation has it been as influential as in foreign affairs. Intellectually, the august credo of American destiny had its origins in the millenarianism of the early Puritans. The secularization of Puritanism led to the setting of what seemed to be more practicable goals than that of a literal rule of the saints. The perfection of man would come about through his conforming to the model established by the perfected elite in American society.

The millenarianism of American diplomacy has not been impractical in its implementation, however. Like the northeastern merchants who sponsored these ideals, more recent exponents have possessed both a hard head for business and a shrewd eye for the realities of power. In the twentieth century, the millenarian authors of our foreign policy have four times persuaded a reluctant and indifferent populace that it should go to war, not for its own interests, but for the interests of Europe, Korea, and Vietnam. The lofty rhetoric of internationalism, world peace, and human rights has been matched in almost every instance by ruthless bargaining for economic, political, and military power. But the pragmatic success of millenarian idealism need not surprise us. It was the very archetype of Puritan millenarianism, Oliver Cromwell, who successfully combined sanctimonious idealism and brutal realpolitik. If millenarianism in politics were to adopt a motto, it could not do better than Cromwell's adage, "Trust in God and keep your powder dry," and Bible-quoting slave traders are not so far removed from modern diplomats who cast tearful eyes on the violations of human rights by our corrupt allies and at the same time measure carefully our trade investments in the Soviet Union and mainland China.

Yet, ultimately, this double face of millenarianism caves in. To construct the City on the Hill, it is necessary to bulldoze the less stately mansions of the earthly realm. In time, with most men, the paradoxical dialectic of millenarianism weighs too heavily. The conscience cannot bear, and the mind cannot reconcile, the brutal (or at least mundane) means by which the final vision is to be realized. So it was with the sensitive consciences and acute, finely educated minds of the American intelligentsia of the 1960s and 1970s. The apparent embarrassment of the Tet offensive, the haunting brutality of My Lai, the toppling of the millenarian heroes of the Kennedy administration by the release of the Pentagon Papers; and the continuous, heckling, unanswerable questions about Vietnam from equally millenarian dissenters all led to the discrediting of the premise on which U.S. globalism had proceeded. Had the Vietnam War been presented to the American populace on its proper grounds—as a strategically necessary conflict against the aggressive forces of North Vietnam and its allies—millenarian ideals would not have been involved. Yet, aside from the question of whether a democracy that wraps itself in millenarian imagery can effectively prosecute a protracted war along cold-blooded geopolitical lines, to have invoked strategic arguments would immediately have led to the questioning of our own strategy of a limited war. If the war were really a struggle against aggression, then why not put a permanent end to the aggressors' ability to make war? Avoiding this unthinkable implication, the authors of our Vietnam policy insisted on defending their course on the grounds that the war was a struggle for democracy, for progress in the Third World, and for the millenarian vision. They could not, of course, sustain this argument, given the realities of our allies and the necessities of counterinsurgency tactics. The only possible defense was that the millenarian omelette required the breaking of several sublunary eggs, and this response immediately exposed the unreality of the final goal.

The result of the Vietnam War in the psychological history of America was the complete discrediting of the millenarian premises of U.S. foreign policy, and with their discrediting there also collapsed any justification for American globalism. Dr. Kissinger, who is possessed of few millenarian illusions, sought to construct an alternate foundation in the balance-of-power realpolitik of his nineteenth-century heroes. But this model was not adequate, as Kissinger himself came to see. It did not reflect the realities of power of the late twentieth century, and, perhaps even more important, it demanded too much of Americans, who disliked its apparent cynicism and the slowness with which it achieved concrete results. In the end, even Kissinger had to admit that Americans were not suited to the pragmatic manipulation of power and privately advised that we reconcile ourselves to a more modest role in world affairs.

The Carter administration also sought to avoid the millenarian illusion of omnipotence, but in its place it developed an ideology of incapacitation. In its view, power, so far from being a bulwark of security, was actually a hindrance and had to be compromised if America were to play an effective role in the world. American power, the academics of the administration told us, had promoted only the jealousy and fears of the Soviets, who had tried to catch up and compete with the United States. Power had made us an object of fear and envy to the Third World as well. The United States should therefore modify its zeal to remain clearly superior to the Soviets in military strength, should seek a more equitable distribution of wealth throughout the world, and should work for an international order composed of cooperating peers rather than one dominated by conflicting giants with their retinues of satellites and clients. This approach to foreign policy also was unsatisfactory, if only because no one could take it seriously. The rejection of power immediately led to results that had been unsuspected by and were unthinkable to most Americans. The devolution of American control over the Panama Canal was disturbing in itself, and it was quickly followed by what its critics had predicted: the escalation of Cuban power throughout the Caribbean. American criticism of the Shah's regime in Iran and its subsequent overthrow in the absence of U.S. support for its ally was followed by a fanatically hostile and far more brutal regime that actually became a threat. American mediation in Africa simply led to more threats of an oil embargo from Nigeria and the loss of initiative throughout the continent. In short, the Carter scheme for the peaceful abdication of American global power did nothing to impress the world and did much to attract hostile reactions. At bottom, the plan ignored a simple law of political physics: power abhors a vacuum, and where one force withdraws, another will enter.

The consequences of the collapse of the millenarian ideal of American foreign policy have been the rejection of the legitimacy and usefulness of national power itself, and with the rejection of power comes the disappearance of respect. What has now come to be called the "new isolationism," defeatism, appeasement, and vacillation that seem to hold sway in our diplomatic counsels derive not from any inherent material weakness of the United States but from the absence of any viable principle that justifies retaining power and exercising leadership.

Yet there is one part of America that has been only minimally affected by the millenarian orthodoxy that has dominated the rest of the country, a part that—according to its critics as well as its apologists—locates its roots and identity in the Old World and has defied throughout its history the efforts of the millenarian vision to envelop it. This, of course, is the South, and no small part of the southern message to America may lie in its instruction on international affairs. Its teaching does not consist in the high arts of diplomacy—though the Foreign Service might learn something from observing the horse traders of the Old South or even the used car salesmen of the New—nor in the content and purposes of policy. What the South offers America in international affairs is a reformulation of the premises with which the United States approaches the world and a reordering of American expectations of the world.

It may be that the United States will decide that it does not want a "dominant position" in international affairs, that its own interests can best be served in a multipolar world with many different, sometimes competing, sometimes cooperating, centers of power. Whether this decision to surrender power would be wise is another question, but if it is taken, Americans must be aware of its consequences and be prepared to bear them. The erosion of American power in the last few years has not been the result of such a decision. Although a modification of American might has been a goal of the Carter Administration, most citizens have not clearly understood it as a goal and have not even begun to explore its consequences. The erosion of power has proceeded from the frustrations, failures, inattentions, and indecisiveness of both the U.S. government and the citizenry and from the collapse of the political formulas that motivated and justified national power. What the South has to offer America in foreign policy is not necessarily either a recovery or a further diminution of power, but rather a different framework of values and institutions through which the United States can approach the world with purpose and coherence.

Southern intellectual history and social institutions have yielded up little millenarianism and few expectations of a New Jerusalem. C. Vann Woodward, in a well-known essay on the southern identity, contrasted the mythology of America with the realities of the American South.[2] America has believed itself (and has been in fact) affluent, in contrast to the historic poverty of the South. America was successful (might we say invincible), and the South was unique in having experienced military defeat, foreign occupation, and the suppression of its institutions. America was innocent, a noble savage pioneering the untrodden solitude of the New Eden, but the South had direct experience and consciousness of sin, in its guilt over the abuse of slavery and racial hegemony. A culture the identity of which is enveloped in poverty, failure, and consciousness of sin cannot easily formulate millenarian ideologies, though a culture mythologized in wealth, success, and innocence can formulate hardly anything else. The cultural identity of the South is thus far closer to that of the Old World than to that of the New, and it approximates the truths of the human condition more accurately. The legacy of the southern identity in foreign affairs is therefore likely to be a far more realistic appreciation of what the rest of the world is like and of what it expects than was implied in the now-shattered millenarianism of the past.

A realism drawn from the southern tradition should not be confused with the realpolitik of modern European diplomacy, however. The realism of the South is based on a pessimism toward man and his works that is affiliated with religious affirmation. This kind of realism tends to distrust power and the ability of statesmen to reorder the world because it ultimately distrusts man himself. Realpolitik of the nineteenth-century European tradition, in contrast, tends to enlarge the ability of human reason to manipulate states and peoples, to divorce human affairs from restraining moral institutions, and to place unproven faith in power. There can be no doubt that America has placed far too much faith in power and that it should regard it more skeptically. At the same time, the problem of

---

2. C. Vann Woodward, "The Search for Southern Identity," in *The Burden of Southern History*, rev. ed. (Baton Rouge: Louisiana State University Press, 1960), 3–26.

American foreign policy has not been the amount of power at its disposal, but the uses to which power has been put. Realism based on the southern, tragic view of man would not hesitate to make full use of power to pursue legitimate national interests—the protection of security, the defense of allies, and the lawful activities of Americans abroad—but it is almost inconceivable that it could lead to the kind of crusades on which millenarianism has several times embarked us or to the expeditions for booty in which realpolitik tends to indulge.

Southerners are able to draw their realism from another source as well, for the South is more similar to the rest of the world than the rest of America is. Poverty, failure, and consciousness of sin may be alien to most of America, but they are the framework in which most of the world lives and has lived since neolithic times. Far more than other Americans, the southerner is in a position to understand the racially dominated and their dominators, the exploitation of undeveloped economies, the persistent tribal and ethnic categories by which most non-Western peoples identify themselves, stratification by status and kinship rather than by class and education, the patterns of deference and the motivations of rebellion. The global complaint against the United States today is that capitalism and industrial technology, democracy and Western liberalism, have undermined traditional cultures, and this complaint—far more than the economics of slavery or the legalisms of the Constitution—also underlay much of the Confederate secession.

A second contribution that the South can make to American foreign policy consists in what may be called its tradition of command. Much has been written about the military traditions of the South— the use of "colonel" as a title, the number of military schools in the South, and the statistics on southern volunteers in the armed forces. These traditions have led some students to speak of southern militarism; yet *militarism* is a term that describes Prussian generals and Third World despots as well. Clearly some distinctions must be made.

The military life is an experience that is most obviously distinguished from a civilian career by its adherence to the principles of obedience and command, and it is probably the continued vitality of this principle in the South—more than any love of violence, ornate uniforms, and marching music—that accounts for the attractions of the military for the southerner. It is difficult to reconcile the images of southern social life—its informalities and laziness—with the ferrous energy of modern militarist organizations. Nor is it easy to reconcile southern forms of violence—most typically, the feud and the vendetta—with the calculated massacres of modern warfare. The principle of obedience and command, however, conforms to the deferential and hierarchical patterns of the historic South. Social stratification in the South can be manifested in dialect, bearing, dress, and manners to a greater degree than in other regions, and it was not until the last generation that black southerners were generally addressed as "Mister," "Miss," and "Mrs." Not merely the military traditions and usages of the South but also the entire hierarchical structure of society have reenforced the tradition of command.

The egalitarian and pacific residues of millenarianism are not present in this tradition, which offers both a moral justification of leadership and restraints on power. In the aftermath of the millenarian collapse, America lacks any justification for its power and any accurate perception of the limitations to what power can accomplish. The lack of leadership in the United States, the unwillingness to make public decisions, the art of making decisions that please everyone, the fear of displeasing, and the dread of hurting and being hurt all point to the absence of any sense of command in American public life and render all efforts to formulate a coherent foreign policy meaningless. The very means by which public men acquire the offices of formal leadership—by pleasing enough people to gain their quadrennial vote—undermines the leaders' ability to face unpleasant realities and communicate them to the electorate. The means of acquiring leadership in contemporary America frustrates the exercise of leadership; the result is a policy of vacillation toward the world and a condition that resembles anarchy internally.

Leadership in southern society, however, has not been the product of amassing votes through cleverly designed and projected images, nor has it resulted from the mere accumulation of property and power. Leadership in the South, of course, has been inseparable from property and power, as it has been everywhere, but they are not the sole sources of command. Given the rudimentary and largely informal political order of the traditional South, it was unlikely that leadership could be acquired through the state. The apparatus of power for southern leaders has historically been located in and virtually identical with the community itself. Church, family, landed property, and neighborhood are both the intermediary institutions of social life and the natural power bases of southern leaders. The means by which influence within and over such institutions is acquired tends to correspond with the necessities of exercising leadership, so that there is no disparity between the art of gaining command and the art of using it.

The zealous scandal mongering of politicians and journalists in the recent past, as well as the scandals that are mongered, strongly suggests that Americans, having lost any justification for their preeminence in the world, have also lost the ability to distinguish between the legitimate uses of power and its abuses. Given the erosion of the purposes of power, this is not surprising. The tradition of command in the South, however, offers instruction not only in the use of power but also in its restraint. A central part of the tradition of command is the idea of the responsibility of the commander. Whether this idea is manifested in General Lee's solicitude for his troops or in the southern housekeeper's paternalism toward sick servants, it implies a limitation in the uses of power and authority and in the privileges that are due the commander. As in every hierarchical relationship, it implies a responsibility for those who are commanded, and their responsibility to obey is communicated to them to the same degree that the commander's responsibility is performed. The origins of power, leadership, command, and authority in the community thus provide legitimation for the exercise of power as well as restraints on its abuses.

The application of the southern tradition of command to foreign policy may not be immediately clear, since the problems of leadership in a localized community are rather different from those of a national or international scale. Yet there are at least two functions that an individual trained to command can provide and will provide by the very nature of his character. First, he can recognize and translate to the community those sacrifices and risks that are always involved in the "important undertakings" of which Tocqueville spoke and which are indeed part of the human condition. The ability to induce one's followers to assume the consequences of their actions, to make sacrifices willingly, and to inflict and endure suffering is virtually a definition of leadership and is not a trait for which mass democracies are noted. The supplying of this trait to America in the past has been no small part of the southern contribution to American history, not only in some of the more attractive of the Founding Fathers and in the Confederate generals, but also in more recent figures of the nature of General Patton. The southern capacity to continue to provide this kind of leadership in the future will be a test to which the aristocratic pretensions of the South may be usefully put. Secondly, the tradition of command can instill some discipline and coherence upon foreign policy itself, not merely within the country at large but also within a particular administration and within the bureaucracy that oversees the formulation and execution of foreign policy. It is not clear how much of our recent foreign policy has been the result of deliberation and how much has been due to the indirect and disguised actions of State Department bureaucrats. A coherent policy cannot exist until the officially recognized leaders have clear control of the policy-making bodies. Moreover, whether America decides to continue the dismantling of its power or to retrieve it, the country must make a deliberate choice and pursue it logically and consistently. It will not do so unless the range of choices and their consequences is made clear, and only highly skilled and trustworthy leadership can clarify these choices.

Finally, America may find useful to the future of its foreign policy the southern ideal of community and the southern concept of a public order. The United States today appears to be in serious danger of social and regional fragmentation.[3] What is often called "divisiveness," the conflict of generations, races, subcultures, or of Sunbelt and Frostbelt, is the manifestation of this fracturing. It has developed from two principal causes. First, since around 1960, several different social categories have developed among themselves an awareness, a cohesion, and an ideology that disciplines them as distinct units of social and political action. Most obviously this is true of blacks, but other sectors—women, youth, students, Indians, ethnics of one kind or another, and homosexuals—have followed

3. See Kevin Phillips, "The Balkanization of America," *Harper's* (May 1978): 37–47, for a discussion of fragmentation.

and emulated blacks. Usually styling themselves "liberation movements," these groups have challenged the conventional institutions
of American society and government, have articulated "alternative
lifestyles" that subvert the conventional American way of life, and
have formulated doctrines and rhetoric centered around themselves,
their own material and political interests, that do not hesitate to
discard any catholic sense of the public interest. Almost all political
leaders, regardless of ideology, now must at least steer around these
liberated collectivities, and many politicians actively pander to them,
recognizing that their votes are many and cheaply had and that their
causes are fashionable.

A second source of fragmentation derives from the increasing
scrabble for economic gain and political largesse. Virtually every
identifiable sector of American society—old people and young,
farmers and city-dwellers, professors and laborers, welfare recip-
ients and corporate executives—makes some special claim for special consideration of their special interest. The regions too have their
special interests and political champions, who press for federal assistance (i.e., for one region to pay for another) in different forms:
land policy, energy allocations, subsidies for construction, education, renovation, or merely for "bail-out."

The result of this fragmentation and internal conflict is the collapse of any general perception of the interests of the public order
and even the denial that there is a public order that has any legitimate claims. While every society is composed of groups that compete for special consideration, no reasonable determination of who
should get what is possible unless all competing groups adhere to a
consensus that affirms the values of some claims over others and
establishes regular procedures for realizing these claims. It is precisely a consensus of this nature that America lacks at the present
time, and the collapse of the dominant millenarian ideology has
only contributed to the confusion. It is doubtful that a new consensus will be established until a particular social force, or a new coalition of social forces, imposes one through its own domination.

The relevance of the fragmentation of America to foreign policy
became obvious during the debate on the Panama Canal treaties in
1977 and 1978. A small but powerful number of banks and established business interests promoted the treaties for some time before

the public became aware of them at all, oversaw their conclusion, and encouraged their ratification. Whether the treaties were good or bad, the immense influence of a narrow and unseen force on a question of national policy revealed the danger of special interests dominating foreign policy with little attention to public desires and interests. The same kind of influence could be demonstrated in the case of a number of economic, ethnic, and regional blocs that have asserted their own influence in foreign affairs for their own perceived interests, and the South, like other regions, has not abstained from this process. Perhaps the South's involvement in this scramble for protection and power should be added to the index of other sins with which it is taxed.

Nevertheless, the South is in a unique position to instruct America in the meaning and importance of a public order, and not simply by trying to dominate in its own interests. The South has had the unique experience of trying to define its existence as a nation and as a subcultural community, legal but in opposition, with special claims. While it would be futile to argue that the content of the southern tradition is of direct use to America, ethical and philosophical problems that the South has sought to define and clarify are those that revolve around the nature of a public order, the legitimacy of its claims, and the legitimacy of the claims of the part as opposed to those of the whole.

The answer to these problems that the southern mind has formulated is that a public order is not the product of rational design but of nonrational and undesigned human activity in time.[4] Hence, the claims of the part—individual or collective—are subordinate to the claims of the whole, although the claims of the whole themselves may recognize the priority of some particular claims. A social unit, community or nation, does not exist through its physical borders or the sum of its individual residents. Its existence is necessarily historical, reaching into the past as well as the future, and any calculation of its particular interests must not omit those of a historical (and therefore not entirely material) nature. In foreign affairs, there-

4. See M. E. Bradford, *A Better Guide Than Reason: Studies in the American Revolution,* Introduction by Jeffrey Hart (La Salle, Ill.: Sherwood Sugden, 1979), for both a discussion and a defense of this view of society in southern and American intellectual history; the *locus classicus,* of course, is Edmund Burke.

fore, it is not enough merely to establish the present material interests of particular sectors; rather, the primary concern in foreign (as in domestic) policy must be the protection of the historic character and identity of the community.

Yet even if the character of the society is known, there is no possibility of formulating and enforcing a policy predicated on it without the support of the community. The particularistic splintering of society has been an important cause of those problems to which Tocqueville pointed, and they are indeed characteristic of a democracy, in which each component is encouraged to pursue its own interests, and no central authority is able to enforce unity, direction, and common purpose. The formulation of foreign policy, then, is by no means a matter solely of "reason of state"—the calculation of the material interests of abstract national blocs—but is rather closely related to the whole range of intellectual, moral, and social institutions that provide a common identity for, and a definition of, a people. The ability to transcend particular concerns and make sacrifices for the whole is the final test of any foreign policy, and without awareness of and loyalty to the whole, there can be no coherent foreign policy at all.

The definition of the identity of a community is not easy, especially if it has been forgotten, but it requires a considerable immersion in the history, letters, and manners of a society. Moreover, the very notion of a public order is alien to most contemporary Americans and is even abhorrent to some. Yet America, for once in its brief and not always glorious history, must try to learn that its own experience is peculiar in world history, that it has been unusually fortunate in coming to maturity in an epoch of untypical peace and prosperity, and that it cannot continue to judge the world by the norm of its own mythology. This lesson is perhaps what the South, and only the South, can teach America, has in a sense always tried to teach it, and has never been able to teach it. The failure of the South in this respect is at least as significant as that other, bloodier, and more dramatic failure that has haunted and informed the region for the past century and more.

Henry Clay and the
Statecraft of Circumstance

Throughout his life, Henry Clay was considered to be something of a ladies' man who, though above moral reproach, enjoyed the intricacies of flattery and flirtation with attractive young belles. In 1850 the charms of a Miss Grace Greenwood, recently arrived in Washington, took his eye, and he sought from her some small evidence of reciprocal attraction. But, wrote Miss Greenwood's hostess, "I do not believe he will succeed in kissing her even once. You would be amused to see how this man's love of subduing extends even to such small matters. He plies all the arts of flattery upon members of Congress and very seldom fails of success."[1]

In few notable figures of American history has the "love of subduing"—*libido dominandi*—been so pronounced as in Henry Clay, and in few has it been so completely unrequited by that most elusive of belles, the American electorate. Three times Clay was nominated for the presidency, and each time he lost. He displayed an interest on other occasions as well, and his wife revealed that the only time she ever saw him in tears was after he lost the election of 1844 to James K. Polk. During his life he held the offices of congressman, Speaker of the House, ambassador, secretary of state, and senator, but that of chief executive was never to belong to him.

Clay failed to win the presidency not because of defects in his character or an incapacity to stir audiences in his support. To win the presidency in Clay's time required an ability to feed the appetites of the established factionalism of American politics, but almost as necessary was the ability to transcend factionalism, to rise above it and appeal to the sentiments and illusions that masked its variegated hungers, gave them direction and restraint, and, in so doing, created a national community of shared values and institutions. It is perhaps for this reason that the most overwhelming electoral victo-

1. Quoted in Clement Eaton, *Henry Clay and the Art of American Politics* (Boston: Little, Brown and Company, 1957), 159.

ries between 1824 and 1844 were won by the popular military heroes Andrew Jackson and William Henry Harrison, who incorporated in their mythical persons the imagery of heroic glory and yeoman simplicity, suggestive of Cincinnatus. This appeal certainly was not to principle—as the wily Thurlow Weed knew, such appeals would lose elections—but it presupposed vague ideals that alone could bring unity to the disparate social forces of the country.

Clay showed himself time and again to be capable of feeding the appetites of faction—this indeed is why he is known today as "The Great Pacificator"—though he never claimed that he could permanently satisfy them. But he was intellectually and emotionally unprepared to transcend the struggle of factions and unite them in a common bond under his leadership. It is this failure to formulate a satisfactory public myth that was the irony of Clay's career as Pacificator, and perhaps the most far-reaching tragedy of early American history.

Henry Clay was born in 1777 to a Baptist minister of Virginia, who died soon after his birth. What education he received was largely under the informal tutoring of George Wythe, one of the great Virginia jurists, who had him read the translated classics. Unlike his colleagues of the Triumvirate, Calhoun and Webster, Clay was never a man of books or ideas. His speeches are by no means unlearned, but the history to which he appealed was largely that of modern Europe, not that of Rome, which, through Livy, permeated the very atmosphere for most of the statesmen of early America.[2] Nor did Clay inherit from his clergyman father a religious orientation. Again, his speeches are full of references to the Supreme Being and to a commitment to the basic tenets of Christianity, but Clay was not a member of a church until his old age, after the death of his son in the Mexican War turned his thoughts to another world. Finally, if Clay inherited little faith or learning from his family, neither did he receive a fortune. His mother remarried while Clay was still a boy, and what meager property survived his father found its way into her hands and those of her husband, who sold it illegally.

---

2. On the Roman Republic as an inspiration of early American statesmen, see M. E. Bradford, "A Teaching for Republicans: Roman History and the Nation's First Identity," *Intercollegiate Review*, 2 (Winter-Spring 1976), 67–82.

Clay, then, had lowly prospects before him in Virginia, and it was no doubt the depressed horizon of a career in that state that led him to migrate to Kentucky in 1797. In Lexington, he quickly won local prominence as a lawyer, especially in criminal law as attorney for the defense, and it was said of him that none of his clients was ever convicted.

In his early life, then, Clay appeared as something of a masterless man, without fortune, education, church, or place. In Lexington, however, he soon found that roots could be implanted. Though he began his political career in the Kentucky legislature as a radical—what he thought was a Jeffersonian—by denouncing the Alien and Sedition Acts and championing emancipation, he discovered that there were more rewarding causes to espouse. He defended the chartered privileges of the Kentucky Insurance Company and supported a movement to translate the capital from Frankfort to Lexington. These positions probably endeared him to the local interests that already had established a predominance in Kentucky politics, and in 1806 he was chosen to fill a vacant seat in the U.S. Senate. He was reelected in 1810, but, preferring a seat in the House of Representatives, he ran for Congress in 1811 and won. In his first term, he was elected Speaker of the House, an office by no means as prestigious or as powerful as it later became, and, by the time he resigned, he had used the office to start a war, remodel the position of Speaker, and, perhaps most remarkable, bridle the oratorical enthusiasm of John Randolph.

But it was Clay's role in pressing for war with Great Britain that first brought him to national attention. Neither the Federalists nor President Madison and the older Jeffersonians wanted the War of 1812, and they had the support of significant economic interests in the North. But other interests did want war. The best known cause of the conflict—British impressment of sailors from American ships—was a popular justification of it, but the depression that afflicted the western and southern United States, expansionist designs on Canada and Florida, and fear of British collaboration with the Indians were at least equally strong motivations. Clay, as a representative of the West, made his reputation as a war hawk and, as Speaker, managed to insert fellow hawks in the relevant committee chairmanships.

What mainly worried Clay about Great Britain was not her impressment of American seamen but the economic threat posed by her Orders in Council. These had been issued by the Privy Council of England as a response to Napoleon's efforts to forbid British trade with the Continent and so force the United Kingdom into economic chaos. Though the Orders in Council were primarily aimed at preventing France from obtaining necessary imports, they also struck at the export trade of American goods. It was this threat to which Clay gave most of his attention in a speech of December 31, 1811; the immediate issue was whether to expand American military forces, but Clay took the opportunity to urge the justice and expediency of the coming war.

Though he gave some attention to the dishonor of impressment and declared that, if there were no war, we would lose "commerce, character, a nation's best treasure, honor," Clay devoted the bulk of his speech to economic grievances. "If pecuniary considerations alone are to govern, there is sufficient motive for the war." America, he said, lost ten million dollars a year by the continuation of peace and the obstacles to exports that the Orders in Council created. The orders of embargo (though in reality aimed at France) were themselves the equivalent of invasion, he argued, and he offered a rather staggering set of statistics to support his charge. Finally, he stated, the argument that Britain was merely responding to Napoleon's economic warfare was only a mask for ulterior motives.

> No, sir; you must look for an explanation of her conduct in the jealousies of a rival. She sickens at your prosperity, and beholds, in your growth—your sails spread on every ocean, and your numerous seamen—the foundations of a power which, at no very distant day, is to make her tremble for her naval superiority.[3]

Clay's line of argument, that is, was that national interest overrode the conventional laws of peace and war. It is arguable that embargoes and impressment are morally justifiable causes of going to war, but moral justification did not appear to concern Clay and the war hawks very much. The threat to the economic well-being of the

3. Henry Clay, *The Works of Henry Clay Comprising His Life, Correspondence and Speeches,* ed. Calvin Colton, Federal Edition, 10 vols. (New York and London: G. P. Putnam's Sons, 1904), 6:38, 40–41.

nation was in itself a sufficient justification, whether life was lost or property destroyed, and the prospect of international rivalry for maritime supremacy was good reason to forestall such competition by force.

The bellicosity of Clay's attitude toward Britain and the nationalistic assumptions of his rhetoric were matched by his earlier defense, in December 1810, of extending the borders of the United States to the banks of the Perdido River in west Florida. He began his oration by a reflection on "the more than Aristidean justice, which in a question of territorial title between the United States and a foreign nation, induces certain gentlemen to espouse the pretensions of the foreign nation."[4] This introductory statement begs the question by assuming what the speech was to prove, that the American claims were indeed just. The sarcastic analogy with Aristides was calculated to embarrass those who actually considered that American claims might be less defensible than the "pretensions" of a foreign country.

In the same speech, however, Clay gave an extensive review of the history of Florida and of the treaties that had governed its disposition. Of course he concluded, on the basis of this historical survey, that America had a right to west Florida. But not content with this careful reconstruction, he elaborated a rather general statement on the nature of national policy.

> I have no hesitation in saying, that if a parent country will not or can not maintain its authority, in a colony adjacent to us, and there exists in it a state of misrule and disorder, menacing our peace; and if, moreover, such colony, by passing into the hands of any other power, would become dangerous to the integrity of the Union, and manifestly tend to the subversion of our laws, we have a right, upon the eternal principles of self-preservation, to lay hold upon it. This principle alone, independent of any title, would warrant our occupation of West Florida.[5]

He then rounded out his remarks by expressing the hope that the United States would embrace all the territory east of the Mississippi, including east Florida, and "some of the territories of the north of us also."[6]

4. Ibid., 13.
5. Ibid., 19.
6. Ibid., 21.

It must be said that Clay was not an early exponent of Manifest Destiny, and when that doctrine became popular, he opposed its implications for Mexico and Texas. Clay did not base his espousal of national expansion on a divinely ordained mission but on solid, material arguments: geopolitics, economics, and national security. Indeed, there is a subtle but increasingly explicit and powerful disengagement of his idea of the national interest from any subordinating moral law. What is in the interest of the nation becomes a law unto itself and, "independent of any title," can be used to justify war and territorial aggrandizement.

Apart from the ethical and practical difficulties to which such a position can lead, there is also a semantic problem: how is "the national interest" to be defined? There were significant sections and forces of American society that did not want to occupy west Florida or wage war against Britain (nor, later, Texas or Mexican territories). How were the interests and wishes of these segments of the nation to be measured against those of other parts that did favor such expansion? And what were the content and meaning of "national interest" when the issues were not as clear as ten million dollars worth of lost exports or the augmentation of national territory? What was the national interest when the issues were tariffs, a national bank, slavery, and the meaning of the Constitution itself? It was around these very issues that Clay's career revolved and on them that his reputation rests. How then do his political realism and his economic nationalism fare when measured on these scales?

Almost from the beginning of his career in national politics Clay had defended protection. An important product of the Bluegrass regions that he represented in the Senate in 1810 was hemp, which faced strong competition from the imported Russian variety. Protection was therefore important to Clay politically, and it also was important personally, for his own estates in Kentucky produced hemp. In the 1840s his son was heavily involved in the hemp trade to Europe. This personal interest was no doubt a strong reinforcement, if not the origin, of his defense of a protectionist tariff, which he espoused from the day he took his seat in the Senate.

The war intervened, however, and it was not until after the Treaty of Ghent that Clay returned to the question of tariffs. Soon after his return from the Peace Congress, Clay contended that the threat of aggression was over. But it was necessary to maintain the military strength that had enabled America to end the foreign threat. The army therefore should be maintained in strength, and the federal government should become actively involved in promoting the national economy.

> In short, I would act seriously, effectively act, on the principle, that in peace we ought to prepare for war; for, I repeat, again and again, that, in spite of all the prudence exerted by the government, and the forbearance of others, the hour of trial will come. These halcyon days of peace, this calm will yield to the storm of war, and when that comes, I am for being prepared to breast it.[7]

To Clay, in this speech, the end of government appears to be the ability to wage war. In peace, we should prepare for war, for we live in a condition of perpetual emergency and incessant threat. Aside from direct military preparations, the maintenance of a standing army in peacetime (a radical departure from the traditional dread of standing armies and military despotism that descended from Cromwell's time), the entire society should be mobilized for conflict. The federal government was to undertake "internal improvements" for the construction of canals and turnpikes; protective tariffs were to be developed to defend American markets and create an economic autarchy; and a system of taxation was to be developed that would produce enough revenue to support this system. The relation of all this to the necessities of war is explicit:

> He would afford them protection, not so much for the sake of the manufacturers themselves, as for the general interest. We should thus have our wants supplied, when foreign resources are cut off, and we should also lay the basis of a system of taxation, to be resorted to when the revenue from imports is stopped by war.[8]

In the twentieth century, this kind of exhortation has not been unfamiliar to Americans. Changes in American domestic policies have frequently been justified by appeals to similar reasoning about "national security," and many Americans in this century have found such arguments plausible with respect to threats from Germany,

7. Ibid., 98.
8. Ibid.

Japan, and the Soviet Union. But in 1816, Clay's apology must strike us as odd. All of Europe from Lisbon to Moscow was exhausted from a generation of wars and revolution. Britain, though victorious, had also been forced into retreat in the conflict just ended. Where then was the threat? From what source did Clay perceive new challenges to American independence? The threat was never specified but was merely assumed and asserted, and Clay never defined "the general interest" or distinguished it from particular interests that would benefit from his proposals.

Clay's "American System" of internal improvements and protective tariffs was not adopted, but in 1824, Clay again returned to his old theme and delivered what became a *locus classicus* of protectionism. Once more he appealed to the needs of the common defense in upholding his plan.

> Its importance, in connection with the general defense in time of war, can not fail to be duly estimated. Need I recall to our painful recollection the sufferings, for the want of an adequate supply of absolute necessaries, to which the defenders of their country's rights and our entire population, were subjected during the late war? Or to remind the committee of the great advantage of a steady and unfailing source of supply, unaffected alike in war and in peace?[9]

But it was in his appeal to the anti-tariff southerners that Clay touched a fundamental idea in his conception of the Union. The South found a protective tariff objectionable because its residents were themselves consumers. It was they who, lacking their own manufacturing centers, would feel the burden of the increased costs of imports that would result. Clay was well aware of this divergence, and he sought to meet it directly.

> Mr. Chairman, our confederacy comprehends, within its vast limits, great diversity of interests: agricultural, planting, farming, commercial, navigating, fishing, manufacturing. No one of these interests is felt in the same degree, and cherished with the same solicitude, throughout all parts of the Union. Some of them are peculiar to particular sections of our common country. But all these great interests are confided to the protection of one government—to the fate of one ship—and a most gallant ship it is, with a

9. Ibid., 292.

noble crew. If we prosper, and are happy, protection must be extended to all; it is due to all.[10]

Clay conceived of American society as a collection of distinct economic interests, correlated with geographical sections. Each interest, and hence each section, found itself in competition and conflict with the others. Unchecked, the rivalry would result in either the dissolution of the Union or the dominance of one sectional interest at the expense of the others. But Clay proposed an alternative to such fierce and suicidal conflict: the federal government would be a judge and arbitrator among the contestants. He outlined the principle by which the judge would reach his decision:

> The inquiry should be, in reference to the great interests of every section of the Union (I speak not of minute subdivisions), what would be done for those interests if that section stood alone and separated from the residue of the republic?[11]

Clay argued that his tariff proposals contained "a case for mutual concession, for fair compromise." It was through "compromise" that the contending economic and sectional interests were to be reconciled: "neither, it is true, gets all that it wants, nor is subject to all that it fears."[12]

Clay conceived of the Union as a kind of mechanism in which each part had a separate functioning from the others. It was a mechanism in which each part was at least discrete and separate from, and often in conflict with, the others. The source of conflict was primarily economic and material, and only a compromise of economic interests could assure the smooth operation of the united machine.

Clay's proposal—and it was a model for his great efforts at later compromises—did not work. It was attractive, simple, and well intentioned, but it ignored certain profound realities for which Clay could find no answer and which he probably never understood. His conception of the Union as a mechanism of separate and dynamic parts had considerable truth in it, but it lacked a dimension that

10. Ibid., 290.
11. Ibid., 290–91.
12. Ibid., 291.

could account for the noneconomic needs of the contending sections. In 1824, the contention over the tariff was largely economic,
but the communities that the tariff problem was creating among
both its advocates in the North and its enemies in the South were
becoming more than economic subcultures. They were in the process of forming separate civilizations, with separate ideas of the
nature and purposes of man and, hence, different conceptions of
the ends of government, law, and social and economic arrangements.
As the two embryonic civilizations differentiated themselves, the
consensus that had originally united them and was the only basis for
political compromise between them began to disintegrate. Clay's
pragmatic and economic nationalism had too little to say to these
two aborning civilizations, too little to speak to their respective
identities and aspirations, to be useful in forging a permanent, compromising settlement between them. All it could offer in the ideal of
Union was a rather purposeless bond that served only as an instrument for mutual concessions. Only the rational calculation of sectional interests would lead each party to limit its appetites and demands, but what Clay's conception did not perceive was that in such
an economic mechanism, rational calculation could just as easily lead
to the conclusion that a section could dominate the others as to Clay's
inference that unless it made concessions, it would be dominated.

   This problem became evident in 1824. Clay argued that his American System offered something for every section. Protection would
not harm the South because the system would encourage domestic
manufactures. Southerners would therefore be able to consume at
the same price domestically what they had previously imported.
The problem was that, in 1824, there was no reason for the South to
compromise. Clay was visibly vulnerable to the charge of "special
interest" himself when his own and his section's hemp interests
were discussed. This in itself jeopardized his self-appointed role as
the designer of a fair compromise. Furthermore, southerners and
other free-traders saw through the claim of the system to impar-
tiality. Churchill C. Cambreleng of New York argued that it would
place the control of all manufacturing in the hands of "capitalists"
(i.e., plutocrats). The centralization implicit in Clay's proposals
aroused old fears of a Federalist crypto-monarchy and rule by vested
financial and manufacturing interests.

The South's hostile reception of Clay's proposals for tariff compromise pointed to the essential weakness of his plan and to the flaw in his ideal of compromise. Given the vigor of the various sectional interests, why should they make concessions? Why should they not push their own interests to the limit, either by nullification, secession, or, if it were open to them, by domination of the federal government? Clay's ideas of the social bond—naked economic self-interest, to be checked suddenly by a mysterious willingness to compromise—could provide no serious answer.

In the event, the Tariff of 1824 passed the House by five votes, was severely watered down in the Senate, and was ultimately signed into law by President Monroe. It satisfied no one—voting was largely along economic lines—and, perhaps for that reason, lasted only until 1828. The South was opposed to it, but New England was not yet committed to support of a tariff or to the industrial economy it was intended to protect. It was in this debate that Daniel Webster made one of the strongest cases ever argued for free trade, a case he repudiated four years later. Compromise, then, was still feasible to some in 1824, but the other aspects of Clay's American System—internal improvements and a national bank—were discarded.

Controversy over protection rose to a height with the Tariff of Abominations in 1828, which protected not only manufactured goods but also the raw materials themselves. Ironically, its advocates hoped to win the North for Jackson by supporting it and to win the South as well when its extreme duties were rejected. Its northern supporters refused to give it up, however, and caused it to be adopted. That result was revealing in itself, for it showed that sectional interest would predominate over a desire for national harmony when the two seemed to conflict and when there was no reconciling principle.

Clay did not support the Tariff of Abominations, but neither did he welcome the crisis that ensued. South Carolina refused to recognize the ruinous duty and claimed the right to "nullify" federal legislation that it found unconstitutional. This response, gathering force since 1828, erupted into a formal Ordinance of Nullification in 1832, when the 1828 duties were not sufficiently reduced by the tariff of that year.

The refusal of northern protectionists to modify the duties of the

Tariff of Abominations in 1828 and the South Carolinian attempt to nullify the moderated duties of 1832 indicate the process of sectional cleavage that was developing within the Union. Jackson's response to nullification would have been to send troops to South Carolina to enforce federal law, but Clay's approach was typically moderate. In 1833, he sponsored a "Compromise Tariff" that succeeded in persuading South Carolina to withdraw its ordinance. Clay's measure called for a gradual reduction of duties over a nine-year period to a maximum level of 20 percent and for additions to the list of imported goods exempt from duties.

Again, Clay sought to mollify both sections by balancing their interests in a common bill. "I want harmony," he declared, on February 12, 1833, in the Senate. "I wish to see the restoration of those ties which have carried us triumphantly through two wars. I delight not in this perpetual turmoil. Let us have peace, and become once more united as a band of brothers."[13] In arguing with those free-traders who objected to a tariff on principle, Clay counseled prudence. The manufacturers would not accept a trade policy that left them exposed to the invasion of foreign imports, and southern refusal to compromise would lead only to the legislative dominance of the manufacturing North.

> But if the measure should be carried by the common consent of both parties, we shall have all security; history will faithfully record the transaction . . . that it was as oil poured from the vessel of the Union to restore peace and harmony to the country . . . here is all the reasonable security that can be desired by those on the one side of the question, and much more than those on the other would have by any unfortunate concurrence of circumstances.[14]

Clay's approach to the tariff controversy is typical of his skeptical, pragmatic, and fundamentally conservative conception of politics.

> It would be vain and foolish to proceed at all times, and under all circumstances, upon the notion of absolute certainty in any system, or infallibility in any dogma, and to push these without regard to any consequences. With us . . . it is a question of mere expediency as to the form, the degree, and the time that the protection shall be afforded. . . . we ought not to over-

13. Ibid., 7:543.
14. Ibid., 545.

look what is due to those who honestly entertain opposite opinions to large masses of the community, and to deep, long-cherished, and growing prejudices.[15]

This is the language of Burke, of what Richard Weaver called the "rhetoric of circumstance," and the Old Whig language of the Framers at their best.[16] To those who identify politics with the approximation of the social order to transcendent truths, it would not be palatable, nor would it be to those who see in this kind of accommodation to circumstances a threat to their own social order. Nevertheless, it is an ancient school of statecraft that, in Henry Clay's time and by his efforts, appeared to be fruitful.

Yet it is not a style that always works. Its success depends upon a set of shared values and common institutions among the contending parties. Only when both sides share fundamental values in common can their differences be reconciled and their separate interests accommodated to each other in a satisfactory compromise. In the 1830s, the North, the South, and the West still shared such a fundamental orthodoxy, and the politics of compromise could work. But it was the weakness of Henry Clay—and it is perhaps the inherent flaw of Burkean or "circumstantial" conservatism—that this style of statecraft could not create or restore such common ground. Burke himself probably understood this problem (hence the pessimism of his later years), but it is doubtful that Clay ever perceived it.

Clay's conservatism, in other words, presumed too much. It took for granted a community of values and interests that defined the United States in the early nineteenth century, and therefore there is, despite its sophisticated and worldly appeal, a naïveté and a parochialism within it that Clay expressed in his summation in 1833.

> Above all, I count upon the good effects resulting from a restoration to the harmony of this divided people, upon their good sense and their love of justice. Who can doubt, that when passions have subsided, and reason has resumed her empire, that there will be a disposition throughout the whole Union, to render ample justice to all its parts? Who will believe that any section of this great confederacy would look with indifference to the pros-

15. Ibid., 557.
16. See Richard Weaver, *The Ethics of Rhetoric* (Chicago: Henry Regnery Company, 1965), chap. 3, and for Weaver's description of Clay as "the archetypal Whig" (78).

tration of the interests of another section, by distant and selfish foreign nations, regardless alike of the welfare of us all? . . . The people of the United States are brethren, made to love and respect each other. Momentary causes may seem to alienate them, but, like family differences, they will terminate in a closer and more affectionate union than ever. And how much more estimable will be a system of protection, based on common conviction and common consent, and planted in the bosoms of all, than one wrenched by power from reluctant and protesting weakness?[17]

Clay never specifically defined the content of the American orthodoxy, which he seems to have regarded as a law of nature. That he believed in such a common, national bond is clear, but at the most it seems to have consisted, in his mind, of a common pursuit of material prosperity and of national independence from foreign threats. The issues with which he was most associated, with the exception of the slavery question, dealt with the material level of affluence: the American System, the national bank, and the tariff controversy. That Clay in his early career was equally concerned over foreign threats is clear from his rather ferocious rhetoric in support of war. But, though his language moderated after the Treaty of Ghent, there persisted in his mind a careful attention to national independence. We have already seen his efforts to relate his American System to a national need for self-defense. In the passage quoted above from his speech on the Compromise Tariff, he again raised the specter of "prostration . . . by distant and selfish foreign nations." And, in his reply to President Jackson's veto of the recharter of the Second Bank of the United States in 1832, he returned to the same theme.

In 1811 Clay had opposed the national bank, but in 1816, he reversed himself and supported it. In 1832 he again supported its rechartering and found himself obliged to account for his reversal. In response to the charge that the foreign interests in the bank would come to dominate American economic life and public policy, Clay argued that, had the bank existed on the same scale during the war as in 1832,

We should have avoided many of the disasters of that war, perhaps those of Detroit and at this place. The government would have possessed ample means

17. Clay, *Works*, 7:561.

for its vigorous prosecution; and the interest of foreigners, British subjects especially, would have operated upon them, not upon us.[18]

"The war and the fatal experience of its disastrous events had changed me," he declared.

> In 1811, I believed a bank of the United States not necessary, and that a safe reliance might be placed on the local banks, in the administration of the fiscal affairs of the government. The war taught us many lessons, and among others demonstrated the necessity of the bank of the United States, to the successful operations of the government.[19]

In Clay's mind, then, the need for national defense colored a variety of issues that ostensibly had nothing to do with military affairs. This is not to say that Clay was a jingoist (after 1815) or a militarist. He was not in favor of the Mexican War, and a theme as constant in his speeches as prosperity or defense was his dread of a Caesarian military state. His first attack on Andrew Jackson, for which the general never forgave him, came in response to Jackson's summary expedition into Spanish Florida in 1818, and Clay portrayed his victim as an insubordinate aggressor who sought to place military above civilian authority.

What then was the point of Clay's persistent concern for national defense when there were no visible enemies and when he plainly did not desire a campaign of imperial acquisition? Clay's conception of American society was that it consisted of a diverse aggregate of sectional, class, and political interests. Each interest had its own aspirations, ideas, values, and ambitions, and each was in opposition to the others. Without compromise, the struggle of factions would destroy the country, either leaving it torn apart or unifying it under the domination of a particular group. Yet, given this perpetual conflict of self-interests, there was no common ground on which the factions could unite. In a conception of society such as this, only a perception of an external threat could bring unity. It was manifestly in the interest of all to unite against the dangers of invasion and conquest or of foreign economic domination. Hence, "national interest" in the pluralistic and appetitive confederacy of factions

18. Ibid., 530.
19. Ibid., 528.

that Clay perceived could be defined only in terms of a common, visible enemy, and the only way to establish harmony and a foundation for fraternal compromise was to emphasize the threat to each and every one of the contending factions.

That there was no such external threat to the United States during the whole of the nineteenth century did not matter a great deal to Clay. What was important was to find a common ground and a common symbol around which all groups and sections could unite. But ultimately the nonexistence of a national threat did matter, for two reasons. In the first place, the symbol proposed by Clay failed to be convincing simply because he could not find a believable threat. In lieu of a common and external real enemy, therefore, the disparate forces that he sought to unite increasingly turned on each other. Secondly, it mattered because, if such a threat had existed, or if its existence had been credible, the measures Clay proposed in the American System and its related concepts would have so transformed the Republic, so offended and threatened it from all sides, that the appeal to a common danger would not have been effective. This had already happened in the War of 1812, when hawks and doves divided along clear factional lines. And it was to recur in the Mexican War. In 1812, some sections had opposed the war because they were convinced it was merely a transparent adventure that would help only their rivals. In the case of Texas and Mexico, the southern case for expansion was again transparently related to the protection of slavery. Thus, the appeal to a common threat as a principle of national reconciliation was not effective and indeed was capable of having the opposite effect, of promoting sectional conflict. The simple truth was that, despite the large element of realism in Clay's view of society as a perpetual contest of factions, there was very little in that view to induce actual compromise, let alone marshal a serious effort by all sides to achieve national harmony.

The Compromise Tariff of 1833 worked in the sense that it induced South Carolina to withdraw the Nullification Ordinance—which it was already looking for a face-saving way to do—and in the sense that it preserved a liveable society for northern protectionists and southern free-traders for the future. But the tariff controversy was almost purely an economic issue and was already becoming stale, though other issues were beginning to arise that could not so easily be resolved.

Clay remained in the Senate until 1842, but his activities were almost entirely devoted to rather transient political questions. There is no great value served by pursuing his feuds with Andrew Jackson and Martin Van Buren, his struggle with Webster and Thurlow Weed to control the Whig party, or his conflict with John Tyler over the bank. The emerging issue of American politics was slavery and its relationship to the future of the Union, and it is in regard to these problems that Clay's activities are remembered.

The importance of slavery in national politics is represented by the debate over the annexation of Texas, which, under its president, Sam Houston, moved closer to the orbit of the United States. Within the country, the question of annexation was directly connected with the question of slavery. The South, seeing an opportunity to expand the number of threatened slave states, was firmly in favor of annexation. The West was divided, and, though the North was not unanimously opposed, the abolitionists were. John Quincy Adams declared that annexation would mean dissolution of the Union, and Daniel Webster also opposed it. Calhoun, of course, was strongly annexationist, and it was he whom President Tyler selected to be secretary of state for the specific purpose of negotiating the treaty of annexation.

Because of the sectional controversy over annexation, it quickly became an issue of the 1844 presidential campaign. The Democrat most likely to carry the party's nomination was Martin Van Buren, and Clay was heavily favored for the Whigs'. This early lead caused Van Buren and Clay to meet privately at the latter's Ashland plantation to establish some common ground, according to Clay, whereby the potentially explosive problem of annexation could be defused. Both therefore declared themselves against the annexation of Texas.

Clay's position, defined in his "Raleigh Letter," was quite simply that annexation would inevitably lead to war with Mexico and that what the country needed was "union, peace, and patience." Van Buren's position was virtually identical, though less strongly worded, and, had he in fact been nominated, the issue might not have excited national attention.

But partly because of his opposition to annexation, Van Buren found himself deadlocked out of the nomination, which was then thrown to James K. Polk, the Speaker of the House, who was an open expansionist. The ensuing campaign therefore came to hinge on the Texas question, and Polk began to cut into Clay's southern support. Faced with the loss of the South, Clay then had to modify the stand he had taken in the Raleigh Letter. He wrote two more letters from Alabama in which he explained that he had no personal objection to annexation but only feared a war with Mexico. This more moderate position, however, while it may have protected Clay's standing in the South, left him open to the abolitionists' attacks in the North. It was in New York that they were able to draw defecting Whigs into their Liberty party, and it was the loss of New York that cost Clay the election.

Clay's effort to articulate a compromise position on annexation that would please both sides illustrates the fundamental weakness of his consensual, equilibrist approach to politics. The only consensus on which compromise could be based was rapidly evaporating. Clay's view of politics did not permit him to make a different approach, however, or to formulate a clear-cut position that would commit him to one side or the other.

The inadequacy of his insistence on harmony is further revealed in his remarks on slavery itself. In 1839 Clay approached the subject in a speech in the Senate. The Constitution, he declared, "never could have been formed upon the principle of investing the general government with authority to abolish the institution at its pleasure." The problem of slavery, he noted, and no doubt correctly, "was happily compromised and adjusted in a spirit of harmony and patriotism."[20] Characterizing the abolitionists as men obsessed with a single abstract idea, he argued against emancipation without defending slavery itself. His arguments were constitutional, economic, and social, but he did not deal directly with the moral foundations of slavery.

> In human affairs we are often constrained, by the force of circumstances and the actual state of things, to do what we would not do, if that state of things did not exist. The slaves are here, and here must remain, in some condi-

20. Ibid., 8:150.

tion. . . . In such an alternative, who can hesitate? Is it not better for both parties that the existing state of things should be preserved, instead of exposing them to the horrible strifes and contests which would inevitably attend an immediate abolition?[21]

More than a century later, the advice of Clay sounds more sensible than it did at the time. The "happy compromise" of the Framers, however, was what we would now call "benign neglect" and was no more possible in the 1840s than it was in the 1960s. The abolitionists appealed to the nature of man and to the ethics of slavery, resting their case ultimately on a "higher law" than the Constitution. This attack pushed Calhoun in 1844 to defend slavery as an institution beneficial in itself. The issue, in other words, had simply moved beyond the gentlemanly spirit of "happy compromise," with a prudent reflection on the disastrous alternatives to the status quo. The argument had become metaphysical, and Clay's skeptical pragmatism had nothing to contribute to such disputations.

Clay—and with him, the system of government and its philosophical presuppositions that had pertained since the drafting of the Constitution—was becoming irrelevant, and the final irrelevance of his politics of consensus and compromise became clear in what, ironically, is commonly regarded as his last and greatest achievement.

The Compromise of 1850, like the Texas question, grew out of the expansionist energies that obsessed the country in Manifest Destiny. The acquisition of vast areas of land from Mexico demanded that this territory be divided into states and brought into the Union. But, as with Texas, the process of division would involve the extension of slavery. In 1846, Congressman David Wilmot of Pennsylvania introduced an amendment to Polk's bill for purchasing the land from Mexico that would have forbidden slavery in any of the new territory. Clearly, the South would oppose doggedly the Wilmot Proviso's disposition of the new land, for it threatened to do away with the Missouri Compromise, which, since 1820, had governed the extension of slavery in the territory of the Louisiana Purchase. Calhoun, sensing that the ensuing battle would be fundamental for the future of the country and especially of the South, girded himself for his final combat, and Clay also returned to Washington for the last time.

21. Ibid., 151.

Clay had retired from the Senate in 1842 and devoted himself to the pursuit of the presidency in 1844. Afterward, he faced for a while financial ruin, the disappointment of his presidential ambitions, the alienation of Kentucky, and the death of his son at Buena Vista. In 1850 Clay was seventy-three years old, but his health and finances had sufficiently improved so that he was able to overcome dissidents in the Kentucky legislature and win unanimous election to the Senate in 1849. His purposes in returning are unclear, but it is doubtful that he sought to reclaim his title as a designer of compromises.

Whatever his motives at this rather grisly age, it was compromise that Clay sought to achieve once he arrived in Washington. The intransigence of both South and North appeared formidable. In Nashville, a convention of southern delegates was about to meet that would discuss the feasibility of secession, and Calhoun declared that if the North sought to exclude all slavery from New Mexico and California, he was for disunion. Horace Mann, on the part of the North, spoke of a servile war as being preferable to the extension of slavery, and the presence of William Seward, a declared abolitionist, as President Taylor's chief adviser seemed to give weight to Calhoun's fears.

It was in this atmosphere then that Clay introduced, in January 1850, eight resolutions designed to give something to each side. California was to enter the Union without restriction of slavery; this meant that it would enter as a free state. The rest of the territory was also to be unrestricted; this could mean anything, but it certainly meant no prohibition of slavery. Second, the dispute over the borders of Texas and New Mexico was to be decided in favor of the latter (thus reducing the size of the slave state), but the federal government was to assume the public debts of Texas. Third, Clay proposed to abolish the slave trade in the District of Columbia but to guarantee slavery itself there as long as it existed in neighboring Maryland. And last, Clay proposed that Congress refuse to tamper with the interstate slave trade and pass a more effective fugitive slave law.

In the course of the ensuing debate, Clay appealed again to the integrity and harmony of the Union. It was then that he pronounced the words that were to be inscribed on his grave: "no South, no North, no East, no West." And a few months later he delivered his most expansive statement on his concept of compromise.

Life itself is but a compromise between death and life, the struggle continuing throughout our whole existence, until the great Destroyer finally triumphs. All legislation, all government, all society, is formed upon the principle of mutual concession, politeness, comity, courtesy; upon these, every
thing is based. I bow to you to-day because you bow to me. You are respectful
to me because I am respectful to you. Compromise is peculiarly appropriate
among the members of a republic, as of one common family. Compromises
have this recommendation, that if you concede any thing, you have something conceded to you in return. Treaties are compromises made with foreign powers contrary to what is done in a case like this. Here, if you concede
any thing, it is to your own brethren, to your own family. Let him who
elevates himself above humanity, above its weaknesses, its infirmities, its
wants, its necessities, say, if he pleases, I never will compromise, but let no
one who is not above the frailties of our common nature disdain compromises.[22]

Clay in this peroration erects his idea of politics into a *Weltan-
schauung*. Compromise is the only means imperfect men have to
achieve a stable and regular way of life; it is a means that is not only
expedient but imbedded in the fabric of the universe, in life itself.
This was the closest to a metaphysical expression and defense of his
political thought that Clay was ever to come.

So certain was Clay that this appeal to the common bond of the
Union would resolve the controversy that he sought a simple and
direct approach. He supported what came to be called the "Omni-
bus Bill," introduced by Henry Foote of Mississippi, which embod-
ied most of his resolutions in one document. Clay assumed that
congressmen would support what they opposed in order to see
passed what they supported. But he underestimated the bitterness
that divided the sections. On July 31, the Senate tore the bill to
shreds when those who disdained compromise took advantage of
parliamentary maneuvering and allowed only the meaningless rump
of the bill to pass. It is said that Jefferson Davis was visibly grinning
and that William Seward actually danced in happiness at the collapse of Clay's bill.

Clay accepted defeat and left Washington to recuperate from the
six-month struggle. But Stephen Douglas saved the measure. Realizing that sectionalism was too strong for Clay's appeal to a common
purpose to work, Douglas resurrected the plan by submitting it piecemeal to different sectional groupings. In other words, Douglas ap-

22. Ibid., 9:418.

parently understood that no basis for a comprehensive compromise existed and managed to steer it through the Senate by taking advantage of different and opposing blocs. Clay had relied on a vestigial sense of national harmony and a presumed willingness to compromise in order to preserve it, and Clay had lost. Douglas abandoned hope for national harmony and accepted sectional conflicts, and Douglas, by September 17, had succeeded in getting the substance of Clay's proposals passed into law.[23]

The way in which the Compromise of 1850 actually passed, therefore, refuted the assumptions on which Clay had based his proposal. He was indeed correct that "all society, is formed upon the principle of mutual concession," but a willingness to make mutual concessions in turn depends on a recognizably shared set of values among the mutually conceding groups. In 1850, there was not sufficient sharing of values between North and South to make Clay's appeal practicable, and by 1861, there would be none at all.

Even if Clay had lived until 1861, and had been preternaturally restored to vigor and political influence, it is doubtful that he could have prevented the schism of the Republic. His failure did not proceed from his defects but from his virtues, primarily from his unshakable, almost childlike, faith in the residual allegiance of North and South to the common Union. In Clay's political vision the United States—and perhaps human society in general—was composed of constantly competing interests—sections, classes, economic and political blocs—that balanced each other and mutually limited the power of any one of them. It was a Madisonian conception, expressed in *Federalist* 51, and Clay more than once hailed Madison as his hero and guide in political thought. But Clay also believed that these separate interests shared a common attachment to the Union, and it was this common denominator that created them a single family, a band of brothers, and gave them the basis for reconciliation, compromise, and harmony. It was the impossibility of realizing perfect justice in an imperfect world, the disastrous consequences that would follow an attempt by imperfect human nature to

23. See David Potter, *The Impending Crisis, 1848–1861* (New York: Harper and Row, 1976), 108–9, for this interpretation and for the foregoing account of the background of the Compromise of 1850.

formulate absolute solutions to public issues, that led him to take his stand, irrevocably, upon the balance of factions and the statecraft of circumstance.

Yet Clay was unable to give a content to his ideal of the Union in any but pragmatic and material terms. He appealed to the economic interests of the composite factions, yet there arose issues for each of them that transcended economics. He appealed to the military dangers of disunion, yet he was unable to identify a convincing enemy, and, as the sectional dispute over expansion developed, one suspects that he feared to push the appeal too far. The threat of a common enemy might too easily have translated into a rationalization for expansion that would upset the sectional balance even further. Finally, Clay appealed to the negative of his proposition: what would happen if the different interests did not unite? The abolition of slavery would lead to racial as well as to civil war; the country would succumb to its foreign enemies; national prosperity would sink into poverty.

But, though Clay was successful in his earlier years in forging compromises that avoided asking the unanswerable questions, he was unable to find a formula that would answer, for all sides, the fundamental question: why should the Union stay together? As different parts of the country began to settle on different goals, and with different rationales for seeking those goals, this question became more and more unanswerable. Clay's pragmatism was incapable of finding a moral unity among these sections, and it was, in different ways, moral unity that the abolitionists and the secessionists each finally created for themselves. When they had formed their own purposes within the Union, when the abolitionists had settled on emancipation and the South had determined on slavery, as the goals around which they would stand or fall, there was no longer any moral or even any material basis for mutual concessions or for allegiance to a common nation. There was only the prospect of dissolution or of domination by one section or the other.

Thus Clay was philosophically unable to bring the two sides together. Had he been able to discover a common loyalty or a public orthodoxy that really encompassed the whole country, and not one that merely tried to satiate the appetites of each part, he might have realized his life's ambition to be president and to create a common national purpose. The "love of subduing" that Miss Greenwood's chaperon saw in him in his later years was doomed to frustration. His efforts at compromise came to be regarded as merely opportunist fence-straddling precisely because he gave no attention to those fundamental principles that he distrusted and on which all others were becoming fixated.

Yet the flaw of Clay's statecraft of circumstance was not his alone. The Madisonian model of checks and balances, formalized in the Constitution and enshrined in the claims of political liberalism, offers no brake by which the perpetual motion of sectional and social conflict can be controlled and reconciled, and neither Clay nor any of his contemporaries can be blamed too much for failing to find or create such a brake. The United States, from its origins as a political society, recognized no such restraint, and it stepped forth into history in the delusion that none is necessary, that balance and compromise through the mutual gratification of economic interests are as natural and stabilizing in society and politics as in the celestial mechanics of the Newtonian universe the Framers inhabited.

In the absence of some common myth—religious, ethical, ideological, national, or racial—that could serve as a framework by which individual and sectional appetites could be governed, and relying solely on a supposititious balance of selfish but enlightened interests, the Republic sooner or later was destined to suffer either dissolution from the centrifugal conflicts those interests engendered or centripetal domination by one or another of the strongest of them. During Clay's lifetime, a balance did indeed endure that permitted the efflorescence of an American civilization and republican liberty through the mutual contributions and antagonisms of different sections, subcultures, classes, and economies. But that balance was an accident of history, not a law of nature. At the end of Clay's life, it was beginning to disappear as subordinate sections began to define themselves as separate civilizations in their own right, and not long after Clay's death, it broke asunder as the two contested for dominance over the Union. The flaw of Henry Clay, then, was not his alone but that of the Republic he sought and failed to govern.

But even as he exited the national stage, there was already another politician, to whom Henry Clay was "my beau ideal of a statesman, the man for whom I fought all my humble life,"[24] who could formulate an orthodoxy of fundamental moral absolutes, however dubious. The doctrine of acquisitive egalitarianism that Abraham Lincoln asserted was not that of the Framers or the early Republic and most certainly not that which Henry Clay assumed to be inherent in the universe. It was, however, better suited to the satisfaction of the *libido dominandi* and the winning of the presidency than anything Clay had imagined, and Lincoln's ambition, far more than Henry Clay's, was what the future president's law partner called "a little engine that knew no rest."[25]

24. Quoted in Eaton, *Henry Clay,* 93.
25. Quoted in Shelby Foote, *The Civil War: A Narrative, Fort Sumter to Perryville* (New York: Random House, 1958), 20.

Message from MARs
The Social Politics of the New Right

The label "New Right" is at best a confusing one. In the first place, what the label represents is not entirely new, since many of its themes, values, and interests have been expounded to one degree or another by the Old Right of the 1950s and 1960s. In the second place, it is not entirely "Right," since other ideals and values associated with it have seldom been expressed by conservatives of any generation. The New Right is perhaps best known for its populism and its heated contempt for elitism and "limousine liberals." Its polemical exchanges with the Left (and even, sometimes, with the Right) often display a bitterness that was lacking in the amiable sparring bouts of Mr. Buckley and Professor Galbraith. Moreover, the New Right voices no small amount of antibusiness (not to say anticapitalist) rhetoric. Bankers, multinational corporations, Big Business, and The Rich occupy a distinct circle in the New Right vision of the Inferno. The symbols of wealth are also important in its demonology: the Ivy League, the country club, and the Trilateral Commission. Orthodox conservatives of the Old Right generally deprecate, smile at, or strain themselves ridiculing such gaucherie.

Yet, if the New Right is often the victim of its own rhetoric, it can, in 1980, lay claim to something that the Old Right can never claim. Political commentators will no doubt debate for years whether the Republican capture of the White House and Senate in 1980 was or was not due to New Right efforts alone, but they have never debated, and never will, whether the Old Right elected Barry Goldwater in 1964—or Robert Taft in 1952—or Herbert Hoover in 1932. The New Right in 1981, and for some years to come, has what the Old Right could never claim: a national constituency, and the clear possibility of political victory, if not political dominance, in the United States for the remainder of the century.

Despite the incoherence of its name and sometimes of its message, the New Right represents far more than a political ideology or an electoral coalition. The New Right is the political expression of a profound social movement that reflects the dynamics of American society and promises to dominate not only politically, but also perhaps socially and culturally. The origins of the New Right in a social movement explain why its political message often appears to be incoherent, contradictory, or simplistic. What the New Right has to say is not premeditated in the inner sanctums of tax-exempt foundations or debated in the stately prose of quarterly or fortnightly journals. The contents of its message are perceived injustices, unrelieved exploitation by anonymous powers that be, a threatened future, and an insulted past. It is therefore understandable that the New Right has less use for the rhetorical trope and the extended syllogism than for the mass rally and the truth squad and that some of its adherents sometimes fantasize that the cartridge box is a not-unsatisfactory substitute for the ballot box.

The social movement that the New Right expresses and whose values, resentments, aspirations, and fears it tries to articulate is composed of what sociologist Donald I. Warren calls "Middle American Radicals"—MARs. This movement, in Professor Warren's description, is less an objectively identifiable class than a subjectively distinguished temperament, yet it possesses verifiable features that set it apart from other social groups and formations. In the mid–1970s, MARs had a family income of three to thirteen thousand dollars. There was a strong presence among them of northern European ethnics, although Italians tended to account for more MARs than other groups. MARs were nearly twice as common in the South as in the north-central states. They tended to have completed high school but not to have attended college. They were more common among Catholics and Jews than among Protestants and among Mormons and Baptists than among other Protestant sects. They tended to be in their thirties or in their sixties and were "significantly less likely to be professional or managerial workers" than to be "skilled and semi-skilled blue collar workers."[1]

Yet these statistical features do not define MARs. What defines them as a movement is an attitudinal quality, and what Warren finds most distinctive of them is their view of government and, in a broader

---

1. Donald I. Warren, *The Radical Center: Middle Americans and the Politics of Alienation* (Notre Dame: University of Notre Dame, 1976), 23–29.

sense, of the "establishment" and their role in it. Unlike adherents of the Left, MARs do not regard the government as favoring the rich, and, unlike adherents of the Right, they do not regard the government as giving too much to the poor. According to Warren,

> MARs are a distinct group partly because of their view of government as favoring both the rich and the poor simultaneously. . . . MARs are distinct in the depth of their feeling that the middle class has been seriously neglected. If there is one single summation of the MAR perspective, it is reflected in a statement which was read to respondents: *The rich give in to the demands of the poor, and the middle income people have to pay the bill.*[2]

This attitude is resonant with significant social and political implications. It points to a sense of resentment and exploitation, mainly economic but also broader, that is directed upwards as well as downwards. It points to distrust of decision-makers in state and economy as well as to fear of the economically depressed. It points also to the frustration of aspirations, to an alienation of loyalties, and to a suspicion of established institutions, authorities, and values.

The economic frustrations of MARs, as represented in the above quotation, spill over into political, cultural, and moral expression. The objective features of the MAR profile, coupled with awareness of MAR political ferocity in New Right protests, from the antibusing movements of the early 1970s to the Panama Canal and anti-ERA mobilizations of 1977–1978, should substantiate the movement as social rather than political in a narrow sense. MARs form a class— not simply a middle class and not simply an economic category— that is in revolt against the dominant patterns and structures of American society. They are, in the broadest sense, a political class, and they aspire, through the New Right, to become the dominant political class in the United States by displacing the current elite, dismantling its apparatus of power, and discrediting its political ideology.

"Ruling classes," wrote Gaetano Mosca, the great Italian political scientist of the early twentieth century, "do not justify their power exclusively by de facto possession of it, but try to find a moral and legal basis for it, representing it as the logical and necessary consequence of doctrines and beliefs that are generally recognized and

2. Ibid., 20–21.

accepted."[3] The current elite in the United States, which has held both political and social power since the 1930s, is no exception. Its ideology or political formula, by which it rationalizes its power, is generally known as liberalism—a set of ideas and values that ostensibly eschews power and upholds equality, liberty, and the brotherhood of man, but which is amazingly congruent with and adaptable to the political, economic, and social interests (the structural interests) of the groups that espouse it.

This elite seized power in the political and economic crisis of the Great Depression. The chief instrument of its rise to power, then and in the following decades, was the state, especially the federal government, and more especially the executive branch. Through the state, it made common cause with certain mass organizations— large corporations, labor unions, universities, foundations, and the media—and has generally favored their expansion and strengthening at the expense of smaller-scale units. In domestic affairs it has supported federally enforced economic planning and social engineering for the purpose (at least ostensibly) of realizing its liberal ideology. In foreign affairs, it has favored international activism through similar large-scale organizations and transnational alliances that seem to promote global fraternity and the disappearance of national distinctions and differences. In political theory it abandoned the ideal of a neutral government based on impartial laws and administering equal justice and associated itself with a concept of the state as intimately involved in social and economic processes and as an architect of desirable social change. This concept of the state has been buttressed by a variety of pseudoscientific ideologies— psychoanalysis, behaviorism, legal positivism, applied sociology, Marxism *manqué,* educational progressivism, etc.—most of which are logically incompatible with liberalism but are nevertheless abridged, distorted, and popularized into congruence with current ideological fixations.

It is in its cultural and social ideologies and life-styles that the new elite has developed what is probably the clearest indicator of

3. Gaetano Mosca, *The Ruling Class (Elementi di Scienza Politica),* ed. Arthur Livingston, trans. Hannah D. Kahn (New York: McGraw-Hill Book Company, 1939), 70.

its dominant position. The life-styles, aspirations, and values of the current elite are bound together, rationalized, and extended by what may be called the "cosmopolitan ethic." This ethic expresses an open contempt for what Edmund Burke called the "little platoons" of human society—the small town, the family, the neighborhood, the traditional class identities and their relationships—as well as for authoritative and disciplinary institutions—the army, the police, parental authority, and the disciplines of school and church. The cosmopolitan ethic, reversing a Western tradition as old as Aesop, finds virtue in the large city, in the anonymous (and therefore "liberated") relationships of de-classed, de-sexed, demoralized, and deracinated atoms that know no group or national identities, accept no given moral code, and recognize no disciplines and no limits. The ethic idealizes material indulgence, the glorification of the self, and the transcendence of conventional values, loyalties, and social bonds. At the same time, it denigrates the values of self-sacrifice, community, and moral and social order. Its most perfect (though extreme) expression is perhaps Mick Jagger, but a more typical and vapid form is portrayed in advertisements that tell us What Kind of Man Reads *Playboy*.

The ideology or formula of liberalism grows out of the structural interests of the elite that espouses it. Liberalism barely exists as an independent set of ideas and values. Virtually no significant thinker of this century has endorsed it. Internally, the doctrines of liberalism are so contrary to established fact, inconsistent with each other, and immersed in sentimentalism, resentment, egotism, and self-interest that they cannot be taken seriously as a body of ideas. Liberalism flourishes almost entirely because it reflects the material and psychological interests of a privileged, power-holding, and power-seeking sector of American society.

In the early twentieth century, the increasing massiveness of American society appeared to demand new organizational forms of control. The imperatives of mass scale in the economy, in government and politics, and in social and cultural life gave rise to a new elite that found its principal power base in bureaucracy. In both the public and private sectors, the bureaucratic organization of power and control appeared to be the only means of ruling modern mass units. In the private sector the evolution of bureaucratic dominance followed the "separation of ownership and control" in the large corporations and took the form of managerial direction of large corporate firms. In government, modern bureaucracy developed in a more sudden and revolutionary way in the crisis of the Great Depression. Yet there was no fundamental difference between the interests of the bureaucrats of the public sector and those of the private sector. Both bureaucratic realms shared a common mentality: a rationalistic faith in administrative and manipulative techniques as a means of holding and exercising power. Both sectors, perhaps more importantly, shared certain common material interests: the more massive the scale of organization, the more imperative the bureaucratic-managerial form of organization and the more power and material rewards that accrued to the elites that controlled such organizations. The same or similar interests and imperatives pertained in all mass-scale organizations, and the same dominant bureaucratic functions developed in control of the mass unions. Similarly, but more recently, the media of mass communication (in almost every form—book publishing, news reporting, entertainment, documentaries, etc.) have displayed the same dynamic of elite formation, and, most recently, the instruments of legitimate force—the armed forces and the larger metropolitan police departments—display it also. Unlike the older, more localized and personal elites of American society, the new elite possesses a more uniform mentality and a more homogeneous interest: the expansion of mass units of organization under the bureaucratic forms of governance, animated by an ideology of manipulative, administrative social engineering.

From its very nature, therefore, the new elite found liberalism a useful and indeed indispensable formula for rationalizing its existence and power. Modern liberalism justified government on a mass scale and bureaucratic manipulation of social and economic processes. Liberalism allowed for an economy led by mass corporations, themselves governed by "progressive" executives whose positions depended on merit and schooling in managerial sciences, and not on inheritance, experience, or the virtues of the Protestant ethic. Liberalism championed schooling itself, especially education (also on a mass scale) that emphasized the practical disciplines of social science, public administration, and modern business management. Finally, liberalism, at its very center, articulated a vision of man that not only rationalized bureaucratic manipulation of the social environment but also laid the groundwork for the cosmopolitan ethic. The great value of this ethic in the rise of the new bureaucratic elite was its discrediting and delegitimization of the formulas and ideologies of its older rivals. Liberalism and cosmopolitanism were able, through their immense appeal to an intelligentsia, to portray localism and decentralized institutions as provincial and a mask for bigotry and selfishness; the small town, the family, class, religious, ethnic, and community ties as backward, repressive, and exploitative; the values of work, thrift, discipline, sacrifice, and postponement of gratification (on which, as values, the moral legitimacy of the older elites rested) as outmoded, absolutist, puritanical, superstitious, and not infrequently hypocritical.

A more direct connection between the material interests of the new elite and the semicollectivist ideology of liberalism exists also. The mass economy of the twentieth century requires a mass level of consumption for the financing of its productive capacities. Due to the inability of lending institutions in the Great Depression to mobilize sufficient credit for the resumption of production, the federal government undertook labor policies, transfer programs, and pension policies designed to insure sufficient demand for the mass economy to function. The immediate beneficiary of these policies, of course, was the impoverished underclass of American society, but the ultimate beneficiaries were the new managerial and bureaucratic elites in corporation and government. The stimulation of demand through government policy—a policy financed by middle-class taxpayers and consumers—insured the existence and dominance of the mass organizations of government, corporation, and union and their managerial elites. At the same time, this policy cemented an alliance, not only among the different sectors of the new elite, but also between the new elite as a whole and the proletariat of American society—against the remnants of the old elite and an exploited and excluded middle class.[4]

4. The alliance of elite and underclass against the middle class—what I have here called the "sandwich strategy"—has been noted by, among others, New Right political theorists Robert W. Whitaker, *A Plague on Both Your Houses* (Washington: Robert B. Luce, 1976), chap. 4; and William A. Rusher, *The Making of a New Majority Party* (Ottawa, Ill.: Green Hill Publishers, 1975), 33.

The new elite, following a pattern that has been repeated many times in human history, also found that the aggrandizement of the federal executive branch was conducive to its revolution. The older elites were based mainly in local and state governments and in the Congress. The Caesarist political style of the new elite made use of the presidency, under Roosevelt and Truman and their successors, to attack, wear down, usurp, and discredit the authority and powers of both state and local bodies and the Congress. In this new political style, the rising managerial elite was following a pattern evident in the careers of Pericles, Caesar, Henry Tudor, Louis XIV, and Napoleon Bonaparte. Older elites, entrenched in established institutions, are attacked by newer social formations that make alliances with charismatic leaders exercising autocratic power and with an underclass that receives material benefits expropriated from the old elite. New, centralized institutions controlled by the new elite develop in place of the localized institutions of the old rulers.

A pattern often associated with this "sandwich" attack on an old elite by an alliance of an underclass and an autocrat who represents an emerging elite is an activist and expansionist foreign policy led by the new men in opposition to the passive, often isolationist policies associated with the old ruling class. Thus, Pericles promoted Athenian imperialism through enfranchisement of the lower-class crews of the Athenian navy and against the interests of the landed, inward-looking Attic oligarchy. Caesar's revolution in Rome, made possible by his patronage of the lower classes, was to be extended in imperial-military adventures in the East, but this was cut short by his assassination. The Tudors, Louis XIV, and Napoleon all embarked on expansionist foreign policies that sought to benefit the aspirations and interests of the new elites on which their own power was based. The older elites oppose expansionism because their own power bases are not equipped to profit from it and indeed are frequently threatened by the rise of new powers and forces in the newly acquired territories.

This pattern also was present in the revolution of the managerial elite of the depression–World War II era. The Old Guard of the Republican party, representing the old elite, was isolationist in both world wars. The new elite found both its economic and political interests benefited by an activist, globalist foreign policy. The new political structures revolving around international and regional blocs, new markets and trade arrangements, and new internal institutions for international relations and conflict were all congruent with the interests of the new elite in government, industry and finance, education, and labor.

It is against this elite—which Irving Kristol and others somewhat belatedly call the "New Class" but which James Burnham more accurately (and much earlier) called the "managerial class"[5]—that the New Right with its MAR social base operates. It would be tendentious to claim that the ideologies and institutions of the managerial elite are purely self-serving while claiming also that those of the MARs are objectively true, public-spirited, in the general interest, and morally pure. The MARs form a sociopolitical force now coalescing into a class and perhaps into a new elite that will replace the managerial elite. As a rising political class, the MARs have their own interests, aspirations, and values, and these are not intended to benefit the nation, society as a whole, or humanity. Nevertheless, the structural interests of the MARs—what is of benefit to them because of their position and functions in American society—may be beneficial to America as well. The MARs, and similar social forces now developing in the Sunbelt, promise a new dynamism in America—economically as well as spiritually—in place of the now decadent and moribund managerial elite. They offer also a discipline, a code of sacrifice for something larger than themselves, and a new purpose that are beyond the reach of the jaded, self-indulgent, increasingly corrupt elite of the present day. The MARs are not better or worse than other human beings in other social formations, but the objective interests of their own formation appear to dictate a social order quite different from, and probably better than, that designed, manipulated, and misruled by the managerial class and its cohorts.

5. See Irving Kristol, *Two Cheers for Capitalism* (New York: New American Library, 1979), especially chap. 2. Kristol's idea of the "New Class" is apparently limited to the public sector and media and does not extend to large corporations. James Burnham, *The Managerial Revolution: What Is Happening in the World* (New York: John Day Company, 1941), despite its age and problems, remains to my mind the most accurate and comprehensive account of the New Class, its ideology, interests, and dynamics. For a fuller discussion of the New Class, see B. Bruce-Briggs, ed., *The New Class?* (New Brunswick, N. J.: Transaction Books, 1979).

What the MARs and the New Right seek, then, is the overthrow of the present elite and its replacement by themselves. This is a revolutionary goal, no less so than the goal of the rising managers of the early part of the century. It is revolutionary not in the sense that its realization will require violent rebellion, mass liquidation, or totalitarian rule—these are not envisioned by the New Right and would be antithetical to MAR interests—but in the sense that the replacement of one elite by another almost always leads to a cultural renaissance, to new and dynamic forces that alter ideas and institutions, and to an efflorescence of material and spiritual life.

Yet the New Right will not be the spearhead of the Middle American Revolution if it is concerned only with politics in its narrow, formal sense. It must go beyond the tactics of electoral coalitions and roll-call votes and develop a strategy for the seizure of real social power. Real power is not limited to control of the formal apparatus of government but extends to the levers by which human societies are controlled—to the media of communication, the means of production, and the instruments of force. At the present time these levers of social control and real social power are almost entirely dominated by the managerial elite or are negated by it. Merely formal control of the political apparatus will not alter this fact. The New Right–MAR coalition must seek to dismantle or radically reform the managerial apparatus of social control, and this objective means a far more radical approach to political conflict and to contemporary institutions. The strategic objective of the New Right must be the localization, privatization, and decentralization of the managerial apparatus of power. Concretely, this means a dismantling of the corporate, educational, labor, and media bureaucracies; a devolution to more modest-scale organizational units; and a reorientation of federal rewards from mass-scale units and hierarchies to smaller and more local ones.

To include the large corporations in the "enemies list" of the New Right may strike many adherents of the Old Right as odd or even as subversive. Yet libertarians have long recognized that large, publicly owned, manager-dominated corporations have interests and political orientations quite different from those of small, privately owned and controlled enterprises. As G. William Domhoff, a radical sociologist, has recognized,

The businesspeople who were most isolationist, antiwelfare and antilabor were more likely to be in NAM [National Association of Manufacturers] and to be associated with smaller and more regional corporations. Those who were more moderate [i.e., more liberal] were more likely to be in CED [Committee for Economic Development] and to manage larger companies. More recently, our study of the corporate interlocks of CED and NAM leaders revealed the same large/small dichotomy. For example, NAM's directors for 1972 had only 9 connections to the top 25 banks, whereas CED had 63. Similarly, NAM had but 10 connections to the 25 largest industrials, while CED had 48. The findings were similar for insurance, transport, utilities and retails.[6]

The present managerial elite, whether in the public or private sector, has a vested interest in centralized decision making and collective organization. The dynamic of MAR interests dictates ultimately a policy of localization and privatization of real social power in both the public and private sectors. Only by unleashing the now over-regulated, overtaxed, and unrewarded MAR social and economic forces can their innovative and productive potential be developed. This unleashing of MAR forces can come about only by dismantling the managerial power structure.

To call the New Right "conservative," then, is true only in a rather abstruse sense. Its social and cultural values are indeed conservative and traditionalist, but, unlike almost any other conservative group in history, it finds itself not only out of power in a formal sense but also excluded from the informal centers of real power. Consequently, the political style, tactics, and organizational forms of the New Right should find a radical, antiestablishment approach better adapted to the achievement of its goals. Ideologically, much in the formulas and theory (in so far as there is any) of the New Right derives from exponents of the Old Right. Yet the premise of almost all Old Right publicists has been that the values and institutions they were defending were part of an establishment that was under revolutionary attack. For much of the period in which the Old Right flourished, this premise was correct. Today, however, and since at least the mid

6. G. William Domhoff, *The Powers That Be: Processes of Ruling-Class Domination in America* (New York: Random House, 1978), 85; see also John Chamberlain, "The New Enterprising Americans," *Policy Review*, No. 13 (Summer 1980): 36, on "the preponderance of small-scale Middle Western enterprisers on the board of trustees" of conservative Hillsdale College, Michigan, and their criticism of Big Business.

1960s, the revolution of mass and managers has triumphed, entrenched itself as a new elite, and indeed has revealed strong signs of ossification and decadence. The Old Right failed to arrest the revolution mainly because it lacked an adequate social base. Its powerful, well-honed, but esoteric critique of liberal ideology appealed to few save the most sophisticated intellectuals and the declining entrepreneurial elite whose interests and values were reflected in conservative theory.

The New Right must consciously abandon much of the inertial conservatism of its Old Right premises. It must cease congratulating itself on its ability to raise money and win elections within the system developed by the present establishment and begin to formulate a strategy for besieging the establishment. With its MAR social base, the New Right is in a strong position to develop such a strategy, and there are signs it is doing so. Some New Right groups have successfully politicized sections of American society. Smaller businessmen, broadcasters, clergy, parent groups, and other institutional representatives have played an active and important role in New Right political campaigns. However, a key element in the success of the New Right will be its ability to focus on how the establishment uses its apparatus of power in the media, corporations, schools, etc., for political domination and exploitation. This has been made reasonably clear with regard to the bureaucracy and the unions, but other institutional supports of the liberal managerial elite need exposure as well.

In economics, the Old Right has consistently defended the free market. While there is much to be said for the renaissance of free market ideas led by Ludwig von Mises, F. A. Hayek, Milton Friedman, Arthur Laffer, and others, it is doubtful that the MAR coalition and its allies in the Sunbelt's entrepreneurial regions will continue to focus on this classical liberal principle. It is more likely that MAR-Sunbelt interests require a strong governmental role in maintaining economic privileges for the elderly and for unionized labor (where it now exists), that they will also require (or demand) subsidization of construction and perhaps of characteristic Sunbelt enterprises (energy, defense and aerospace industries, and agriculture). One New Right tactic would be payment of these subsidies and privileges out of the proceeds of taxing the Frostbelt and reorienting economic policy and legislation toward the South and West. For the New Right to embrace such a tactic openly (as well as a more favorable attitude toward protectionism) would be a frank recognition that the classical liberal idea of a night-watchman state is an illusion and that a MAR elite would make use of the state for its own interests as willingly as the present managerial elite does. MAR resentment of welfare, paternalism, and regulation is not based on a profound faith in the market but simply on the sense of injustice that unfair welfare programs, taxes, and stifling regulation have bred. The central focus of MAR–New Right political economy is likely to be economic growth, a value often confused with, sometimes encompassing, but not identical to the free market.

Clearly, economic growth involves the lifting of most legal and administrative restraints on enterprise—the demise of environmentalist legislation, OSHA, the sale of federally owned land in the Far West, etc. But it would also include government assistance to dynamic but underfed sectors of the economy—e.g., the space program and new technology forms. The role of government in stimulating growth is no less inconsistent with free market ideals than its role in retarding growth, and since the social forces of the New Right would have a strong interest in the former role, there is little value in their adherence to a strict laissez-faire ideology.

The promotion of a "no-growth" cultus by powerful elements of the current liberal managerial elite is strong evidence of its decadence and ossification. The "selective isolationism" in foreign policy, the withdrawal from the Third World and the conflict with the Soviets, and the guilt experienced for our past foreign policy are also indications of decadence. The fundamental reason for the fall of Vietnam, the U.S. retreat from Angola, the betrayal of Somoza, the desertion of Taiwan, and the collapse of the Shah (as well as the weakening of our commitments to other Third World allies) lies in the inability of our present elite to deal effectively with the often brutal realities of the Third World, in the failure of the liberal formulas of the elite to rationalize necessary and desirable policies for dealing with these realities, and in a preference by the elite to deal with other elites similar to itself in developed regions (Japan, Western Europe, and the Soviet Union). The rationalistic, administrative, and technical skills on which the power of the managerial class is based are of little value in underdeveloped regions, especially where violent resistance to planning and manipulation requires a more coercive response than managerial ideology can justify.

Moreover, the material interests of the elite, as well as its psychic interests and ideological orientation, impel it toward the developed world. Ideologically, the current elite distrusts nationalism and favors internationalist and regionalist units of organization (the United Nations, the Common Market, the British Commonwealth, the Atlantic Community, etc.). This preference is in accord with its cosmopolitan ethic, but it also is consistent with the economic interests of the large corporate entities. Free trade, the integration of international markets, and the stabilization of international relations all reflect the interests of the transnational elites that dominate in the developed countries. In contrast, smaller producers situated in the Sunbelt require protection against cheap imports and access to the raw materials and resources of the Third World, and they are less committed to international stability than to the continued predominance of the United States.

The foreign policy of the New Right, then, reflecting the interests and values of its MAR-Sunbelt-neo-entrepreneurial base, is likely to endorse a new nationalism that insists on the military and economic preeminence of the United States, on international activism (and even expansionism) in world affairs, on at least some measure of protection for domestic producers, and for more resistance to Third World arrogance, aggression, and barbarism. The controversy over the Trilateral Commission, whatever its merits, reflects this conflict over foreign policy between the social forces of the dominant elite and those of the New Right. The commission is essentially the forum of the elite and its multinational components; as such, it has become a symbol of the resentments of MARs and the forces of the Sunbelt.[7] Moreover, the nationalism of the New Right will probably replace the anticommunism of the Old Right as a focus of foreign policy. While the Soviet Union, Cuba, and their allies remain the principal threat to the United States and our predominance, New Right elements are likely to focus on the threat itself rather than the ideologi-

7. Thomas Ferguson and Joel Rogers, "Another Trilateral Election?" *Nation* (June 28, 1980): 783–84.

cal origins of the threat. The distinction between the nationalist focus of the New Right and the anticommunist orientation of the Old became clear in the opposition to the Panama Canal Treaty. While Old Right anticommunists sought to portray Panamanian dictator Omar Torrijos as a Marxist, this was a far less effective tactic than Ronald Reagan's New Right, nationalist slogan on the canal—"We built it, we paid for it, and it's ours."

The nationalism of the New Right points to what is perhaps its best-known characteristic, the rejection of the cosmopolitan ethic of the managerial elite and a thunderous defense of moral and social traditionalism. The most offensive component of cosmopolitanism to MARs is its abstract universalism, its refusal to make any distinctions or discriminations among human beings. The brotherhood of man, egalitarianism, the relativization of moral values, and the rejection of conventional social and cultural identities as obsolete and repressive all derive from this universalist tendency. In its place, the central formula of the rising MAR-Sunbelt elite is likely to form around what may be called a domestic ethic that centers on the family, the neighborhood and local community, the church, and the nation as the basic framework of values. The values associated with the domestic ethic will contrast sharply with those of cosmopolitanism: the duty of work rather than the right of welfare; the value of loyalty to concrete persons, symbols, and institutions rather than the cosmopolitan dispersion of loyalties; and the social and human necessity of sacrifice and deferral of gratification rather than the cosmopolitan-managerial demand for immediate gratification, indulgence, and consumption. The domestic ethic may also lay the basis for a more harmonious relationship between employer and worker, since the place of work itself can be portrayed as an institution no less central than the family or the local community. The common interest of workers and employers in opposing the restrictive, stagnationist policies of the managerial elite is one element of New Right rhetoric that could develop into this harmony, and the explicit approach to blue-collar workers by recent New Right candidates appears to confirm this trend.

Out of the structural interests and residual values of the MARs, and similar forces in the Sunbelt and in new entrepreneurial forces throughout the country, the New Right can construct a formula or ideology. This formula will reflect the demands for economic growth, a more aggressively nationalistic foreign policy, and an assertion of traditionalist ethics and loyalties. It will not be conservative although it will encompass some ideas of the Old Right and reject others. It will, in fact, be a radical formula, demanding changes not only in the formal appearance of power but also in the realities of the distribution and uses of power in its social forms. As a radical movement, representing rising social forces against an ossified elite, the New Right must abandon the political style of the Old Right. That style, based on the premise that the Old Right represented an establishment, sought to defend the intermediary institutions against the Caesarist, leveling forces of the new managerial elite. The managerial class, however, has long since become the establishment and shows signs of abandoning the executive branch as a spearhead of its power-seizure. The New Right, therefore, should make use of the presidency as its own spearhead against the entrenched elite and should dwell on the fact that the intermediary bodies—Congress, the courts, the bureaucracy, the media, etc.—are the main supports of the elite. The adoption of the Caesarist tactic by the New Right would reflect the historical pattern by which rising classes ally with an executive power to displace the oligarchy that is entrenched in the intermediate bodies.

Jeffrey Hart has suggested this idea of a New Right–Caesarist style based on the presidency, but apparently without attracting broad support.[8] While the New Right can expect to make gains in Congress and state and local governments, only the presidency—as Nixon and Agnew showed—has the visibility and resources to cut through the intractable establishment of bureaucracy and media to reach the MAR social base directly. Only the presidency is capable of dismantling or restructuring the bureaucratic-managerial apparatus that now strangles the latent dynamism of the MAR-Sunbelt social forces. The key to this Caesarist strategy is that the New Right does not now represent an elite but a subelite, that it must acquire real social power and not preserve it in its current distribution. The intermediate institutions of contemporary America—the bureaucracy, the media,

8. Jeffrey Hart, "The Presidency: Shifting Conservative Perspectives?" *National Review* (November 22, 1974): 1351–55.

the managerial hierarchies of the mass unions and corporations, the universities and foundations, the urban conglomerates—are not allies of the New Right and are not conservative influences except in the sense that they serve to protect established powers. Hence, the New Right should not defend these structures but should expose them as the power preserves of the entrenched elite whose values and interests are hostile to the traditional American ethos and as parasitical tumors on the body of Middle America. These structures should be levelled or at least radically reformed, and only the presidency has the power and the resources to begin the process and to mobilize popular support for it.

The characterization of the New Right presented in this essay is unconventional and will perhaps be controversial. The New Right is not merely an electoral coalition concerned with winning elections and roll calls; it is the political expression of a relatively new social movement that regards itself as the depository of traditional American values and as the exploited victim of the alliance between an entrenched elite and a ravenous proletariat. Viewed in this sociopolitical perspective, the New Right is not a conservative force but a radical or revolutionary one. It seeks the displacement of the entrenched elite, the discarding of its ideology of liberalism and cosmopolitanism, and its own victory as a new governing class in America. The New Right is able to aspire to these ambitions because, unlike the Old Right, it has a viable social base in the Middle American Radicals and in the dynamic economy of the Sunbelt.

If the New Right is not conservative, it should be clear that it will need a new ideology, formula, or political theory that can win the loyalties and represent the interests of its social base and rationalize its quest for social and political power. The primary justification of its quest for power must be the corruption, decadence, incompetence, oppressiveness, and alienation of the old elite that it is seeking to displace. This elite—identified here as the managerial class that rose to power in the government bureaucracy, large corporations, and other modern mass-scale organizations since the 1930s—is clearly foreign to the bulk of the nation in its life-style, values, and ideals. Yet these life-styles, values, and ideals cannot be simply discarded by the old elite; they represent a logical outgrowth of its own structural interests: large, social engineering government in alliance with corporations, universities and foundations, the mass media, unions, and other bureaucracies. Only the cosmopolitan ethic and liberal ideology described above can rationalize these structural interests of the entrenched elite. The fundamental problem is not the ethic or ideology of the elite but the elite itself, and it is the elite and its apparatus of power that must be the main targets of New Right attack.

The principal values to which the New Right should appeal in this attack differ from those defended by the Old Right as well as from those articulated by the managerial elite. In place of the free market of the Old Right or the "stabilization" of the present elite, the New Right should center its economic aspirations on the concept of economic growth. Clearly, the concept of growth involves a dismantling of bureaucracy, regulation, fiscal and environmentalist policies, and a decentralization and privatization of economic forces, but this reorientation toward a freer economic climate is incidental to the central idea of economic growth, expansion, and dynamism. In place of the strictly anticommunist foreign policy of the Old Right or the selective isolationism of the decadent managerial class, the New Right should assert a foreign policy founded on a new activist and expansionist nationalism—a policy that would necessarily encompass Old Right anticommunism but would also respond to rising noncommunist threats. In place of the hedonistic, pragmatist, relativist, and secularized cosmopolitanism of the present elite, the New Right should expound without compromise the ideals and institutions of the American ethos: hard work and self-sacrifice, morally based legislation and policies, and a public commitment to religious faith. In place of the faith in congressional supremacy and established intermediary institutions that characterizes both the Old Right and the entrenched managerial elite, the New Right will favor a populist-based presidency able to cut through the present oligarchical establishment and to promote new intermediary institutions centered on Middle America.

The conflict into which the New Right is entering is a complex one. Because of its complexity, the political expression of the MARs cannot take forms that are entirely consistent in ideology or calculated to please everyone within its own ranks. Because the issues and values are real and not the product of abstract cerebration, there will probably be no monolithic movement under the New Right aegis. There will be a coalition that will often find itself split, and the opponents of the New Right will of course seek to take advantage of these splits. Hence, the political movement requires, more than is customary in American political history, a discipline, a leadership, and a formula that will promote its cohesion, its electoral advantages, and its objectives.

The late Carroll Quigley argued that new civilizations form themselves around dynamic, innovative social forces, which he called "instruments." As these instruments develop, they acquire vested interests that retard their dynamism and slow their innovative capacities. The instruments then become ossified "institutions" that oppose the rise of new forces and, unless challenged, lead to civilizational decay.[9] The managerial elite as described in this essay began its history as an "instrument" and is now in a stage of what Quigley would call "institutionalization." In its youth it was a force for much innovation, expansion, and cultural dynamism. In its senescence it is a force only for itself and for the cultivation of self-indulgence, both material and psychological. Its power is being challenged by a new force, also described above; if victorious, no doubt the MARs themselves will exploit their rivals and, like all men, have much to answer for. No doubt also the new elite that they will form will someday degenerate and itself be challenged by new dynamic forces. But the choice between the present elite and its challengers is not merely between one power and another. It is a choice between degeneration and rebirth, between death and survival, for survival is not a right or a gift freely granted by the powers that be. Survival, in the jungle or in political societies, is a hard-won prize that depends ultimately on power itself. In this world, wrote Goethe, one must be the hammer or the anvil. The essence of the message from MARs is that the messengers want to work the forge.

9. Carroll Quigley, *The Evolution of Civilizations: An Introduction to Historical Analysis* (New York: Macmillan Company, 1961), 73–74.

Prophet of the Heartland

The conservative movement in the United States has come a long way, politically and intellectually, since the death of Willmoore Kendall in 1967. Although the successes of conservatism could not easily have been predicted in the early 1960s, when Kendall's thought flourished, they would not have surprised him, for it was the essence of his political thought that the American people were profoundly committed to conservative principle and deeply hostile to liberalism and ideological experimentation with their lives and government. On the other hand, certain recent trends in conservative thought and politics—a seeming preoccupation with "respectability" and "credibility" and an inclination to dilute the expression of its commitments in return for acceptance by the establishment—would surely have angered him. Kendall called himself an "Appalachians-to-the-Rockies patriot,"[1] and he was both temperamentally and philosophically incapable of living in peace with the dominant structures of the Northeast. Nor, were he living today, would Kendall have been silent about such trends. In his last years he was working on a book that was to deal with the contemporary "sages" of the renaissance of conservative thought in the 1950s (Russell Kirk, James Burnham, and William F. Buckley, Jr., among others), and what we know of this project suggests that he had some critical, even unkind, things to say about his colleagues. There is a legend about Kendall that at *National Review* he was never on speaking terms with more than one associate at any one time. He was not a man to allow personal friendship to stand in the way of what he took to be philosophical truth and political rectitude, nor would he have permitted political success to deflect his perception of truth and rightness.

Kendall's understanding of what constitutes conservatism is often described as "populist," and it is true that the persistent theme throughout most of his work is that the locus of political virtue in

1. George H. Nash, *The Conservative Intellectual Movement in America since 1945* (New York: Basic Books, 1976), 242.

the United States resides in the American people and is expressed in their majority will through the deliberate processes of the Constitution. Only in his last years did he incline to the view that a "select minority" must keep the people virtuous, and to the natural rights theory put forward by Leo Strauss. Despite these flirtations, the characteristic of Kendall's political thought is his unrelenting defense of the historic mainstream, the heartland, of American society against a radical and basically un-American establishment, and the value of his ideas for political conservatism today is that they offer a framework for attacking the establishment. It is likely that Kendall, a Rhodes Scholar and Ivy League professor, knew the temptations of celebrity and accommodation to which intellectuals, whether conservative or not, are particularly susceptible and that that is why his polemics with his conservative colleagues were so fierce and his criterion of true conservatism so strict.

Yet if his standard was strict, it was not narrow. It was not Kendall's intention to exclude from conservative ranks everyone but himself, and indeed much of his criticism of rival conservative theorists dwelled on what he took to be their own idiosyncratic, dogmatic, and narrow doctrines that effectively ostracized everyone but themselves. "I make no sense," he wrote,

> of calling "Conservative" the man who takes a dim view of his country's established institutions, feels something less than at home with its way of life as it actually lives it, finds it difficult to identify himself with the political and moral principles on which it has acted through its history, dislikes or views with contempt the generality of the kind of people his society produces, and—above all perhaps—dissociates himself from its Founders, or at least holds them at arms' length.[2]

Indeed, the key to Kendall's thought is contained in the phrase about a "country's way of life as it actually lives it." "All political societies," he wrote,

> all peoples, but especially I like to think our political society, this "*people of the United States,*" is founded upon what political philosophers call a *consensus;* that is, a hard core of shared beliefs. Those beliefs that the people

---

2. Willmoore Kendall, *The Conservative Affirmation* (Chicago: Henry Regnery Company, 1963), ix.

share are what defines its character as a political society, what embodies its meaning as a political society, what, above all perhaps, expresses its understanding of itself as a political society, of its role and responsibility in history, of its very destiny.[3]

It was in terms of the "way of life," or public orthodoxy, of a country, its ethos, identity, or consensus, that Kendall defined conservatism, the disposition, articulated by intellectuals or not, to defend and conserve the fundamental identity of a society, including its political institutions and government. It was because of this way of life and the threats presented to it by its enemies that congressional committees for the investigation of activities outside and hostile to it were justified. It was because of the existence of the public orthodoxy that Kendall understood that the United States is not an "open society," a society that remains officially and perpetually uncommitted to all principles and values and suspends judgments as to whether some principles are true or false, but rather a society that holds, as Kendall put it, "at the very moment of its birth," the truth of some principles to be self-evident and is therefore closed to the serious consideration of, or even to very much tolerance for, principles and parties that challenge such publicly acknowledged truths. And it is because of the way of life of a society that those who claim "rights" and drastic alterations in law and government from a society in which such claims are hitherto unknown are not only out of line with its fundamental ethos and identity but also are, implicitly or explicitly, proposing to change or even to destroy the society.

To understand conservatism as "a country's way of life as it actually lives it" is to reject those versions of conservative thought that depend upon abstract principles, to which a society should conform in its institutions and policies. Thus Kendall rejected the formulations advanced by libertarians, who identify the principle of individual freedom as the abstraction to which our way of life should accord, as well as those of Christian conservatives who, like Frank S. Meyer, argued that "the Christian understanding of the nature and destiny of man is always and everywhere what Conservatives strive to conserve." These principles were included in the traditional American way of life but were not the whole of it, and as part of the whole

3. Ibid., 74.

they acquired a meaning different from the meaning they acquired in abstraction. By themselves, these principles are at best only partial visions of the way of life, and their defenders have extracted them from a selective reading of various documents and events in the nation's history that ignores the mainstream of that history, of how the country actually lives its way of life.

Yet alternative concepts and definitions of conservatism were not, to Kendall, the main problem. Such alternatives were not in themselves powerful enough to threaten the public orthodoxy significantly. The principal threat came from liberalism and what Kendall called the "Liberal Revolution," a crusade against the traditional beliefs and practices of the United States that, through the presidency, the executive bureaucracy, the courts, and the institutions of education and the mass media, had declared war against the public orthodoxy, intended to destroy it, and planned to substitute an alternative design in its place. The central principle to which liberalism adheres and which is the foundation of its social and political design is egalitarianism:

> Liberal proposals do involve a common principle—one moreover which, once you grasp it clearly, appears on the face of it as revolutionary because it looks to the overthrow of an established social order. The principle in question is the *egalitarian* principle. . . . It says that men are not merely created equal, are indeed not created equal at all, but rather ought, that is have a right, to be *made* equal. That is to say equalized, and equalized precisely by governmental action, so that if they end up other than actually equal—in political power, in wealth, in income, in education, in living conditions—no one shall ever be able to say that government has spared any effort that might conceivably have made them equal.[4]

Ostensibly founded on the equality clause of the Declaration of Independence, liberal egalitarianism appeals to a selective, false, and distorted interpretation of the American way of life in order to justify its imposition of equality. This appeal to a false tradition is a necessary political tactic for liberalism, for if it appealed to the real sources of egalitarian ideology— ideas that have nothing to do with and in fact postdate the formation of the United States as a political order—it would expose itself as an alien and revolutionary force.

4. Ibid., 17–18.

Kendall viewed liberalism as literally revolutionary in the threefold sense that

> give the Liberals their way and the American social order will not bear even a cousinly resemblance to that which is traditional among us; revolutionary, because the revolution must go on and on forever, since if you are in the business of making people equal there is and can be no stopping-place; revolutionary, finally, because the job cannot be done by a government of limited powers—any more, to use James Burnham's phrase, than you can use an automobile to dig potatoes.[5]

To base conservatism on a defense of a way of life, a concrete and historical manner of thinking and living, rather than on an adherence to various abstract ideals and principles, involves at least two important presuppositions. First, Kendall's view of conservatism involved an understanding of American history and of its major documents and events as incorporating and expressing the traditional public orthodoxy. Although he did not live to complete the full development of his interpretation of the American past, he frequently alluded to or expanded upon it in his articles and reviews, and his interpretation is developed more fully in his posthumous *The Basic Symbols of the American Political Tradition,* completed by his friend and colleague George W. Carey.[6] Thus, Kendall did not share the liberal interpretation (increasingly common among some conservatives today) that the Declaration of Independence called for egalitarianism and the remolding of American institutions in accordance with the doctrine of equality. The egalitarian principle of liberalism, Kendall wrote, is

> not the equality principle of the Declaration of Independence, which "holds" merely that all men are created equal. That is, as I understand it, are created with an equal claim to be treated as persons (though by no means necessarily as equal persons), with an equal right to justice, and an equal right to live under a government limited by law (and constitutionally excluded from concern with certain major spheres of human endeavor).[7]

5. Ibid., 18.
6. Willmoore Kendall and George W. Carey, *The Basic Symbols of the American Political Tradition* (Baton Rouge: Louisiana State University Press, 1970).
7. Kendall, *Conservative Affirmation,* 17.

Nor did Kendall share the liberal affection for Abraham Lincoln, whom he regarded as a perverter of the American tradition, "dedicated . . . to egalitarian reforms sanctioned by mandates emanating from national majorities,"[8] a dedication that Kendall regarded as completely alien to and destructive of the constitutional tradition and political thought of the Framers.

Kendall's understanding of the public orthodoxy thus required historical grounding in order to show that it was the country's actual way of life. And, for the public orthodoxy to retain its legitimacy, it must be shown that the American people continue to live by its norms. Failing this demonstration, Kendall's "way of life" becomes simply a form of political antiquarianism, a judgment of contemporary political issues by the standard of what once was thought but which now has been abandoned. Liberals also, because they profess to take their principles from the democratic consent of the people rather than from ideological abstractions, must claim popular support for their policies. Hence they point to the "mandates" obtained by presidents as legitimizing the democratic character of their policies.

Kendall's response to the liberal claim to popular consent involved a challenge to the criterion of presidential elections and the fiction of the mandate as the sole standards by which liberals allow themselves to be tested and an emphasis on the persistence of institutions and beliefs that liberals oppose. Writing in the 1960s, Kendall pointed to the inability of liberals to abolish the House Un-American Activities Committee, the seniority system in Congress, and the electoral college; the congressional defeat of President Kennedy's proposals; and the continuing control of Congress by basically conservative elements. He was fond of pointing out that, despite much liberal invocation of the "tradition" of freedom of speech in America, opinion polls, the actual history of censorship in the United States, and the actual practices and beliefs of most Americans in regard to school prayer, censorship, and tolerance for Communists showed a very limited commitment to the "open society." "One begins to suspect," he wrote, "that the true American tradition is less that of our Fourth of July orations and our constitutional law textbooks, with their

8. Ibid., 252.

cluck-clucking over the so-called preferred freedoms, than, quite simply, that of riding somebody out of town on a rail."[9]

It is possible to criticize Kendall's understanding of popular allegiance to the public orthodoxy on the grounds that since he wrote in the early 1960s the American people have significantly defected from or have chosen to alter that orthodoxy. Congressional investigating committees were abolished in the 1970s, and it seems unlikely that they will be restored to perform their traditional functions. The seniority system has been reformed. If Kennedy's programs were rejected, those of Lyndon Johnson were enacted overwhelmingly, and the counterculture and the New Left of the late 1960s have apparently affected the way most Americans—even conservatives— think about social, political, and moral issues and relationships. Moreover, while Kendall was willing to grant liberalism its presidential claims, he insisted on the inherently conservative disposition of the Congress. Since 1968, however, the American presidency has displayed conservative inclinations that are well to the right of what most members of Congress are willing to support. This development appears to contradict Kendall's understanding of how the electorate and its representatives manifest the political aspects of the traditional public orthodoxy.

It is possible to circumvent many of these objections, however. Many of the gains of the liberal revolution since Kendall's death have not been made through submission to the judgment of the American people. They have been pushed through by the most undemocratic institutions in the American system—the courts and the federal bureaucracy—and have been defended mainly by institutions that are not at all responsive to popular control—the mass media and the universities. The acceptance of the civil rights legislation of the 1960s was based on a misunderstanding that conceived of civil rights as an essentially moderate step. The social revolution implied in these laws and in the movement that promoted them quickly became apparent, however, in efforts at forced busing, affirmative action, and the continuing imposition of egalitarian reforms (as Kendall noted, the revolution must go on and on forever). When these implications became clear, the electorate overwhelmingly and resolutely rejected

9. Ibid., 82.

them, and the efforts of conservatives since then have been directed at finding ways in which civil rights laws could be denuded of their radical consequences. Thus far, these efforts have not been very successful.

Indeed, it is quite possible to argue that the whole political revival of conservatism since 1980 is a confirmation of Kendall's central contention that the American people remain faithful to the main body of their traditional way of life and that politicians who propose measures very far out of line with that orthodoxy are likely to have short careers. The cast of Kendall's conservatism was thus essentially optimistic, and he shunned the thought of pessimistic conservatives who saw liberalism, retreat, and decadence as the dominant forces in the United States and the West. In its optimism and in its reliance on popular confrontation with the liberal establishment, then, Kendall's ideas deserve to be better known among New Right activists and strategists.

Yet Kendall emphasized the resistance of the mainstream to the forces of liberalism, and he did not dwell on the institutional entrenchments of liberalism in bureaucracy, universities, media, and corporations. He did not live to suggest strategies by which the American heartland can counterattack and regain the ground lost to these encroachments, and there is little suggestion in most of his work that there was any great need to reverse what liberals had, by the 1960s, succeeded in imposing. Kendall leaves the impression that liberalism had succeeded in very little of its crusade. There is absent from his thought the sense of apocalyptic catastrophe that is strongly present in the thought of Whittaker Chambers and James Burnham.

Kendall's optimism thus expresses a sense that the American polity is basically sound and faces no challenge, internal or external, that cannot be met within the framework of the traditional public orthodoxy and traditional political institutions. One must wonder today if he was correct in his optimism, which is too easily transmuted into complacency. Are there not challenges, of both a material and spiritual nature, that the American people and their leaders seem reluctant to recognize and meet? Americans no doubt remain overwhelmingly anticommunist, but are they prepared to make the sacrifices and to sustain the long-term commitments that the destruction of aggressive, totalitarian empires demands? Americans remain deferential to and respectful of the legitimate and traditional authorities of church, state, and the social order, but when these authorities have been captured by radical forces that manipulate the best instincts of the American people to dispossess them of their heritage, does this deference and respect allow for the kind of militancy that is needed?

The last decade has seen the proliferation of militant anti-liberal groups and leaders that do reject the liberalism of the establishment, and this rejection is based upon an understanding of and allegiance to a traditional public orthodoxy that underlies our national institutions and values. Yet, as Kevin Phillips has suggested, there is a danger that this "New Right" will be or has been co-opted by a national political and intellectual leadership that neglects and misunderstands its basis and which seeks to use it to gain the rewards of the establishment rather than challenge it directly. While Willmoore Kendall's political thought remains indispensable for the resurgence of a militant popular conservatism, it also contains little that would justify a counterrevolution against the establishment, and it is possible that Kendall exaggerated the counterrevolutionary impulses that the mass of the American people harbor. Kendall would surely have rejected any accommodation with the liberal establishment and would have sought to develop a theoretical framework for a popular counterrevolution against it, but his untimely death at the age of fifty-eight prevented him from developing such a framework on a systematic basis. It is perhaps the greatest tragedy of American conservative thought in the 1950s and 1960s that he did not live to complete his work and to witness and comment upon the incipient resurgence of the heartland that underlies the conservatism of the 1980s.

The Harmless Persuasion

Irving Kristol,
Reflections of a Neoconservative:
Looking Back, Looking Ahead

Irving Kristol is the most articulate, the most learned, and probably the best known exponent of the body of ideas and opinions that
has come to be called neoconservatism, a label that Mr. Kristol,
unlike several other writers in this movement, accepts. His most
recent collection of essays and journalism is therefore a valuable
book, not only for its intrinsic merits of learning and style, but also,
since it does accept this label, because it may long serve as a representative text of what neoconservatism is and what its exponents
believe.

Although there is considerable overlap between neoconservatism
and the philosophical conservatism of the Old Right, the two are
distinct from each other both in their theoretical presuppositions
and practical applications as well as in their historical and political
origins. The Old Right, or, in George Nash's phrase, the "conservative intellectual movement," originated largely as a protest against
the statism of the New Deal, the internal and external threat of communism, and the danger to traditional institutions and values (including private property and its uses) presented by modern liberalism in government, economy, and society. The Old Right in the
United States took its bearings from the American experience, especially from the constitutional tradition, and was reinforced by European thinkers such as Eric Voegelin and Leo Strauss, who drew attention to the medieval, classical, and biblical roots of the American
tradition. Socially, the Old Right tended to be Roman Catholic or
High Protestant in religion; German, Irish, or southern Celtic in
ethnic identity; and midwestern or southern in geographic and cultural roots.

Neoconservatism, on the other hand, originated in northeastern,
urban universities and periodicals in the late 1960s. Its exponents

have been most notably Jewish and Eastern European in religious and ethnic identity and urban, academic, and northeastern in origins. The political impetus for neoconservatism was, first, the threat to the integrity of universities and American intellectual life presented by the militancy of the New Left and the barbarism of the counterculture of the late 1960s; secondly, the threat to Jewish academic and professional achievements in America presented by the quotas and affirmative action programs of the Great Society; and thirdly, the development of serious anti-Semitism on the Left and the Soviet alliance with radical anti-Western and anti-Israeli Arab regimes and terrorists. Like the prospect of being hanged, these phenomena have tended to concentrate the Jewish mind wonderfully. Historically associated with the liberalism and the Left in American and European history, American Jews have moved demonstrably to the right in the past fifteen years, not only intellectually but also politically. In 1980 Ronald Reagan won some 40 percent of the Jewish vote.

The differences between the Old Right and the neoconservatives in political origins and social composition largely account for the differences in political style and values between the two movements. The Old Right was anti-liberal as well as anticommunist; the neoconservatives are noticeably reticent in their opposition to the welfare state and their critique of liberal ideology, and their anticommunism is largely directed toward the Soviets and their surrogates (Communist China is of far less importance to them than to the Old Right). The Old Right was committed to conserving what it took to be the unique historic identity of American society as a continuation of the Anglo-Saxon political tradition and the Western European Christian tradition in social, moral, and aesthetic values. The neoconservatives appear to have little interest in conserving the historic realities of the American tradition and indeed show little sympathy for the Christian heritage beyond a highly selective amalgamation of Judaism and Calvinist Protestantism.

In place of an appeal to the ancient norms of the Western and American traditions, Mr. Kristol in these essays articulates a defense of what he variously calls "bourgeois civilization," the "commercial society," or "liberal capitalism." The United States, for him, is the embodiment of bourgeois civilization, the principles of which were first articulated by the Anglo-Scottish Enlightenment of David Hume, Adam Ferguson, and Adam Smith in distinction to the Continental Enlightenment of Voltaire, Diderot, and Rousseau. "Out of the traditions of the Anglo-Scottish Enlightenment," Mr. Kristol tells us, "there merged a sociopolitical order that defines an important epoch in human history: the 'bourgeois' epoch, in which we Americans, at any rate, still live, though with increasing unease." Between the American Revolution (which Mr. Kristol tends to see as the Anglo-Scottish Enlightenment in arms) and the Founding on the one hand, and the discontents of the 1960s and 1970s on the other, there is barely any reference to American history in these essays. For Mr. Kristol, American history as a concrete experience (as opposed to an abstraction) appears not to exist or to be unimportant.

The bourgeois order that Mr. Kristol defends "roots itself in the most worldly and common of human motivations: self-interest," and it "assumes that, though only a few are capable of pursuing excellence, everyone is capable of recognizing and pursuing his own self-interest." Hence, bourgeois society is characterized by a capitalist economy, a democratic-republican political order, and a liberal ethos that tolerates and legitimizes a high degree of private differentiation (i.e., an "open society"). In its classic form, however, bourgeois society is also characterized by what Mr. Kristol calls "republican morality" or "civic virtue," a moral code that, while acknowledging the usefulness and value of material acquisition, imposes an ethic of self-restraint on the bourgeoisie that prevents it from degenerating into a collection of plutocrats and hedonists. Bourgeois society, he says, is "the most prosaic of all possible societies," eschewing the heroic, the transcendent, and the romantic-utopian, and the "bourgeois ideal is much closer to the Old Testament than to the New—which is, perhaps, why Jews have felt more at home in the bourgeois world than in any other."

Yet Mr. Kristol's defense of the bourgeois ideal and its institutions is not total: "The attitude of neoconservatives to bourgeois society and the bourgeois ethos is one of detached attachment" or of "*modest* enthusiasm" in recognition that "liberal-democratic capitalism" is not the best of all imaginable worlds but "only the best, under the circumstances, of all possible worlds." He recognizes the flaws of bourgeois society—what its enemies call philistinism—and its tendencies to degeneration, and his principal criticism of American society today is that it has abandoned the republican morality that the Anglo-Scottish theorists of the bourgeois ideal and their alleged disciples, the Founding Fathers, took for granted. Mr. Kristol's constant lament throughout these essays is that this moral code of bourgeois society has eroded. "The challenge to our urban democracy is to evolve a set of values and a conception of democracy that can function as the equivalent of the republican morality of yesteryear. This is our fundamental urban problem." Without a set of constraining and directing values, bourgeois society degenerates under the temptations of mass affluence. "Crime and all kinds of delinquency increase with increasing prosperity. Alcoholism and drug addiction also increase. Civic-mindedness and public-spiritness are corroded by cynicism. . . . The emphasis is on the pleasures of consumption rather than on the virtues of work . . . 'fly now, pay later' becomes, not merely an advertising slogan, but also a popular philosophy of life."

Mr. Kristol is undoubtedly correct in his critique of the degeneration of the bourgeois order, but it is the irony of these essays (and indeed of neoconservatism) that he nowhere suggests either a means of restoring the moral code of a healthy republic or of formulating a new code that would be viable for a postbourgeois society. He is partially correct in suggesting that the defense of bourgeois society distinguishes neoconservatism from "the Old Right and the New Right—both of which are exceedingly suspicious of it." As a social and political movement, Old Right conservatism was an extension and a defense of the bourgeois forces that came to dominate the United States between the Civil War and the depression, but intellectually the "traditionalist" wing of the Old Right argued that America was not, in its essence and origins, a bourgeois society and that the Old World roots of the American order, manifested most clearly in the traditional values and institutions of American society, predated the ideals and disciplined the appetites of bourgeois forces. Russell Kirk and the neo-Burkeans, Richard Weaver and the Southern Agrarians, *Triumph* and the Catholic Right, and Leo Strauss and his school argued with each other over the precise nature of the American order, but all were equally critical of the modernist forces that, from the Civil War to the Great Society, successfully subverted and redesigned that order. It is true, as Mr. Kristol claims, that there is an element of nostalgia in Old Right political thought, and perhaps it is true that the Old Right was impractical in much of its restorationist critique. Yet the fact remains that the Old Right not only formulated a far more sophisticated body of ideas than the neoconservatives but also perceived the inherent weaknesses and tendencies of bourgeois society more profoundly than neoconservatism.

As Mr. Kristol acknowledges, "For many generations capitalism was able to live off the accumulated moral and spiritual capital of the past" but was unable to produce such capital itself. The "prosaic" nature of bourgeois ideology and values was precisely the reason for this failure, and it finally resulted in the disintegration of the bourgeois ethos and the discontents of the present day. As Mr. Kristol is also aware, the very material and organizational success of bourgeois society led to the triumph of technocratic and bureaucratic elites—what he calls the "corporate revolution" but which is largely identical to what James Burnham much earlier called the "managerial revolution"—and to the transvaluation of the "civic virtue" of the early republic by the managerial ideologies of collectivism, social engineering, and mass hedonism. Mr. Kristol therefore understands the flaws of bourgeois society and its ideologies, but nowhere does he firmly argue that these flaws are inherent in that society; nowhere does he develop a basis for resisting or rejecting these flaws; and nowhere does he seem aware that the corrective for them lies in the heartland of America, far from the northeastern urban academies and salons where the bourgeois pathology is bred. It is Mr. Kristol's basic error that he exaggerates the importance of bourgeois ideology in the revolution, the country's founding, and the American experience and thus, by portraying America as in the main a bourgeois order, creates a selective and distorted picture of our national identity. If, furthermore, America is and was in its origins mainly a bourgeois society, then it contains no corrective for the inherent degenerative tendencies of that order, and those who wish to resist the mortal consequences of these tendencies must go outside the American tradition.

Mr. Kristol may be correct that bourgeois society, "under the circumstances," is the best possible world, but it is not self-evident that it will long remain possible at all. The ideological and institutional fabric of the bourgeois order has already been subverted by the "New Class" of managers and verbalists in both the private and public sectors, and it is doubtful that a defense of bourgeois values will appeal to many outside a dwindling and declining social class. If there is a future for the American Right, it lies in the heartland of Middle America, which is fundamentally neither bourgeois nor New Class in its values and life-styles and which remains the only part of contemporary American society capable of mobilizing "heroic" virtues and "transcendent" myths to overcome and correct our present distempers. In any case, Mr. Kristol's lukewarm, circumstantial endorsement of bourgeois society can do nothing to ensure its survival. To paraphrase Whittaker Chambers, who can imagine a Marine wading ashore at Tarawa with *Reflections of a Neoconservative* in his pocket?

The most frequent criticism of neoconservatives by the Old and New Right is that they are more "neo" than conservative and that, when things come to the crunch, they retreat into elegant reprimands of the establishment rather than advance to a principled confrontation with it. This criticism is generally sustained by a reading of Mr. Kristol's reflections, for at no place in them is there a clear break with liberalism and its works. Indeed, Norman Podhoretz, who with Mr. Kristol himself is probably the leading exponent of the movement, has suggested that a more appropriate name for the neoconservatives would be "neo-liberals." According to Mr. Kristol, "A conservative welfare state—what once was called a 'social insurance' state—is perfectly consistent with the neoconservative perspective," and he describes the Soviet Union not as a malevolent force for global expansion but merely as an unpleasant "great power whose interests often conflict with those of the United States." If Old Right conservatism was, in Clinton Rossiter's phrase, a "thankless persuasion," neoconservatism is simply a harmless one, and there is no reason for the Establishment Left to drive the neoconservatives into academic and journalistic exile as it succeeded in doing to the Old Right. The neoconservatives may, in fact, be seen as the right wing of the New Class that they criticize so much, engaged in an effort to moderate its collectivist and utopian dynamic with a strong dose of bourgeois liberalism.

Some years ago, in an exchange with the neoconservative sociol-

ogist Peter Berger, James Burnham remarked that although the neoconservatives had formally broken with liberal ideology, they retained the "gestalt of liberalism," its emotional, psychic, and moral
reflexes. The reason they retain these reflexes is that the neoconservatives are the products, socially and intellectually, of the northeastern urban academic establishment that is the natural habitat of
both the declining bourgeoisie and its pathologies and of the new
managerial-verbalist class that is succeeding the bourgeois order.
Irving Kristol's most recent book shows that he, for one, still retains
these reflexes and many of the intellectual and political ambiguities
that attend them and that these ambiguities account for the tepid
and often shallow precepts that the neoconservatives offer. It is one
thing for the American Right to accept the neoconservatives as political allies, but this acceptance must be balanced by recognition
that their ideas are not an adequate substitute for a more far-reaching critique of the bourgeois order and its legacies.

Neoconservatism and
the Managerial Revolution

The emergence in the 1970s of the political and intellectual movement known as "neoconservatism" is generally regarded as a response to the failures of conventional liberalism to deal effectively with the challenges of that decade. Neoconservatives, in Irving Kristol's well-known definition, are "liberals who have been mugged by reality"—persons whose lifelong commitment to liberalism was unsettled by the patent contradictions that political and social realities began to present to the articles of liberal doctrine. College students who burned libraries and attacked their professors and high school graduates who were illiterate violated the liberal faith in education as an instrument of human improvement. Communist regimes that refused to converge with the West and consistently betrayed their international commitments mocked the liberal preference for negotiation over force as a means of settling global conflicts. Third World states that did not develop economically or politically and indulged in orgies of racism, genocide, and terrorism challenged the liberal ideal of a Western democratic mixed economy as the goal of human progress. Minorities that would not or could not be assimilated by liberal policies raised questions about the feasibility of social engineering and the reliability of environmentalist explanations of inequality. An economy that exhibited hyperinflation, exorbitant fiscal burdens, and declining standards of affluence contradicted the prescriptions of Keynesian orthodoxy. At the level of national and international policy and in the most visible currents of contemporary society, the poverty of conventional twentieth-century liberalism became manifest to an increasing number of American intellectuals.

The failure of liberalism was thus the immediate historical occasion of the emergence of neoconservatism. Almost none of the adherents of this movement came from what is now generally called the Old Right; almost all approached it from the Left, usually the moderate Left, but sometimes from rather far on the Left. Yet whenever a sizeable portion of a social formation such as an intellectual class begins to change or modify its beliefs and ideology, there is more involved than a purely cerebral process. Social and political forces express ideas and values that reflect their interests and perform functions for them in their efforts to keep or acquire power. This is true for neoconservatism no less than for the Old and New Right and the Old and New Left, and whatever the strength, attractiveness, or truth of the ideas of these movements, no explanation of them can be complete if it neglects their aspirations and interests and their relationships to dominant and declining social and political forces.

The twentieth century, for the United States as well as for the rest of the world, has been an age of revolution of far more profound transformational effect than any the modern world has ever experienced. Perhaps not since neolithic times has mankind undergone simultaneous changes in economic, social, political, and intellectual relationships of such far-reaching consequences. Some aspects of this transformation are obvious and have been explored by countless analysts—the rise of totalitarianism, the intellectual revolution precipitated by Einstein and Freud, the decline of the Euro-American civilization and the rise of non-white power centers, the evolution of a "postindustrial" technology and economy in place of agricultural and manufacturing sectors. Yet for all the theories, explanations, and accounts of the twentieth-century revolution, there is no better perspective from which to view this transformation than James Burnham's theory of the managerial revolution, formulated in 1941. Despite many flaws, inaccurate predictions, and overstatements, Burnham's theory perceives the essential core of the twentieth-century revolution and contains the elements by which the complex political and intellectual ramifications of our age can be explained.

Although in a narrow sense Burnham's theory sought to explain the civilizational impact of the "separation of ownership and control" in the corporate economy and the rise of large corporations directed by professional managers rather than by traditional individual owners and partnerships, in a broader sense his theory applies to political and social, as well as to economic, organizations. The characteristic feature of twentieth-century history has been the vast expansion in the size, scale of transactions, and complexity and technicality of functions that political, social, and economic organizations exhibit. This expansion, which Pitrim Sorokin also noted under the label "colossalism," was itself made possible by the growth of mass populations and by the development of technologies that could sustain the colossal scale of organization. Just as business firms expanded far beyond the point at which they could be operated, directed, and controlled effectively by individual owners and their families, who generally lacked the technical skills to manage them, so the state also underwent a transformation in scale that removed it from the control of traditional elites, citizens, and their legal representatives. Just as in the mass corporations a new elite of professional managers emerged that replaced the traditional entrepreneurial or bourgeois elite of businessmen, so in the state also a new elite of professionally trained managers or bureaucrats developed that challenged and generally became dominant over the older political elites of aristocrats and amateur politicians who occupied the formal offices of government. Both in the economy and the state, organizations began to undertake functions for which a smaller scale of organization was not prepared and which the traditional elites of aristocratic and bourgeois society were unable to perform. A similar process occurred in labor unions, professional associations, churches, educational institutions, military organizations, and the organs of mass communication and cultural expression. In all sectors of twentieth-century industrial society, the growth of mass organizations brought with it an expansion of functions and power, a new elite wedded by its material interests and psychic and intellectual preparation to continuing expansion, and a metamorphosis of the organizations themselves as well as of the social and political orders they dominated.

The rise of mass organizations and the new, managerial elites that controlled them involved also the evolution of new social and political ideologies—indeed, a new world view—that rationalized the functions and power of the new elite. Traditionalist and bourgeois ideologies, centering on the individual as moral agent, citizen, and economic actor, could not provide justifications for the managerial economy and the managerial state. Managerial society involves the collective organization and disciplining of huge masses of workers, citizens, soldiers, and consumers, and the political and economic individualism of the bourgeois era offered little predicate for such collectivist coordination. Traditional social relationships, especially the inheritance of leadership and property through family and community bonds, became irrelevant in the large corporation, controlled by managerial "meritocracies" and not by the owners of property. The units of the economy—corporations and mass unions—themselves became closely integrated with the mass state and dependent on the state for legal privileges, subsidization, and the regulation of aggregate demand through fiscal and monetary policy. Bourgeois economic theory, enshrined in the laissez faire thought of the classical economists, offered no conceptual framework for the new interdependence of state and economy that characterized managerial society and the managerial system. In the state itself, the bourgeois ideal of a neutralist, minimal government by law was replaced by a managerial political ideal that involved a bureaucratic, social engineering state actively intervening in and altering by design the economic, social, and even intellectual and moral relationships of its subjects. Outside economic and political relations, the social fabric of traditional and bourgeois society—localized, private, centered on self-contained communities and kinship networks—acted as a constraint on the development of the colossal scale of managerial organizations. Hence, it was in the interest of the new elites to dissolve the old social fabric, to break up local community and family bonds, and to reorganize the members of such institutions into the massive political and economic structures under their own control. The new ideology of the managerial regime thus involved a cosmopolitan, universalist, and egalitarian myth that challenged the localized and traditionalist loyalties and moral values of bourgeois society and offered a rationalization for the dominance of managerial organizations and their elites.

The ideology of the emerging managerial regime in the United States came to be known as "progressivism" and later as "liberalism," though a more appropriate label might be "managerial humanism." The ideology articulated a view of man as the product of social and economic environment and thus susceptible to amelioration or perfection by a scientifically trained elite with power to redesign the environment. It involved a collectivist view of the state and economy and advocated a highly centralized regime largely unrestrained by traditional legal, constitutional, and political barriers. It rejected or regarded as backward, repressive, or obsolete the institutions and values of traditional and bourgeois society—its loyalties to the local community, traditional religion, and moral beliefs, the family, and social and political differentiations based on class, status, and property—and it expressed an ideal of man "liberated" from such constraints and re-educated or redesigned into a cosmopolitan participant in the mass state-economy of the managerial system.

The evolution of the new order and its ideology was not, of course, the result of a conspiracy or a conscious design on the part of its founders, but rather the product of an almost irresistible process by which new technologies, new forms of organization, and new ideas joined together to challenge and replace old forms that were unable to sustain or accommodate the immense scale of human numbers and their interactions. Those who gained from this process—the new managerial elites—encouraged it instinctively from a combined sense of their personal and group interests and their unquestioned faith in their self-serving ideology.

Yet the managerial regime did not evolve nor its elites become dominant in the economy, government, and mass society without a struggle. From the early twentieth century to the present, the social and political forces that resisted the formation of the managerial regime and the implementation of its agenda constituted a conservative, at times reactionary, influence. Small businessmen and entrepreneurs, the more parochial sectors of American society, lower middle-class elements, and groups that found the fiscal burden and social effects of the new regime a threat to their economic status and cultural identity provided the political base of the conservative resistance to managerial forces and ideas. The members of this base saw in the fusion of state and economy a threat to their own independent standing, endangered by the labor unions, regulations, and intervention imposed by the new managerial state in partnership with mass corporations. They saw their own values and institutions denigrated and undermined by the cosmopolitan ethic and egalitarian policies of the new elite. They suffered from the inflation and exorbitant taxation that financed the managerial state and from the crime and social dislocation that resulted from its social policies, by which the managerial regime subsidized an urban proletariat as its own political base. They were offended and often frightened by the globalist and, in their view un-American, international policies of the elite, which involved permanent intervention in world affairs, expensive foreign aid programs, the prospect of global war, and the renunciation of national interests in return for a cosmopolitan "one-world" that they regarded as both illusory and dangerous.

The conservative and essentially bourgeois resistance to the managerial regime was uncoordinated and largely ineffective until the death of Franklin Roosevelt (under whom the managerial revolution achieved its most dramatic and far-reaching victories) and the end of the depression and World War II. In the years following 1945, however, the resistance began to revive with a new political and intellectual movement that actively challenged the managerial agenda in Congress, in presidential elections, and in verbal and intellectual conflicts. The intellectual movement that for the most part provided the ideological underpinnings of American conservatism has been chronicled by George H. Nash,[1] and though its more sophisticated exponents were not usually directly involved in practical politics, the movement as a whole was antimanagerial and probourgeois in its thrust and was aware, to one degree or another, that it represented a force that was in the process of being dispossessed by a revolution.

The perception of the revolutionary impact of managerial liberalism was implicit in Whittaker Chambers's explanation of contemporary history.

> I saw that the New Deal was only superficially a reform movement. I had to acknowledge the truth of what its more forthright protagonists, sometimes defiantly, averred: the New Deal was a genuine revolution, whose deepest purpose was not simply reform within existing traditions, but a basic change in the social, and, above all, the power relationships within the nation. It was not a revolution by violence. It was a revolution by bookkeeping and law-making. In so far as it was successful, the power of politics had replaced the power of business. This is the basic power shift of all the revolutions of our time. This shift *was* the revolution.[2]

1. George H. Nash, *The Conservative Intellectual Movement since 1945* (New York: Basic Books, 1976).
2. Whittaker Chambers, *Witness* (New York: Random House, 1952), 472.

Frank S. Meyer, one of the most influential and representative voices of postwar American conservatism, in 1958 also pointed to the revolutionary implications of managerial liberalism:

> In a fundamental sense the dominant forces in American life today are revolutionary, that is, they are directed towards the destruction of the principles of Western civilization and the American tradition. The politics of New Dealism, Fair Dealism, and New Republicanism are directed towards the strengthening of the State and the diminution of the person. The prevalent quasi-Marxist and Keynesian economics are directed towards the substitution of a state-controlled, ever less "mixed," economy for the free economy of capitalism. The positivist and materialist philosophy of our educational theory and practice, of our radio and television and press, of our academic and intellectual circles, eats away at the fabric of principle and belief which is Western civilization. Everywhere the same revolutionary spirit expresses itself. For the conservative to compromise with it is to give up his reason for being. . . . Its contemporary political forms were described . . . sixteen years ago by James Burnham, who called it "the managerial revolution." Its historical and philosophical meaning has been drawn forth and powerfully presented by Eric Voegelin, who calls it "gnosticism."[3]

Willmoore Kendall also spoke of the "Liberal Revolution," though he did not link its political ideology with any particular social force and appears during most of his life to have believed that it had made limited progress in practical political achievements. James Burnham, in a series of books, explored the political and intellectual consequences of the emergence of the managerial elite and its ideology.[4]

On a practical level, conservative resistance to and hostility toward the new managerial regime was expressed in the political movements led in the 1950s by Robert A. Taft, Joseph R. McCarthy, and later by Barry Goldwater, Ronald Reagan, and, to some extent, George Wallace. While the right wing of the Republican party expressed the traditional entrepreneurial ideology and values of the old bourgeois elite, the left wing of the Republicans and the mainstream of the Democratic party became the political vehicles of the managerial class. Any examination of the advertisements carried by conserva-

3. Frank S. Meyer, *The Conservative Mainstream* (New Rochelle, N. Y.: Arlington House, 1969), 85–86.
4. For an account of Burnham's political thought in terms of his theory of the managerial revolution, see Samuel T. Francis, *Power and History: The Political Thought of James Burnham* (Lanham, Md.: University Press of America, 1984).

tive periodicals of the 1950s and 1960s shows that the economic base of the conservative movement lay largely in smaller-scale, privately owned and operated, and locally oriented firms, and not in the multinational, managerially controlled corporations. One of the principal sources of weakness of the conservative movement in this period lay precisely in the limited financial resources, small numbers, and lack of cultural sophistication that typified the elements of its political and economic base and derived from the declining fortunes of the bourgeois elite in an age of managerial ascendancy.

Yet the revitalization of conservatism in the postwar period was paralleled by an equally significant change in the ideology of liberalism. In the early part of the century, managerial ideology had been radical in its thrust. It challenged the legitimacy of traditional values and institutions, advocated far-reaching reforms in political and economic arrangements, and aggressively used the executive branch of the state, allied with the lower- and working-class masses, to impose its ideological demands for more federal regulation, more equality, and more mass democracy. With the consolidation of its political, economic, and cultural power in the course of the New Deal and World War II era, however, the new elite began to mute or retreat from the radical and progressivist content of its ideology. The challenging of established authority was no longer useful to the managerial elite in the bureaucracy of the central government, the management of large corporations, and the intelligentsia of mass universities, foundations, and organs of mass communication and cultural and intellectual expression, as it had been to the same forces when their goal was to acquire power. Once the managerial elite had itself occupied the positions of established authority, its interests lay in defending and conserving these positions and the legitimacy of the processes by which they gained power. Certainly it was not the first time in history that a new elite had compromised the radicalism of its ideology and transformed itself into a conservative force. The bourgeoisie in Western Europe and America in the eighteenth century had originally articulated a radical critique of the *ancien régime* in the ideology of classical liberalism, but in the course of bourgeois dominance in the nineteenth century, the ideology was transmuted into an essentially conservative framework.

American liberalism in the late 1940s and 1950s began to exhibit a similar tendency. "Liberalism," wrote Eric F. Goldman of the late 1940s, "turned into a form of conservatism,"[5] and during the 1952 presidential campaign, Adlai Stevenson actually called himself a conservative. Liberal intellectuals—Arthur Schlesinger, Jr., and Reinhold Niebuhr, most prominently—began to reformulate liberalism in a way that muted the radical, progressivist, egalitarian, and utopian premises of the Progressive Era and to talk about "original sin," the inherent irrationality of human nature, and the limitations of political solutions to intractable problems of the human condition. The themes of "pluralism," "consensus," and "the end of ideology" characterized the mainstream of American liberalism from the 1940s to the end of the 1960s.

"Consensus liberalism"—what the New Left later called "corporate liberalism" because of its positive and uncritical concept of corporate capitalism—in fact reflected the new position and power of the managerial elite and the mass organizations it controlled. Each of the three principal sectors of the managerial regime—the bureaucratized apparatus of the federal government, the large corporations, and the media of mass communication and education—played a special role in the "consensus" or "pluralistic" order that postwar liberalism advocated and defended. Liberalism endorsed and rationalized the evolution of the "Imperial Presidency" that presided over the regulatory and interventionist bureaucracy, the globalist diplomacy, and the military managers of the mass state. Its most articulate representatives made their living and acquired an unprecedented degree of political and cultural influence in the academic and mass communications establishments that increasingly resembled and were intertwined with the bureaucratized structures of the state and corporations. The corporations themselves were defended by consensus liberalism, which regarded them as an essential part of the "pluralist" managerial system.

> After the war the crisis of capitalism had failed to make its expected reappearance, and unprecedented prosperity began eroding the old antagonism toward big business. Here the representative figure was the Harvard econo-

5. Eric F. Goldman, *Rendezvous with Destiny: A History of Modern American Reform,* rev. ed., abrdg. (New York: Alfred A. Knopf, 1956), 334.

mist John Kenneth Galbraith. . . . Large corporations were not the enemies
of economic efficiency but the promoters of technological progress.[6]

and

> Intellectual liberals unashamedly asserted the benevolence of large corpora-
> tions and defended the existing distribution of wealth and power in Amer-
> ica. Political liberals assumed corporate hegemony and pursued policies to
> strengthen it. The quintessential corporate liberal was John F. Kennedy, who
> never pretended to be otherwise and for whom the good opinion of big
> business was the highest political priority.[7]

Despite the conservative, stabilizing, and establishmentarian appearance of consensus liberalism, however, the managerial system
is incapable of stabilization. The dynamic of managerial capitalism
involves a continuing erosion of the social and cultural fabric through
the mass consumption and hedonism, social mobility, and dislocation that it promotes and through the obsolescence of hard private
property, under the control of individual and family ownership,
that corporate and collective property and governmental regulation
encourage. The managerial state obtains its *raison d'être* from continuing intervention, activism, and social engineering, as became
clear in the War on Poverty, the civil rights revolution, and the Great
Society programs. The intellectuals, technocrats, and professional
verbalists of the managerial intelligentsia and communications elite—
what Kevin Phillips has called the "mediacracy"—are committed by
their material interests and their ideological predispositions to the
design and implementation of continuing social change, the rejection and destruction of the bourgeois constraints on their functions
and power, and the defense and extension of the apparatus of the
managerial system. The rhetoric of conservatism did not alter the
basic reality of the managerial regime and its continuing revolution,
and the reality came to the surface again in the utopian imagery of
the "New Frontier," "Camelot," and "Great Society" of the 1960s
and even in the planning of the Vietnam War. Lyndon Johnson and
his advisers projected a "TVA on the Mekong" that would "solve"

---

6. Allen J. Matusow, *The Unraveling of America: A History of Liberalism in the
1960s* (New York: Harper & Row, 1984), 6–7.
    7. Ibid., 33.

the environmental problems that, in their view, lay at the root of communism, and the "McNamara Revolution" in the Defense Department carried through the managerialization of war and the technocratic transformation of the military services. Few large corporations supported Senator Barry Goldwater's rather quaint evocation of bourgeois beliefs in the 1964 presidential campaign, and most corporate donations accrued to the Johnson-Humphrey ticket.[8] The "conservatization" of managerial liberalism in the postwar era was intended to legitimize the managerial regime by lending it the appearance of continuity and respectability and to check the tendencies of the ideological Left to push the regime beyond what the elite wanted and required, but it did not significantly slow or reverse the radicalizing and antibourgeois mechanisms of the regime and its system of social dominance by the managerial elite.

The conservatism of managerial liberalism was thus entirely distinct from the bourgeois conservatism of the Old Right. The former sought merely to conserve, rationalize, and legitimize the new managerial establishment in state, corporations, and mass media and cultural institutions. The Old Right conservatives sought to conserve and restore at least the principles and values if not the actual institutions of the premanagerial bourgeois order and the social, moral, and religious traditions that formed the substratum of bourgeois society. The two "conservatisms" were, in fact, incompatible, and much of the literature of 1950s liberalism concerned itself with proving that it, not bourgeois conservatism, was the true representative of the American tradition.

The claim of consensus liberalism to be the true conservatism was buttressed by an impressive and elaborate interpretation of American history and society articulated by such historians as Daniel Boorstin, Louis Hartz, Richard Hofstadter, and David Potter and by sociologists such as Daniel Bell, Arnold Rose, Talcott Parsons, David Riesman, Nathan Glazer, and Seymour Lipset. The aggressiveness of the McCarthy movement and the efflorescence of serious anti-liberal thought in *National Review* and among the writers associated with it in the 1950s required a response from consensus liberalism. The very existence and popularity of such movements suggested

8. Ibid., 151.

that there was something else in the American tradition besides a "liberal consensus" and a teleological movement toward the New Deal and its legacy.

The response that consensus liberals gave to the rise of the political and intellectual Right of the 1950s was the theory of "status anxiety," most notably formulated in an anthology of essays, *The Radical Right,* edited by Daniel Bell with contributions from Glazer, Hofstadter, Parsons, Lipset, and other representatives of 1950s liberalism.[9] The gist of the theory of the anthology was that McCarthyism represented the frustrations of the mass man and the resentments of socially dislocated strata of American society against traditional upper-class leadership of the northeastern "establishment" as symbolized by banking and manufacturing elites, prestigious universities, and the foreign service and its ideology of "one-worldism," or globalism. The political meaning of the collection, stripped of its verbal and social science camouflage, was that the American Right of the 1950s was, in Hofstadter's term, "pseudo-conservative" and that it had no legitimate or important place in the liberal "consensus" or indeed in the American political mainstream. This interpretation of the political Right also involved the ascription of economic motivations to the financial supporters of the movement and the use of the "authoritarian personality" model developed by Theodor Adorno and the Frankfurt School; and the social and political base of the American Right was perceived as essentially identical to that of European totalitarian movements.

Subsequent empirical research seriously challenged this interpretation of "McCarthyism" and the right-wing movements of the 1950s. There was, to be sure, at least in the grassroots components of the Right, a hostility toward newly established elites, their upper-class collaborators (Franklin Roosevelt had been a "traitor to his class") and their ideology and institutions, as well as a visible sense of frustration. It is likely that traditional and bourgeois elements in the movements of the Right accurately perceived the revolutionary implications of the managerial elite and its quite narrow "consensus" ideology and that their frustrations and resentments were the prod-

---

9. Daniel Bell, ed., *The Radical Right: The New American Right Expanded and Updated* (Garden City, N. Y.: Doubleday & Company, 1964).

uct of thwarted economic interests, threatened social and cultural values, and political weakness.

What was missing from the psychological explanation of the American Right was any effort to apply the same methodologies and concepts to liberalism and its social and political context. This one-sided use of social science was characteristic of the environmentalist and relativist sociology that the reformers and intellectuals of the Progressive movement had developed. As Eric Goldman has written,

> When they [the reformers] said that all ideas must be related to economic interest, they did not really mean *all* ideas; they meant only their opponents' ideas. So conservatism became a rationalization of greed, while the tenets of progressivism were "scientific," "objective," and "moral," the same kind of absolute Truth and Good that has immemorially given men enthusiasm for a cause. [10]

Historian Allen Matusow has also suggested the political motivations involved in the transformation of American liberalism from a faith in mass democracy to an elitist pluralism:

> The groups accused of status anxiety and of practicing McCarthyism (e.g., urban Catholics and midwestern farmers) belonged to the same "masses" whom the intellectuals had romanticized in the 1930s. Traumatized by McCarthyism, many intellectuals began to reassess the assumptions that had once supported their faith in these masses and in popular democracy. The result of their reflections was the so-called New Conservatism, or as political theorists called it, pluralism. [11]

The one-sidedness and political convenience of the consensus liberal interpretation of the American Right reveals the ideological functions that the social sciences performed for its exponents. In their hands, sociology, economics, psychology, political science, and history operated not as disciplines to explain reality but as political weapons.

The consolidation of managerial control of the mass organizations of the central state, corporations and unions, and the larger

---

10. Goldman, *Rendezvous with Destiny,* 155.
11. Allen J. Matusow, ed., *Joseph R. McCarthy* (Englewood Cliffs, N. J.: Prentice-Hall, 1970), 131–32.

organs of mass communications, education, and culture established the framework for the "consensus" to which managerial liberalism appealed. Despite its claim to "pluralism," however, the consensus effectively excluded and denied intellectual and political legitimacy to all nonliberal ideas and movements—to the American Right as well as to the Left. The consensus nevertheless served an important function for the managerial intelligentsia, for it legitimized intellectuals and verbalists as the mind as well as the conscience of the new elite, and the managerial system offered considerable material and psychic rewards to the intellectuals who designed its public policy agenda, explained and justified the agenda to the mass population, instructed new generations of managers in the skills and techniques as well as in the articles of faith of managerial rule, and debated and interpreted the specific policies and activities of the system. As Richard Hofstadter acknowledged,

> Social scientists . . . had special reason for a positive interest in the reform movements. The development of regulative and humane legislation required the skills of lawyers and economists, sociologists and political scientists, in the writing of laws and in the staffing of administrative and regulative bodies. Controversy over such issues created a new market for the books and magazine articles of the experts and engendered a new respect for their specialized knowledge. Reform brought with it the brain trust.[12]

Nevertheless, the era of liberal-managerial "consensus" of the 1950s and early 1960s did not last. The political and cultural schisms of the late 1960s, from both the Left and the Right, and the evident failures and crises of the colossal managerial apparatus, disrupted the functioning of the system and discredited its formula of consensus liberalism. On the one hand, the New Left and the counterculture rejected and ridiculed the complacency of consensus liberalism and demanded an acceleration of the managerial agenda far beyond what the elite in government, corporations and unions, and the educational and communications establishment was willing to grant. The New Left demands for social and economic equality and its hatred for traditional and bourgeois values and institutions were

12. Richard Hofstadter, *The Age of Reform: From Bryan to F.D.R.* (New York: Random House, 1955), 155.

all consistent with the earlier progressivism of managerial liberalism but were incompatible with the interests of the managerial elite and with the mass organizations they directed. There was no way for the managerial intelligentsia to express its antipathy for New Left ideology and aims without betraying its own professed beliefs and revealing the self-serving nature of its ideology, and the New Left and its countercultural allies insistently hammered away at the vulnerabilities of consensus liberalism and the managerial system it served.

On the other hand, the Wallace movement and the embryonic New Right of the 1970s also rejected the liberal consensus and much of the managerial system. In fact the New Right was far more radical and threatening to the system than the New Left. When Wallace railed against "bureaucrats," "intellectuals," and the "media," he did not, like the New Left, limit his passion to the military arm of the managerial state (in which he had little interest) but meant its whole social engineering apparatus, its allies in the intelligentsia, and even its corporate sector. His following cared little for the bourgeois slogans of the "free market" and constitutionalist integrity but was concerned mainly with the "social issues," the protection of their own social, cultural, and economic standing, and the rejection of managerial cosmopolitanism and social engineering. Moreover, Wallace and the New Right drew their votes and much of their financial support from the core of the political base of the managerial system in the white, urban, working and lower middle class. While the political challenge from the New Left dwindled after the McGovern campaign of 1972, the militancy and success of the New Right in the following years continued the challenge to the managerial system and successfully questioned the social, economic, and foreign policies of the system in a series of highly visible and salient issue campaigns—the opposition to busing, the Equal Rights Amendment, the Panama Canal treaties, the extended regulation and interventionism represented by such agencies as the Occupational Safety and Health Administration (OSHA) and the Environmental Protection Agency (EPA), and in the tax revolt of the late 1970s.

By the mid 1970s it was evident to a sizeable portion of the intellectual and verbalist class that consensus liberalism in its pristine form was no longer functional, that intellectuals and verbalists were being drawn into an "adversary culture" of the Left, that large segments of American society were attracted to New Right movements, and that a new or revised formula had to be developed if the managerial system was to retain legitimacy. The result of that realization was neoconservatism, which rejected both the explicit collectivism, utopianism, and anti-Americanism of the New Left that frightened and offended most Americans as well as the more radical implications of the New Right.

Neoconservatism rejected all forms of extremism and all suggestions of a need for far reaching change. "The basic credo of us Neo-conservatives, or whatever you want to call us," stated Ben Wattenberg in 1980, "is that society moderately and gradually self-corrects."[13] Moderation, gradualism, empiricism, pragmatism, centrism became the watchwords of neoconservatism, whereby confrontation with the fundamental mechanisms and tendencies of the managerial system and fundamental changes suggested by either the Right or the Left were avoided. In the neoconservative view of America, there was nothing seriously wrong with the society and government that had developed between the New Deal and the Great Society, and it was the goal of neoconservatives to communicate the soundness of the managerial system to the adversary intellectuals of the Left and to co-opt the militant activists of the New Right.

Neoconservatism was thus the heir of the consensus liberalism of the 1950s and 1960s and served the same stabilizing and legitimizing functions for the managerial regime. Norman Podhoretz acknowledged as much in the late 1970s:

> These intellectual adversaries of the adversary culture were often called "neo-conservatives," a designation happily accepted by some (like Irving Kristol) but rejected by most others, who continued to think of themselves as liberals. "Neo-liberal" would perhaps have been a more accurate label for the entire group than neo-conservative, except for the fact that its liberalism was old and not new—that is, it derived from the New Deal and not from the New Politics.[14]

13. *Objections to Conservatism* (Washington: Heritage Foundation, 1980), 59.
14. Norman Podhoretz, "The Adversary Culture and the New Class," in B. Bruce-Briggs, ed., *The New Class?* (New Brunswick, N.J.: Transaction Books, 1979), 30–31.

Indeed, a number of neoconservatives—Daniel Bell, Nathan Glazer, Seymour Lipset—had themselves been architects of consensus liberalism and had been associated with or had strongly influenced others such as Podhoretz and Irving Kristol. Some, like Jeane Kirkpatrick, Ben Wattenberg, Elliott Abrams, and Carl Gershman, had been close associates of Hubert Humphrey, Lyndon Johnson, Henry Jackson, and other political leaders of the managerial state.

To be sure, neoconservatism retreated from or modified the conventional liberal emphasis on the state as the proper instrumentality of progressive social change, but it is difficult to find in the body of neoconservative thought any principled rejection of this role of government.[15] Thus Irving Kristol, one of the most conservative of the neoconservatives, has written equivocally of the "nostalgia" of the free market ideas of F. A. Hayek and Milton Friedman and has endorsed the essential structure of the managerial state:

> In economic and social policy, it [neoconservatism] feels no lingering hostility to the welfare state, nor does it accept it resignedly, as a necessary evil. Instead it seeks not to dismantle the welfare state in the name of free-market economics but rather to reshape it so as to attach to it the *conservative* predispositions of the people. This reshaping will presumably take the form of trying to rid the welfare state of its paternalistic orientation, imposed on it by Left-liberalism, and making it over into the kind of "social insurance state" that provides the social and economic security a modern citizenry demands while minimizing governmental intrusion into individual liberties.[16]

It is difficult to tell what this passage means, except that neoconservatism has little interest in dismantling or radically restructuring the welfare state, and it does not explain how, in a mass democracy, the demands of a "modern citizenry" can be restricted to basic "social and economic security" or indeed in what such security consists. In short, the neoconservative idea of the welfare state leaves open the possibility of the continuing expansion of central government and its resumption of its social engineering functions, and it thus supports a principal pillar of the managerial regime and agenda.

15. Neoconservatives were at first more critical of large and active government than they later became in the course of the Reagan administration and afterwards.

16. Irving Kristol, *Reflections of a Neoconservative: Looking Back, Looking Ahead* (New York: Basic Books, 1983), xii.

The preferred instrument of progress for neoconservatives is the managerial corporation and "democratic capitalism," which, in neoconservative Michael Novak's view, engenders a "continuous revolution" resulting in increasing levels of material affluence and cultural "openness" in place of the confining institutions and values of traditional and bourgeois society.[17] While neoconservatism formally recognizes the importance of religion, family, morality, community, and patriotism in creating and preserving a free society, it has generally emphasized social conservatism less than foreign policy, defense, and economic issues. Thus, Ben Wattenberg has indicated the priorities of neoconservative policy, as well as its basic shallowness:

> The central notion that Senator [Daniel Patrick] Moynihan has been pursuing these many years might be characterized as "the Russians are coming and they are threatening human liberty"; and the central notion that Phyllis Schlafly has been pursuing in recent years is: "unless we stop ERA there will be men in women's rest rooms." Then I would ask you to consider the following statement by Mr. Gilder: "Phyllis Schlafly is better at defining national priorities than is Daniel Patrick Moynihan." If you think ERA is a greater threat to our civilization than the Soviet buildup, then you have your candidate.[18]

Aside from Mr. Wattenberg's trivialization of the content and goals of the anti-ERA movement, the non sequitur of his conclusion, and the probability that Mrs. Schlafly's voting record, were she a member of the Senate, would compare favorably with that of Senator Moynihan on conservative defense and foreign policy issues, what Mr. Wattenberg apparently does not perceive is the strong connection between the integrity and health of social institutions, such as the family, which Mrs. Schlafly sees threatened by the ERA and ideological feminism, and the will of a nation to meet foreign threats and preserve its security. Mr. Wattenberg's apparent obliviousness to the values of social conservatism is entirely consistent with the concentration of managerial ideologies on purely material and "pragmatic" issues and their neglect of moral, social, and spiritual concerns.

17. Michael Novak, *The Spirit of Democratic Capitalism* (New York: Simon and Schuster, 1982), 171–72.

18. *Objections to Conservatism,* 59; Mr. Wattenberg's remark was made in the context of a debate with George Gilder.

In foreign policy itself, there appears to be a strong overlap between neoconservatism and consensus liberalism. Both are anticommunist, but both also serve the managerial system and its globalist and cosmopolitan tendencies and interests by emphasizing a Wilsonian global democratism as the proper response to the Soviet Union and the appeal of communism (and indeed as the central purpose of U.S. foreign policy). Under the Reagan Administration, neoconservative Wilsonianism was manifested in the National Endowment for Democracy and in increasing neoconservative sympathy for sanctions against South Africa, the ratification of the Genocide Convention, measures against the Pinochet government in Chile, the ousting of Philippine President Marcos, the promotion of Jose Napoleon Duarte over Roberto D'Aubuisson in El Salvador, the invocation of human rights against anticommunist allies of the United States, and a general preference for an untested and impractical social democracy over the pro-Western and anticommunist authoritarian regimes of the Third World. Despite formal acceptance of the "national interest" as the proper measuring rod of American foreign policy (including a neoconservative journal of that name), in practice the neoconservative interpretation of national interest reduces to the integration of the United States into a global and cosmopolitan world order. The most insulting epithet in the neoconservative lexicon of foreign affairs is not "anti-American," "one-worlder," or "pro-communist," but "isolationist." Democratic capitalism, combined with political and social democracy, is intended by neoconservatives to solve the political and economic problems of Third World states in the same way that consensus liberalism intended foreign aid and managerial reconstruction to develop the political and social democratic institutions of such countries.

The principal "enemy" for neoconservatism is what it calls the "New Class," which consists, in Irving Kristol's description, of "scientists, lawyers, city planners, social workers, educators, criminologists, sociologists, public health doctors, and so forth—a substantial number of whom find their careers in the expanding public sector rather than the private."[19] The New Class, in Mr. Kristol's view, is "far less interested in individual financial rewards than in

19. Kristol, *Reflections,* 211.

the corporate power of their class" and sees in ideological themes drawn from the New Left a means of rationalizing and extending its class power. The neoconservative idea of the New Class, as Mr. Kristol once acknowledged, was influenced by James Burnham's theory of the managerial elite, though for Mr. Kristol the New Class does not include corporate managers and the technically skilled groups that John Kenneth Galbraith terms the "technostructure," the concept of which was also influenced by Burnham's theory.[20] The exclusion of the corporate managerial elite from the neoconservative idea of the New Class is all the more striking in view of Mr. Kristol's acknowledgment of what he calls the "corporate revolution" and his understanding that "the large corporation has gone quasi-public, that is, it now straddles, uncomfortably and uncertainly, both the private and public sectors of our 'mixed economy.' "[21]

The distinction and even the antagonism that Mr. Kristol draws between the New Class, adversarial in its ideology and located in the public sector, and the corporate managers is, in fact, necessary to neoconservative theory and its ideological functions. To include the corporate branch of the managerial elite within the New Class would contradict the neoconservative view of the corporation as an alternative instrument to the state. If the same social force were seen as being in control of the state as well as the corporation, there could be little differentiation in the elites that direct each sector and hence little difference between their goals and activities. Managerial capitalism could not then be presented in neoconservative ideology as the benevolent agent of progress through "voluntary" action. Moreover, to acknowledge that corporate managers are part of the New Class and that both are derived from Burnham's managerial elite would jeopardize the distinctions neoconservatives draw between the "good" liberalism of the New Deal era and the "bad" liberalism of the late 1960s. Neoconservatism, if it is to function as an effective legitimizing ideology for the managerial regime and to preserve the regime from radical alterations by the Left, cannot acknowledge that the managerial elite in the corporation is essentially

20. Irving Kristol, "The 'New Class' Revisited," *Wall Street Journal,* May 31, 1979, 24; John Kenneth Galbraith, *The New Industrial State,* 3d ed., rev. (New York: New American Library, 1978), 107–9, 107, n. 6.

21. Kristol, *Reflections,* 204, 216.

the same as the New Class in the public sector, nor can it acknowledge that both groups share essentially the same interests, world
view, and agenda—the transcendence of bourgeois institutions and
values and the extension of the collectivist and cosmopolitan forms
of the managerial regime—or that the New Class and its agenda
were not the products of the 1960s but of the managerial revolution
of the early part of the century. To use the theory of the managerial
revolution to link the New Class enemy with a corporate elite that is
a neoconservative ally and to see both the New Class and the corporate elite as products of New Deal–Great Society-era liberalism
would implicate the "bad" liberalism with the "good" liberalism of
the New Deal.

Neoconservatives are, in fact, involved in what their liberal critic
Peter Steinfels calls the "war for the New Class."[22] Nowhere in their
analysis and critique of the New Class do neoconservatives urge or
even insinuate its abolition or the radical restructuring of the mass
organizations that the New Class directs and on which its position
and interests depend, and the concept of the New Class is less a sociological than an ideological construct. In neoconservative discus-
sions of the New Class, individuals appear to be included in this
category not on the basis of their social position but rather because
of what they believe. Neoconservatives object mainly to what the New
Class thinks, not to its existence, its position, its power, or the processes by which it holds power, and, as Steinfels points out, the neoconservatives are themselves part of the New Class.[23] In this sense,
the neoconservative sociology of the New Class is really a pseudo-
sociology, reminiscent of the use of social science as a political and
ideological weapon by the reformers of the Progressive Era and the
consensus liberals of the 1950s.

Neoconservatives genuinely reject the New Left orientation of
some elements of the New Class because they understand that the
radical acceleration of social and political change that this orientation advocates would destabilize and perhaps destroy the managerial system. New Left radicalism would thus be counterproductive,

---

22. Peter Steinfels, *The Neoconservatives: The Men Who Are Changing America's Politics* (New York: Simon and Schuster, 1979), chap. 11.
23. Ibid., 285–86.

or, as many neoconservatives think of it, reactionary, in jeopardizing
the gradual and more realistic means of implementing the managerial agenda that neoconservatism contemplates. What neoconservatives want, therefore, is not to disperse the New Class or to dismantle the mass structures of the managerial regime in which the
New Class occupies a position of power but rather to persuade the
radical elements of the New Class that their true ideological goals
and group interests are better served by neoconservative ideology
and methods than by New Leftism. Hence, neoconservatives habitually address themselves not to grassroots audiences or to Old Right
constituencies but to the New Class itself. Virtually all of the journals under neoconservative influence—*Commentary, Public Interest, National Interest, This World, New Criterion,* the editorial
page of the *Wall Street Journal, Policy Review, American Spectator*—are intended for "elite" audiences; and "elite" in contemporary America means the New Class and the managerial establishment. The transformation of the *American Spectator* from the
right-wing, antiestablishment, irreverent, and occasionally radical
Alternative of the early 1970s into the solemn and pontifical neoconservative journal for yuppies that it is today is of interest in this
regard. The advertisements once carried by the *Alternative* (aside
from those for local small businesses) generally quoted insulting
descriptions of the magazine from establishment journals and spokesmen, to communicate to potential readers the contempt in which
the editors of the magazine held the establishment. Today the *Spectator* sports ads listing the Important People who read it. In the
early 1980s, the magazine moved from its original base in Bloom-
ington, Indiana, to Washington, D.C., a geographical transition that
conveniently symbolizes the magazine's evolution from the antimanagerial to the managerial Right.

If neoconservatives seek to provide a new managerial ideology
for the New Class or managerial elite in place of New Left ideas, they
also seek to co-opt and mute the radical antimanagerial impetus of
the Old and New Right. Efforts by the political Right to challenge
the managerial establishment—to nominate M. E. Bradford rather
than William Bennett for the chairmanship of the National Endowment for the Humanities in 1981 and to develop a serious conservative presence among university students through right-wing news-

papers and a conservative group called Accuracy in Academia—have been vigorously opposed, resisted, and undermined by neoconservative leaders (even to the point, reportedly, that neoconservative foundations threatened to terminate support for conservative groups that did not toe the line). Unable to build a grassroots political constituency or electoral coalition themselves, neoconservatives welcome New Right activism for providing a political base that can elect a conservative or moderate President, but they seek to obstruct the agenda of such constituencies if it threatens or interferes with their own rather different agenda and interests.

While there is, to be sure, a certain overlap between the ideas and agendas of neoconservatism and those of the Old and New Right, and while each can be politically and intellectually helpful to the other, ultimately the two movements seek incompatible goals. Neoconservatives seek to rationalize, legitimize, defend, and conserve the managerial regime—what conservatives have usually called the "Liberal Establishment"—because the regime provides the social force to which they belong with its social functions and power. The Old and New Right have historically opposed the managerial regime and have developed an ideology, an analysis of public policy, and an electoral strategy by which the regime can be challenged and dismantled or radically reformed. The goals of the radicalism of the Old Right are not the overthrow of the government and the destruction of society in pursuit of an imaginary utopia, but the conservation, in institutionalized forms, of the traditional beliefs that inform Western and American civilizations in both their ancient and bourgeois manifestations. If neoconservative co-optation, and the dynamics of the continuing managerial revolution, deflect the American Right from this goal, the result will not be the renaissance of America and the West but the continuation and eventual fulfillment of the goals of their most committed enemies.

The Case of George Will

George F. Will,
Statecraft as Soulcraft:
What Government Does

Few writers who apply the label "conservative" to themselves
have acquired so prominent a position in establishment media as
George F. Will. A nationally syndicated columnist who regularly
appears in the *Washington Post* and *Newsweek,* a fixture on national
television discussion programs, and a winner of the Pulitzer Prize,
Mr. Will has traveled a long way since he wrote articles for the *Alternative* in the early 1970s. With the possible exceptions of Patrick J.
Buchanan, James K. Kilpatrick, and William F. Buckley, Jr., it is difficult to think of any other self-described conservative publicist who
has so strikingly "made it."

The secret of Mr. Will's success is only in part attributable to his
many merits—his willingness to explore controversial areas of public life in a manner remarkably free of popular cliché and conventional wisdom, his learning in the literary and philosophical classics, and his habitual articulateness. His success is due also to the
general thrust of his distinctive formulation of conservatism and the
way in which he applies his ideas to public matters, for it is evident
in much of his writing that Mr. Will is at considerable pains to separate himself from most Americans who today regard themselves as
conservatives and to assure his readers that there are important public institutions and policies, usually criticized by conservatives, with
which he has no quarrel.

Statecraft as Soulcraft is Mr. Will's first real book, as opposed to
collections of his columns, and its purpose is to develop in a rather
systematic way his political beliefs and to explain how these beliefs—
"conservatism properly understood"—are different from and superior to the ideas to which most American conservatives subscribe.
The most distinctive difference, he tells us in the preface, appears to
be his "belief in strong government." "My aim," he says, "is to recast

conservatism in a form compatible with the broad popular imperatives of the day, but also to change somewhat the agenda and even the vocabulary of contemporary politics. To those who are liberals and to those who call themselves conservatives, I say: Politics is more difficult than you think."

Despite his assertion that today "there are almost no conservatives, properly understood," the principal line of argument of *Statecraft as Soulcraft* will be familiar to most and largely congenial to many American conservative intellectuals. It is Mr. Will's argument that modern political thought from the time of Machiavelli forward has ignored or denied the ethical potentialities of human nature and has concentrated on passion and self-interest as the constituent forces of society and government. Modern politics therefore seeks to use these forces, rather than to restrain or elevate them, in designing social and political arrangements in such a way that passion and self-interest will conduce to stability, prosperity, and liberty. "The result," he writes,

> is a radical retrenchment, a lowering of expectations, a constriction of political horizons. By abandoning both divine and natural teleology, modernity radically reoriented politics. The focus of politics shifted away from the question of the most eligible ends of life, to the passional origins of actions. The ancients were resigned to accommodating what the moderns are eager to accommodate: human shortcomings. What once was considered a defect— self-interestedness—became the base on which an edifice of rights was erected.

The Founding Fathers also subscribed to the modernist school of political thought, particularly James Madison, whose "attention is exclusively on controlling passions with countervailing passions; he is not concerned with the amelioration or reform of passions. The political problem is seen entirely in terms of controlling the passions that nature gives, not nurturing the kind of character that the polity might need. He says, 'We well know that neither moral nor religious motives can be relied on.'"

The result of political modernism and its concentration on the lower elements of human nature has been the loss of ideals of community, citizenship, and the public moral order. With its emphasis on "self-interest" and the proper arrangement or equilibrium of passions and appetites rather than their reform and improvement, modernism has opened the door to the privatization of politics, distrust of public authority, the pursuit of material and individual self-interest, and the proliferation of individual rights in the form of claims against government and society.

> Once politics is defined negatively, as an enterprise for drawing a protective circle around the individual's sphere of self-interested action, then public concerns are by definition distinct from, and secondary to, private concerns. Regardless of democratic forms, when people are taught by philosophy (and the social climate) that they need not govern their actions by calculations of public good, they will come to blame all social shortcomings on the agency of collective considerations, the government, and will absolve themselves.

Contemporary American conservatism, in Mr. Will's view, as well as contemporary liberalism, are both derived from political modernism.

> They are versions of the basic program of the liberal-democratic political impulse that was born with Machiavelli and Hobbes. Near the core of the philosophy of modern liberalism, as it descends from those two men, is an inadequacy that is becoming glaring. And what in America is called conservatism is only marginally disharmonious with liberalism. This kind of conservatism is an impotent critic of liberalism because it too is a participant in the modern political enterprise. . . . The enterprise is not wrong because it revises, or even because it revises radically. Rather it is wrong because it lowers, radically. It deflates politics, conforming politics to the strongest and commonest impulses in the mass of men.

For Mr. Will, then, the proper corrective to the degeneration of democracy and the substitution of private indulgence for the public good is the restoration of ancient and medieval political and ethical philosophy and its vindication of the role of government in constraining private interests in deference to the public moral order and in inculcating virtue—in other words, "legislating morality." "By the legislation of morality I mean the enactment of laws and implementation of policies that proscribe, mandate, regulate, or subsidize behavior that will, over time, have the predictable effect of nurturing, bolstering or altering habits, dispositions and values on a broad scale." Such policies would clearly distinguish a "real conservatism" from the fake American version:

> The United States acutely needs a real conservatism, characterized by a concern to cultivate the best persons and the best in persons. It should express renewed appreciation for the ennobling functions of government. It should challenge the liberal doctrine that regarding one important dimension of life—the "inner life"—there should be less government—less than there is now, less than there recently was, less than most political philosophers have thought prudent.

Despite Mr. Will's predilection for putting down contemporary conservatives, the theoretical dimensions of his argument will come as no great shock to many of them. It has been articulated in one form or another by a number of American writers since the 1940s—Russell Kirk, Leo Strauss, and Eric Voegelin, to name but a few. Mr. Will is quite correct that the libertarian and classical liberal faction of American conservatism will dissent vigorously from his thought and that they are not conservatives in the classical sense of the term. Yet many prominent libertarians have resisted and rejected being called conservatives, and it is hardly fair to criticize them for not adhering to a body of ideas with which they have never claimed any connection.

But it is hardly fair for Mr. Will to categorize all conservatives or even the mainstream of American conservatism as libertarian. Although this mainstream has been oriented toward the defense of the bourgeois order as expressed in classical liberal ideology, its principal exponents have generally been aware of the moral and social foundations of classical liberal values and have accepted at least some governmental role in the protection and encouragement of these values. Conventional American conservatism is in effect a reformulation of the Old Whiggery of the eighteenth century and has sought to synthesize Edmund Burke and Adam Smith, order and liberty, in what was ascribed to its most representative voice, Frank S. Meyer, as "fusionism."

There are of course serious philosophical problems in effecting this synthesis, and the problems have never been satisfactorily resolved; but the efflorescence of conservative thought around these problems in recent decades shows that American conservatives are neither as simple-minded nor as illiterate as Mr. Will wants us to believe. In the last decade conservative political efforts have increasingly emphasized moral issues in campaigns against pornography, abortion, and the dissolution of the family and community, and in favor of public support for religious faith. It is therefore simply a gross error to claim that the American Right, old or new, is oblivious to the role of government in sustaining morality.

Mr. Will, moreover, knows this, because he is himself a well-informed man and because he was at one time an editor of *National Review* and has had close intellectual and professional connections with the conservative movement. Yet at no place in *Statecraft as Soulcraft* is there any acknowledgment of the richness or variety of contemporary conservative thought, any appreciation for the intellectual and political contributions of serious conservatives to sustaining and reviving premodern political ideas, nor indeed any reference at all to any contemporary conservative thinker. There is only a constant barrage of patronizing and often contemptuous generalization about "*soi-disant* conservatives," "something calling itself conservatism," and " 'conservatives.' "

Although the traditionalist and most antimodern orientation within American conservatism will probably experience little discomfort at Mr. Will's development of his ideas, it may have more problems with some of his applications of his philosophy to contemporary policy. Although Mr. Will is consistent in his strong support for the illegalization of pornography and abortion, he also tries to use premodern or classical conservatism to endorse the welfare state and to justify the civil rights legislation of the 1960s, both of which are the principal creations of modern liberalism and constitute revolutionary engines by which the radicalizing dynamic of liberalism is built into contemporary American government.

Although Mr. Will acknowledges that the "almost limitless expansion of American government since the New Deal . . . was implicit in the commission given to government by modern political philosophy: the commission to increase pleasure and decrease pain," he also believes that "the political system must also incorporate altruistic motives. It does so in domestic policies associated with the phrase 'welfare state.' These are policies that express the community's acceptance of an ethic of common provision." He cites Disraeli and Bismarck as conservative architects of the welfare state and regards as the conservative principle underlying welfare the idea "that private economic decisions often are permeated with a public interest and hence are legitimate subjects of political debate and intervention."

Mr. Will is certainly correct in his assertion of this principle, but the centralized, redistributive welfare apparatus created by liberalism and resisted by conservatives is not legitimately derived from the principle. The classical conservative vision of society as an organic, hierarchical, and authoritative structure of reciprocal responsibilities implies a social duty to the poor, but it also implies a responsibility on the part of the poor that the liberal "right to welfare" denies. Moreover, the virtue of charity endorsed by classical conservatives presupposes an inequality of wealth and an ideal of *noblesse oblige* that the architects of liberal welfare states abhor. Nor is the classical conservative ideal of public welfare necessarily or primarily restricted to a centralized apparatus or even to government, but rather allows for social provision of support through family, community, church, and class obligations as well as at local levels of government.

Finally, the classical conservative welfare state usually developed in nondemocratic societies in which the lower orders who received public largess did not also possess votes that gave them electoral control of the public leaders who dispensed welfare. The mass democratic nature of the modern welfare state ensures the indefinite expansion of necessary and desirable public provision into a socialist redistribution of wealth that reduces the public order to a neverending feast for the private interests and appetites of those who benefit from welfare. Yet even as they feast, the modern welfare system also destroys lower-class families and communities. The system encourages the mass hedonism that characterizes bureaucratic capitalism and enserfs the welfare class as the political base of the bureaucratic-political elite in the state. The modern administrative apparatus of the centralized welfare state thus supports a bureaucratic and social engineering elite that devotes its energies to the further destruction and reconstruction of the social order.

Mr. Will offers some suggestions "for a welfare system that supports rather than disintegrates families" and which "will use government to combat the tendency of the modern bureaucratic state to standardize and suffocate diversity." Frankly, it is not easy to see how this can be accomplished, since governmental welfare replicates, usurps, and thus weakens the functions of the family and community and must necessarily proceed along uniform legal and administrative lines. Indeed, Mr. Will's defense of the welfare state suggests no awareness of the important differences between the concept and actual functioning of the classical conservative welfare state and those of modern liberalism. An important part of his case is the pragmatic argument that conservatives must accept the welfare state or find themselves consigned to political oblivion. "A conservative doctrine of the welfare state is required if conservatives are even to be included in the contemporary political conversation" and the idea of the welfare state "has now come and is not apt to depart."

"Conservatism properly understood," then, accepts the premises and institutions of contemporary liberalism and must not challenge them if it is to enjoy success and participate in dialogue with a dominant liberalism. Hence, any discussion of the very radical and unsettling reforms that would be necessary to construct a welfare state consistent with genuine classical conservatism, as opposed to the abridged, expurgated, and pop version presented by Mr. Will, would defeat his pragmatic purpose by alienating and frightening the very liberal and establishment elites he is trying to impress.

Similarly, Mr. Will's defense of the civil rights revolution in terms of classical conservatism is an erroneous application of a traditionalist principle.

> But the enforcement of law by making visible and sometimes vivid the community values that are deemed important enough to support by law, can bolster these values. . . . Of course, nothing in a society, least of all moral sentiment, is permanent and final. Indeed, there have been occasions when the law rightfully set out to change important and passionately held sentiments, and the law proved to be a web of iron.

One such occasion, he argues, was the abrogation of the right of owners of public accommodations to deny service to blacks, enacted in the civil rights legislation of the 1960s. The exercise of this right became "intolerably divisive" and therefore had to be abridged by congressional action.

> The most admirable achievements of modern liberalism—desegregation, and the civil rights acts—were explicit and successful attempts to change

(among other things) individuals' moral beliefs by compelling them to change their behavior. The theory was that if government compelled people to eat and work and study and play together, government would improve the inner lives of those people.

Mr. Will is correct that "moral sentiment" does indeed change, but absolute moral values do not, and only if we believe that egalitarian values are superior to the rights of property can we accept the legislation Mr. Will is defending as legitimate. Nor is it clear that the civil rights revolution has really improved our "inner lives" or even changed our external conduct to any great degree, and if it has, the change has derived not only from government but also from social and nonpublic sanctions as well. It is quite true that "stateways" can make "folkways," that imposition of beliefs through coercion by an apparatus of power can eventually alter patterns of thinking and conduct. The Christian emperors of Rome after Constantine certainly used the coercive power of the state to alter beliefs and values, as did Henry VIII and his successors in the English Reformation.

What the conservative wants to know, however, is by what authority a state undertakes such massive transformations and whether what is gained compensates adequately for the damage that is inevitably done. In the case of the suppression of paganism and its replacement by Christianity, Christian conservatives will have little doubt of the authority and ultimate value of the revolution. The processes by which the civil rights revolution was accomplished are more questionable. It is not clear they have led or will lead to more justice and tolerance or to greater racial harmony. They certainly did damage to the Constitution by allowing the national judicial and legislative branches to override state and local laws. They also damaged the political culture by popularizing and legitimizing the idea that every conceivable "minority" (women, sexual deviants, the handicapped, and all racial and ethnic groups) may use the federal government to satisfy its ambitions at the expense of local jurisdictions, the public treasury, and the social order. Nor is it clear on what authority Congress overrode traditional property rights to impose new rights. The exploitation of the national government to abrogate and create rights by which the ambitions and private dogmas of a faction may be satisfied is no less an instance of the degeneration of modernism than the abuse of government by the constituencies of the welfare state. The civil rights revolution and the welfare state are not, then, reactions against the tendencies of modernism as Mr. Will presents them, but rather their fulfillment.

Indeed, for all his expostulations in favor of the highminded and aristocratic enforcement of virtue, Mr. Will repeatedly expresses his deference to the conventional and the popular. The rights of proprietors in 1964 "had become intolerably divisive," so "conservatism properly understood" accepts the demands of those who initiated the division. "An American majority was unusually aroused," so authority must follow the majority. The welfare state is an idea whose time "has now come," so conservatives must accept the idea and must not resist the times. "If conservatism is to engage itself with the way we live now," it must adapt itself to current circumstances, and perish the thought that we might really change the way we live now by rejecting the legacies of liberalism, dismantling its power structure, and enforcing and protecting the real traditions of the West. In place of that disturbing thought, Mr. Will invites us to indulge his elegant pretense that such a conservative radicalism is really what he supports, even as he snorts his open contempt for the only force in American politics that has ever seriously proposed it.

Throughout Mr. Will's articulation of what he takes to be conservatism there is an ambiguity or confusion between the respect for tradition and a given way of life that animates genuine conservatives, on the one hand, and the desire to impose upon and "correct" tradition by acts of power, on the other.

> The primary business of conservatism is preservation of the social order that has grown in all its richness—not preserving it like a fly in amber, but protecting it especially from suffocation or dictated alteration by the state. However, the state has a central role to play. The preservation of a nation requires a certain minimum moral continuity, because a nation is not just "territory" or "physical locality." A nation is people "associated in agreement with respect to justice." And continuity cannot be counted on absent precautions.

And similarly, "Proper conservatism holds that men and women are biological facts, but that ladies and gentlemen fit for self-government are social artifacts, creations of the law." Once again, Mr. Will's premise is unexceptionable, but there is no clarification of what the role of the state, government, and law might properly be. The state is certainly not the only agency that enforces morality, and while it is true that "ladies and gentlemen" are indeed social artifacts, it is untrue that they or many other social artifacts are "creations of the law."

Mr. Will is again correct that "the political question is always which elites shall rule, not whether elites shall rule," but elites do not always rule by means of the formal apparatus of the state. They also hold and exercise power, provide leadership, enforce public morality, and inform culture through nongovernmental mechanisms in the community, in business, in patronage of the arts and education, and in personal example. Only in the managerial bureaucratic regimes of modernity have elites relied on the state for their power, and they have done so only because the roots of their power and leadership in society have been so shallow that they possess no other institutions of support. That government has an important and legitimate role to play in enforcing public morality no serious conservative will doubt, but it is nevertheless a limited role and one that is performed mainly not by government but by the institutions of society.

Mr. Will defines no clear limits either as to how far government may go in enforcing moral improvement or how much man can be improved, and on more than one occasion he appears to confuse the legitimate role of the state in protecting the moral order with a kind of environmentalist Pelagianism. Thus, he speaks of "the ancient belief in a connection between human perfectibility and the political order," although few ancients, pagan or Christian, and no conservative of any time or faith ever believed in the perfectibility of man. By failing to clarify the limits and precise functions of the state in enforcing moral norms, Mr. Will fails to define classical conservatism adequately or to formulate a theoretical basis for distinguishing the legitimate and proper role of the state that conservatism justifies from the statism and social engineering of the Left.

Mr. Will's embrace of the modern bureaucratic state as a proper means of encouraging "soulcraft" is neither realistic nor consistent with the classical conservatism he purports to espouse. It is not realistic because the bureaucratic state of this century is predicated on and devoted to a continuing dynamic of moral and social deracination and cannot merely be adjusted to protect and sustain the moral and social order. It is inconsistent with classical conservatism because classical conservatism flourished in and upheld an aristocratic and limited state that operated on predicates completely different from those of its bloated, abused, alien, suffocating, and often ineffectual modern descendant—"bureaucracy tempered by incompetence," as Evelyn Waugh described modern government.

Mr. Will's ideology is consistent, however, with the agenda of liberalism and the structures that carry out its agenda, and his self-professed aim "to recast conservatism in a form compatible with the broad popular imperatives of the day" is in fact an admission of his acceptance of and deference to the liberal idols that modern statecraft adores. Although Mr. Will is sometimes called a neoconservative, he is not, actually. Neoconservatives typically try to derive more or less conservative policy positions from essentially liberal premises. Mr. Will in fact does the opposite: he seeks to derive from more or less unexceptionable premises of classical conservatism policy positions that are often congruent with the current liberal agenda. It is because he accepts, and wants to be accepted by, the "achievements" of modern liberalism and their champions that he ignores or sneers at the serious conservative thinkers and leaders of our time who have sought to break liberal idols and voices no criticism of the powers that support these idols. It is therefore not surprising that his commentary is welcomed in and rewarded by liberal power centers. They have little to fear from him and his ideas and much to gain if his version of "conservatism" should gain currency. He enjoys every prospect of a bright future in their company.

The Other Side of Modernism
James Burnham and His Legacy

James Burnham died of cancer at his home in Kent, Connecticut, on July 28, 1987, at the age of 81. Debilitated since 1978 by a stroke that impaired the functioning of his memory, he had long since ceased to write the fortnightly column "The Protracted Conflict" in *National Review,* on the masthead of which his name had appeared since its first issue in 1955. A reticent man by nature, Burnham by the time of his death was not well known in either the national intellectual community or even in the conservative movement with which he had worked since the 1950s, and many today who are pleased to call themselves conservatives confessed their ignorance of who he was or what he had done. Although Burnham from the 1930s to the 1950s was a highly visible star in the New York intellectual constellation and continued his luminescence among New York conservatives until his stroke, his death elicited barely a twinkle from either the Right or the Left save among friends and former colleagues. The indifference is all the more striking since President Reagan had seen fit to award Burnham the Presidential Medal of Freedom in 1983 and issued a laudatory tribute to him after his death.

The neglect of Burnham by liberal and even mainstream media is explained by many conservatives as the response to be expected from those whose incantations to the broad mind and the open mouth are belied by their contempt for those who dissent from their canons. Yet Burnham was also neglected by many conservatives, who knew him best through his column and his classic *Suicide of the West,* repeatedly reprinted since its first publication in 1964. George H. Nash in his monumental *The Conservative Intellectual Movement in America since 1945* acknowledges Burnham's importance in the emergence of conservative anticommunism in the 1940s and 1950s, but neither Mr. Nash nor most other students of American conservatism have fully appreciated the significance of Burnham's political ideas or their potential for constructing a serious and critical political theory for the contemporary American Right.

129

Burnham did not generally socialize with the conservative movement. He was not a member of the Philadelphia or Mont Pelerin societies, rarely contributed to conservative periodicals other than *National Review,* and seldom or never participated in the seminars and summer schools of the Intercollegiate Studies Institute or Young Americans for Freedom. His aloofness was probably in part a personal choice, but it also reflected an incongruity between his mind and that of the mainstream of American conservatism as it has developed since the 1940s. Burnham and his more percipient readers were aware of the incongruity, which served to keep him at a distance from many of his professional collaborators on the Right, while, ironically, causing the Left to concentrate its fire on his writings to a greater degree than on those of any other conservative intellectual figure of our era.

Until fairly recently, the mainstream of American conservative thought could be divided into two camps, generally called libertarian and traditionalist. The former centered on individual rights and the limitations of the state and emphasized the free market as a means of solving social and economic problems. The traditionalist wing of conservatism focused on the duties of men in a historic continuum and emphasized authority, order, and religious and ethical virtue. Although subsidiary and eclectic bodies of opinion flourished, and though some like the late Frank S. Meyer sought to formulate a "fusionist" school that bridged the contradictions between libertarians and traditionalists, these were the generally predominant currents among American conservatives until the 1970s. At that time, with the rise of the New Right and neoconservatism, which are less schools of political thought than political and policy movements, the clear dual framework of conservative thought began to break up.

James Burnham belonged to neither the libertarian nor the traditionalist category, though his thought was not merely a bridge between them. He often endorsed governmental action in the economy and was strongly criticized by libertarians such as Murray Rothbard and Edith Efron for his fundamental ideas of man and society. Yet while these ideas emphasized order, authority, and power, they were rather clearly distinct from those expressed by orthodox traditionalists.

The religious and ethical orientation of traditionalism has led it to look to premodern thought, classical and medieval, for its ideas on social and political order. Indeed, traditionalist conservatives generally identify themselves in opposition to what they call "modernity" and its legacy. As traditionalist Stephen J. Tonsor defined the concept in a noted address to the Philadelphia Society, later reprinted in *National Review,* in 1986:

> By "modernity" I mean that revolutionary movement in culture which derived from a belief in man's radical alienation, in God's unknowability or non-existence, and in man's capacity to transform or remake the conditions of his existence. The thorough-going secularism, the attack upon the past, religious and social, aristocratic or bourgeois, the utopian dream of alienation overcome and innocence restored are all linked together in the modernist sensibility. . . . The Romantic Satanic hero is the same man as the Prometheus of Shelley and Marx, the Zarathustra of Nietzsche.[1]

"Modernism" in the view of Dr. Tonsor and other adherents of traditionalist thought (most notably, Eric Voegelin, Russell Kirk, Richard Weaver, and Leo Strauss, among others) cuts man off from the transcendent. Hence, modernism denies or ignores God and concentrates on secular knowledge and action. Human knowledge can be only empirical; moral statements can be only relative or factual, there being a dichotomy between fact and value; and human action cannot be modeled on transcendent or spiritual goods that either do not exist or cannot be known. Hence, science, the amoral and empirical description of nature, is the characteristically modern way of knowing, and technology, the application of science to practice, is the typically modern way of doing.

While traditionalists bring philosophical and religious arguments against modernism, their major practical argument against it is its political implications. Denying the absolute and transcendent sources of moral values, modernism has no grounds for resisting tyranny or controlling anarchy. In Dr. Tonsor's view, "We can see that the denial of the existence of order as the ground of being, and the rejection of the transcendent, are a one-way street to Dachau. If everything is permitted and the will to power is the only reality, then the

1. Stephen J. Tonsor, "Why I Too Am Not a Neoconservative," *National Review,* June 20, 1986.

Gulag is as logical as an Euler diagram."[2] Modern political thought from the time of Machiavelli and modern liberalism from the time of Mill have rejected the idea of an absolute moral order to which social and political institutions should conform and in the absence of a basis for firm moral judgments are unable to distinguish between dissent and subversion, friend and enemy, right and wrong, or to exercise power in the interests of justice and a morally based social order.

What is striking about the political thought of James Burnham, however, is that it is distinctively modernist. This was true not only of his post-Marxist period in the early 1940s, when he published *The Managerial Revolution* and *The Machiavellians,* but also of his final period from the mid–1950s onward, when he was identifiably conservative. In *The Machiavellians,* which remained the fundamental statement of his general theoretical political framework, he explored the school of political thought extending from Machiavelli to his positivist heirs of the nineteenth and twentieth centuries, Vilfredo Pareto, Gaetano Mosca, Roberto Michels, and Georges Sorel. The conclusion of the book was that there exists a "science of power" that can describe the general laws of human political behavior based on inferences from historical experience. "The recurring pattern of change expresses the more or less permanent core of human nature as it functions politically. The instability of all governments and political forms follows in part from the limitless human appetite for power."[3]

Burnham's emphasis on "the limitless human appetite for power" places him in the camp of moderns such as Nietzsche and Alfred Adler (and of later sociobiologists who write of the "imperial animal" and "instincts of dominance") and of other exponents of an essentially irrationalist depiction of human nature such as Dostoevsky, Conrad, Freud, and Pareto himself. The "science of power" that discovers and explores this human appetite is itself a product of empirical observation. It was through such observation, either of the historical past or of contemporaries, that Machiavelli and his

2. Ibid.
3. James Burnham, *The Machiavellians: Defenders of Freedom* (New York: John Day Company, 1943), 63.

heirs constructed this science, and, unlike the medieval Dante, with whom Burnham contrasts Machiavelli, they did so by eschewing the "formal" for the "real." "By 'real meaning,'" wrote Burnham, "I refer to the meaning not in terms of the fictional world of religion, metaphysics, miracles, and pseudo-history . . . but in terms of the actual world of space, time, and events."[4]

The predominant elements of Burnham's thought separate him from the ethical absolutes around which premodern and contemporary traditionalist ideas center. Whereas the latter sought to constrain power and the human appetites by ethical precepts and religious institutions, Burnham was specific in rejecting this effort:

> The Machiavellians are the only ones who have told us the full truth about power . . . the primary object, in practice, of all rulers is to serve their own interest, to maintain their own power and privilege. . . . No theory, no promises, no morality, no amount of good will, no religion will restrain power. Neither priests nor soldiers, neither labor leaders nor businessmen, neither bureaucrats nor feudal lords will differ from each other in the basic use which they will seek to make of power. . . . Only power restrains power. . . . when all opposition is destroyed, there is no longer any limit to what power may do. A despotism, any kind of despotism, can be benevolent only by accident.[5]

Burnham thus harbored no illusion that a particular form of society—agrarian, theocratic, or feudal, much less socialist, liberal, or democratic—could adequately restrain the appetite for power. What could restrain it was a balanced distribution of power among various social and political forces that mutually checked the power of each other and in the conflict of which both political freedom and the level of civilization could flourish. Although his idea of balance derived from Machiavelli, Mosca, and Pareto, it had its roots in classical thinkers like Cicero and Polybius; but Burnham's adherence to what Ralf Dahrendorf would call a "conflict model" of society, like that of Machiavelli, Hobbes, and Marx, is more distinctively modern than the "consensus model" of most classical and medieval thinkers

4. Ibid., 9–10. In the 1963 edition of *The Machiavellians* (Chicago: Henry Regnery Company, 1963) Burnham changed the word *fictional* to the more ambiguous *mythical* (11).

5. Burnham, *The Machiavellians* (1943), 246–47.

such as Aristotle, Plato, and Aquinas, as well as Burke. In the latter concept of society, men form society because they are naturally sociable, and a shared consensus, based on religious and moral beliefs and transmitted through tradition, provides a restraint on human conduct. In the conflict model, consensual elements are at best subordinate, and consensus itself is a product of conflict and eventually of domination by one social force. Thus, for Machiavelli, religion is imposed on the citizens by the legislator or prince for the purpose of internal discipline, and Marx's "ideology," Pareto's "derivations," Sorel's "myth," and Mosca's "political formula" are analogous concepts.

It might be argued that a book published in 1943, when Burnham was not yet forty years old, bears only tangential relevance to his later thought. Yet there is no clear break between Burnham of *The Machiavellians* and his later books and articles. Indeed, the same themes, though less bluntly stated, are found in most of his later work. The last book review that Burnham published[6] in 1978 was a highly favorable account of the autobiography of A. J. Ayer, a leading logical positivist, and in his obituaries of André Malraux and Pablo Picasso in *National Review,* Burnham specifically invoked Nietzsche's "will to power":

> What defines the essence of the superman (or merely, "superior man," as the German can also be translated) is his creation of his own values, thus also his rejection of, or indifference to, all values the origin and authority of which are external to himself in custom, church, tribe, or state. . . . For Nietzsche, the supermen were not the conquerors and rulers, who were in fact often as much slaves of convention and prejudice as the servile masses, but above all the supreme poets and artists, the prophets, and the wilder of the saints. . . . Supermen are more dangerous than H-bombs. The world can't digest very many of them, but it would be a drearier place if there weren't any.[7]

Burnham developed a similar theme of power expressed in art (and religion) in a column of 1961, where he saw Piero della Francisco's

6. James Burnham, "Mind and Manner," review of A. J. Ayer, *Part of My Life, National Review* (March 3, 1978):287–88.

7. "Pablo Picasso, RIP," *National Review* (April 27, 1973):456; the obituary is unsigned; I owe the fact of Burnham's authorship to *National Review* editor Joseph Sobran; see also Burnham's signed obituary of André Malraux, *National Review* (December 24, 1976):1392–93, where Nietzsche is also invoked.

fresco of the Resurrection as an allegory of the decline of the West, symbolized by the sleeping Roman sentries and the emergence of a triumphant enemy symbolized by Christ,

> a Christ that has none of the physical weakness or effeminacy with which He is so often painted. Piero's risen Christ has thrown His shroud, like a cloak, over His shoulder, to reveal a spear-slashed breast that, though gaunt, is strong and hard-muscled; in His right hand He holds the standard of an unfurled white banner, quartered by a red cross; His glance, directed straight out, is majestic, terrible, almost—through the effect of those eyes that seem to stare to infinity without particular focus—obsessive. . . . What we are looking at in Piero's picture, among so many other things, is the power and wealth and luxury of Rome gone soft and sluggish, asleep instead of alert and on guard. The closed eyes of the sentries in their handsome dress cannot see, do not even try to see, the fierce Phoenix rising from the gathering ashes of their world.[8]

In both *Congress and the American Tradition* and *Suicide of the West,* Burnham focused on the irrational and mythic forces of tradition and ideology, and throughout his work he analyzed the basic social and political conflict between an ascendant managerial elite, using Marxist and liberal ideology as a vehicle of its power, and a declining bourgeois class expressing "conservative" and "classical liberal" ideas to resist managerial dominance. In one of the last columns he wrote prior to his stroke, he again eschewed the moralism and ideology that characterized both the Left and the Right:

> The primary goals at which I aim in this column, as in most of the books and articles I have written, are fact and analysis. I do not accept any theory of class, national, ethnic, partisan, or sectarian truth. If conclusions I reach are true, they are just as true for Russians as for Americans, for pagans as for Christians, and for blacks as for whites.[9]

Burnham, then, represents modernism in a dimension very different from that depicted by Dr. Tonsor and other orthodox antimodern traditionalists. While this school is correct in pointing to one side of

---

8. James Burnham, *The War We Are In: The Last Decade and the Next* (New Rochelle, N. Y.: Arlington House, 1967), 309–10; the column is entitled "Sleeping Sentries," published in *National Review* (June 17, 1961):377–78, 381.

9. James Burnham, "No Entangling Alliances, Please," *National Review* (September 15, 1978):1132.

modernist thought as a vehicle for revolutionary and secular millenarian ends, there is also another side to modernism, represented by
Machiavelli himself, Montesquieu, Hume, and Madison, to name but
a few of its early representatives. Although this body of thought is
modernist in its general secularism, its reliance on empirical and
historicist rather than metaphysical or rationalistic methods of inquiry, its avoidance of moral absolutism, its pessimistic and skeptical portrayal of human irrationality and the inherent appetitive
forces of human nature, and its elaboration of a theory of "balance"
rather than transcendence or moral virtue as a means of restraining
human nature, it very clearly rejects the possibility of what Tonsor
calls "man's capacity to transform or remake the conditions of his
existence" and the chiliasm attendant on it. Such secular transfor-
mationalism, "immanentization of the eschaton," in Voegelin's
phrase, is, in fact, an importation from secularized Judeo-Christian
thought and, as not only Voegelin but also James Billington and the
late Frances Yates have shown, lies at the root of modernist revolutionary totalitarianism. The other side of modernism that James
Burnham represented leads not to Dachau and the Gulag but to the
classical republicanism that originally informed the Framers of the
American republic.

Burnham's modernism alienated those traditionalist conservatives
who were aware of it. Their minds tend to center on the more ethe-
real regions of religion, ethics, metaphysics, and aesthetics, rather
than on the sociological analysis of political conflict and the geopolitics of global struggle, and they are not attracted to and are often
repelled by a worldview that centers on conflict, power, and human
irrationality. Whittaker Chambers, whose own mind reflected a ten-
sion between modernism and antimodern elements and who expressed deep admiration for Burnham, nevertheless criticized him
for his "prudent, practical thinking." "The Fire Bird," wrote Chambers, "is glimpsed living or not at all. In other words, realists have a
way of missing truth, which is not invariably realistic."[10] The "Fire
Bird" refers to the classical myth of the phoenix, a bird composed

---

10. Whittaker Chambers, *Odyssey of a Friend: Whittaker Chambers' Letters to
William F. Buckley, Jr., 1954–1961,* ed. and with notes by William F. Buckley, Jr.
(New York: G. P. Putnam's Sons, 1969), 155, January 23, 1957, Chambers to Buckley.

of fire that, since it was consumed by flames as it flew through the air, left no body. Its existence therefore could not be proved empirically, by finding its body; it had to be seen alive or not at all. Chambers's meaning is that Burnham's worldview demanded empirical proof for things that by their nature could not be proved but were nevertheless known to be true by those who had seen—or felt or intuited—them.

If both contemporary conservative traditionalists and libertarians were at odds with the contours of Burnham's thought, the Left found itself attracted to it and yet at the same time repelled. Burnham's *The Managerial Revolution* was strongly criticized by C. Wright Mills, Ralf Dahrendorf, and other sociologists of the Left, who saw its thesis as a direct threat to their own Marxist and neo-Marxist analyses of contemporary power relations in capitalist society. George Orwell also wrote long essays on Burnham in which he sought to deflect the criticisms that Burnham, from his perspective of modernist realism, raised against the utopian formalism of the Leftist mind. Similar critiques greeted Burnham's analysis of the Cold War and communism, until, in the early 1950s, his refusal to denounce Joseph McCarthy led to his virtual expulsion from northeastern intellectual circles. Yet the Left, unlike much of the Right, recognized Burnham's preeminence, and in 1950 David Riesman could write in *The Lonely Crowd* of "Marx, Mosca, Michels, Pareto, Weber, Veblen, or Burnham" in the same sentence.[11] The Left perceived that Burnham's inversion of modernism was a far more serious threat to it than the antimodern traditionalism that many conservatives represented, since Burnham's counter-modernism threatened to remove the philosophical grounds from under the feet of the Left and leave it with no basis for its political ideology.

The American Right, for all its intellectual sophistication and political progress, has yet to come to terms with or make use of the implications of Burnham's thought. Libertarianism is a modernist ideology, but it does not turn modernism away from the interpretation the Left has imposed on it. Neoconservatism, as Tonsor argues,

---

11. David Riesman, with Reuel Denney and Nathan Glazer, *The Lonely Crowd: A Study of the Changing American Character* (New Haven: Yale University Press, 1950), 252.

is also modernist, but it too refuses to challenge the conventional drift of modernism. Neoconservatives rely on an eclectic assimilation of liberal, libertarian, and traditionalist ideas, and seek only to achieve "piecemeal" or gradualist changes within a conventionally modernist framework. Most of the journalism and propaganda that has issued from the New Right and neoconservatives cannot be taken seriously as political and social thought. Orthodox traditionalism rejects modernism, but does so in a manner that is largely alien and inexplicable to the modern mind and tends to degenerate into cultism. Among contemporary conservatives only James Burnham offered a theoretical framework and a practical application of modernist political ideas that challenge the conventional modernist categories as defined by the Left. When the American Right begins to understand and accept his legacy, it will begin to glimpse a more enduring victory in the protracted domestic and global conflict in which Burnham was enlisted.

The Evil That Men Don't Do
Joe McCarthy and the American Right

His is probably the most hated name in American history. Other villains—Benedict Arnold, Aaron Burr, Alger Hiss, Julius and Ethel Rosenberg—today evoke merely the esoteric passions of the antiquarian or the interminable controversies of partisans. Only Joe McCarthy has given his name to an enduring term of political abuse, and in American politics today there is literally no one who would publicly defend him. When he died, eminent public men could find no good to say of him. Vandals in Appleton, Wisconsin, have repeatedly desecrated his grave, and nearly thirty years after his death, his ghost continues to haunt us, called up only by his old enemies to frighten us of what we once became, to warn us of what we might become again.

It is not immediately clear why so much hatred should endure so long, especially when it is recalled that the senator was never accused or convicted of any crime, never betrayed his country, caused no wars, perpetrated no atrocities, and after 1946 never even lost an election. The reason usually given for the hatred of McCarthy is that he did and said so many evil things. That he has a reputation for doing and saying evil cannot be denied. We are told that McCarthy made reckless accusations of treason, and he often or always failed to substantiate his charges. He made vitriolic attacks on his opponents and publicly challenged their good faith and integrity. He interfered with the workings of the State Department and the army. He sent his aides on a junket to Europe, where they made fools of themselves and embarrassed the United States. He ruined the careers of many—hundreds, thousands—of innocent people. He encouraged mass hysteria, played on fear and resentment, and harmed the cause of responsible anticommunism. He violated the rules of the Senate as well as the standards of common decency. He physically attacked Drew Pearson. He lost his temper, bullied witnesses, talked dirty, and drank too much. He insulted such devoted public servants and stalwart patriots as Dean Acheson, Adlai Stevenson, Harry

Truman, Dwight Eisenhower, and George Marshall. He tried to link Stevenson with Alger Hiss, and he made attorney Joseph Welch cry on national television. Perhaps worst of all, when journalists or other senators called McCarthy a liar, a criminal, an extremist, a homosexual, or a fraud, he paid them back in the same coin with his distinctive gift for invective. Joe McCarthy said and did all these things and more, and the evil that inheres in them lives after him and recoils upon us to this day in the hatred that attaches to his cursed name.

Once in a while, however, someone who marches to the tune of a different drummer points out that Joe McCarthy did not do some of the evil things that were done in and around his era. He did not, for example, make solemn commitments to anticommunist allies of the United States, as Franklin Roosevelt did to Chiang Kai-shek, and then violate those commitments at the first opportunity. He did not, like General Eisenhower, initiate "Operation Keelhaul," in which untold numbers of anticommunist Russians were delivered to the Soviets at the point of American bayonets in the aftermath of World War II. He did not make agreements with Joseph Stalin that consigned an entire subcontinent to communism and then announce the Yalta agreements as an act of prudent statecraft. He did not send American troops to Korea, and later to Vietnam, and then deny them the full support of American military power while their death tolls mounted. He did not allow the Hungarians who revolted against communist domination to be shot or rounded up by Soviet tanks and Mongolian troops. He did not sponsor an invasion of communist Cuba, withdraw promised air support at the last minute, and leave the invaders to be slaughtered by Castro's armies. He did not countenance the overthrow and murder of President Diem and his brother, plunge an anticommunist ally into chaos from which it never recovered, and later sign a peace treaty that ensured communist control of South Vietnam and make excuses while the Communists ignored the treaty, conquered the ally, and defeated the United States for the first time in its history. He did not embark on foreign and defense policies that permitted the most savage and aggressive tyranny in world history to become the equal of the United States in strategic weapons and pronounce it a step for a generation of peace. Perhaps most of all, McCarthy did not, in the wake of Alger Hiss, the *Amerasia* case, the Rosenbergs, and other lesser treasons, ignore, ridicule, scorn, and work against those Americans who knew the extent of communist infiltration in the federal government and obstruct most substantial measures to expose it and bring it to an end.

Joe McCarthy did not do any of these things, which were usually done or authorized or approved or supported by many of the persons and institutions he attacked, and they, like much of what McCarthy did, were also evil, among the most evil things in our history, and most of us have forgotten them and even wonder if they really happened or if anyone really did them. The evil that never happened, that other men didn't do, died with them and lies interred with the bones of its victims—not hundreds or thousands but millions—whose ghosts are never invoked and who have largely disappeared from human memory; but if there is a Bar of Justice beyond this world and beyond human memory, I would rather stand before it and answer for the evil that Joe McCarthy did than for the evil that he didn't do.

The real reason for the hatred borne by the name of Joe McCarthy has little to do with the evil that is attributed to him or with his uncompromising anticommunism but rather with what he discovered about the forces—the people, ideas, and institutions—that by 1950 had come to dominate American government and public discourse and with what he communicated and exposed to the American people about those forces. McCarthy not only claimed that a communist presence had entered into the federal government but also that noncommunist or ostensibly anticommunist elements in the government and more broadly in the national elite were in some sense "soft" on or sympathetic to communism and, consequently, that they lacked the resolution to extirpate the internal communist presence and deal effectively with communism abroad. Even more, he suggested that the connection between the elite and the forces of subversion and aggression was in itself an indictment of the elite, regardless of whether its members were formally affiliated with communism, whether they had actually committed espionage or treason in a legal sense, or whether they verbally espoused opposition to communism. McCarthy, in other words, was not principally concerned with the issue of communism in government but with the relationship between communism and the elite, or establishment, and because his concern necessarily involved a militant challenge to and a rejection of the elite, it launched a massive political and verbal counterattack upon him, crushed him and the movement he created, and transformed him into the demonic embodiment of evil that moves among us even today.

McCarthy's contention about the dominant forces in American society was, of course, never presented explicitly or in general terms and was usually expressed in hyperbole and ad hominem. It is quite true that McCarthy often exaggerated and overdramatized the connections between the establishment and the more clearly subversive forces, but it was precisely that dramatization that enabled large numbers of Americans to perceive the connection at all. It is probably also true that McCarthy himself did not think of his rhetoric as a device for political and didactic purposes but that he accepted his own dramatization as literal truth. Taken literally, however, much of what McCarthy habitually said was absurd. His notorious attack on Adlai Stevenson—"Alger, I mean Adlai"—linked two men who had little real association and who were quite distinct on a literal level. Yet it was the point of his attack that Adlai and Alger did share some important things in common besides their stuffiness. The great virtue of McCarthy consisted precisely in his ability to communicate to the average American what the bonds were that connected establishment liberals like Stevenson and crypto-Communists like Hiss. McCarthy's rhetoric pointed directly to what they shared, isolated it, and held it up, squirming and screaming, for all the American nation to see. And what the nation saw, it did not like.

Between approximately 1930 and 1950 the United States experienced a social and political revolution in which one elite was largely displaced from power by another. The new elite, entrenching itself in the management of large corporations and unions, the federal bureaucracy, and the centers of culture, education, and communication, articulated an ideology that expressed its interests and defended its dominance under the label of liberalism. Although liberalism formally defines itself in opposition to communism, in fact it retains and incorporates some of the basic premises of Marxist doctrine—in particular, the idea that human beings are the products of their social environment and that by rationalistic management of the environment it is possible to perfect or ameliorate significantly the human condition and indeed man himself. The environmentalist and ultimately utopian premises of liberalism are the justification for the expansion of state and bureaucracy, the regulation of the economy, the redistribution of wealth, and the imposition of progressive education and egalitarian experiments on traditional institutions and communities by liberal agencies and policies. In foreign affairs, the premises of liberalism hold out the prospect of an "end to war" through the transcendence of nationalism and international rivalry and the evolution or conscious design of a cosmopolitan world order in which war, empire, sovereignty, and significant national and cultural differentiations among peoples have disappeared. It so happens that the ideology of liberalism, for all its contempt for "special interests," coincides very conveniently with the political, economic, and professional interests of the bureaucrats, social engineers, managers, and intellectuals who believe in it and who are most zealous in pressing for its agenda. Without liberalism or some such formula under another name, these groups cannot easily explain or justify the power, prestige, and rewards that they hold. By the late 1940s, due to the crises and power vacuums created by the Great Depression, two world wars, and the advance of technical knowledge and skill, this complex of special interests and its ideology had secured an essentially dominant, though not exclusive, influence in the strategic power centers of American society. In a word, the rising liberal elite had become a liberal establishment.

The environmentalist premises of liberalism, its social engineering methods, and its utopian or meliorist implications are not fundamentally distinct from those of communism, and indeed the two ideologies share common roots in the pleasant fantasies of the Enlightenment as well as in what Whittaker Chambers called "man's second oldest faith," the promise of which "was whispered in the first days of the Creation under the Tree of the Knowledge of Good and Evil: 'Ye shall be as gods.' "[1] Given the common premises and roots shared by members of the new elite and by Communists, it is not terribly surprising that they could work together in administrations and institutions committed to the premises. Nor is it surprising that liberals often failed to recognize the Communists among them or, when their presence was pointed out, that they often failed

1. Whittaker Chambers, *Witness* (New York: Random House, 1952), 9.

to see them or the significance of their presence or even to express very much concern about it. Finally, it is not surprising either that some who began as liberals found themselves frustrated by the compromises and slow pace of conventional politics and, faced with the emergencies of global war and economic chaos, were ineluctably drawn toward and into support for the more muscular tactics of Lenin and Stalin. Liberal ideology and the expectations it creates in the minds of those who believe it do not conduce to caution, nor do they discourage the mental habit of dividing the world into the simple dichotomies of the Manichean under the labels of "progressive" and "reactionary." "Thus," wrote Chambers, "men who sincerely abhorred the word Communism, in the pursuit of common ends found that they were unable to distinguish Communists from themselves, except that it was just the Communists who were likely to be most forthright and most dedicated in the common cause."[2]

The discovery of communist infiltration, then, was not the principal meaning of McCarthy's activities, although it cannot be doubted that he did indeed discover and expose Communists in sensitive positions and, more importantly perhaps, the indifference of the new elite in government to their presence. On February 23, 1954, for example, Mrs. Mary Stalcup Markward, who had worked for the FBI as an undercover informant in the Communist party in Washington, D.C. and had had access to party membership files, testified under oath before McCarthy's Permanent Subcommittee on Investigations and identified Mrs. Annie Lee Moss, a civilian employee of the Army Signal Corps, as having been to her knowledge a member of the Communist party. Mrs. Moss, testifying under oath also, later denied this accusation and, because she appeared to be almost completely uneducated, was believed by many to be a most unlikely Communist. The Markward testimony was thus not widely credited at the time, and the incident appeared to be an embarrassment for Senator McCarthy.

In the course of her testimony, however, Mrs. Moss had mentioned her address as "72 R Street, S.W.," Washington, D.C. In 1958 the Subversive Activities Control Board (SACB), weighing the credibility of Markward as a witness, obtained access to the membership

2. Ibid., 472.

files of the Washington-area Communist party, which had been seized by the FBI. These files, the authenticity of which the party did not challenge, contained a record of one Annie Lee Moss, living at 72 R Street, S.W. in Washington. Although the SACB, in a ruling of 1959, found that "Markward's testimony should be assayed with caution," this reassessment by the board had nothing to do with the Moss case. Nor did it involve an insinuation of lying or unreliability on the part of Markward but rather a conflict of interpretation of how she had been compensated by the FBI. Moreover, even while urging caution in regard to Markward's testimony, the SACB concluded that a finding that Markward "palpably lied or that she testified in this or other proceedings to a deliberate series of falsehoods" would not be warranted and that "in the few instances relied upon, Markward is, with two minor exceptions, corroborated by other credited evidence."[3] Given Markward's unequivocal identification of Moss as a party member, the substantiation of the identification by a bipartisan and independent board through the discovery of Moss's name and address in party membership files, and the absence of any reason to believe that Markward had lied, the conclusion that Moss was a Communist is inescapable.

Another such case made public by McCarthy is that of Edward M. Rothschild, an employee of the Government Printing Office, who was described under oath by his fellow worker James B. Phillips on August 17, 1953, as having attended meetings in 1938 for the purpose of forming a Communist party cell in the GPO. Mrs. Markward also testified under oath the same day that she had known Rothschild's wife, Esther, as a member of the Communist party. Rothschild himself had earlier acknowledged that he was in a position at the GPO to obtain access to classified information that was being printed and assembled there, but he had denied actually having done so. The witness Phillips related an incident in which he had observed another employee try to steal classified data. When asked if they were Communists, both Mr. and Mrs. Rothschild took the Fifth

---

3. U.S., Subversive Activities Control Board, *Reports,* 4 vols. (Washington: Government Printing Office, 1966), 1:93–94, 99; see also the account of the Moss case in Thomas C. Reeves, *The Life and Times of Joe McCarthy: A Biography* (New York: Stein and Day, 1982), 548–50, 567–69, 767–68, n. 12. Reeves states, "Either Mrs. Markward or Mrs. Moss was lying" (568).

Amendment. There was no reason to doubt the testimony of Phillips and Markward, and because of McCarthy's hearing Rothschild was discharged from his position in the GPO.[4]

In neither the Moss nor the Rothschild case was a major espionage investigation involved. Their significance is not that Moss and Rothschild were equivalent to Alger Hiss or Kim Philby but that the information publicized by McCarthy's hearings had been presented to the appropriate security authorities by the FBI some years before. In the case of Moss, the FBI had offered a witness against her to the Army and to the Civil Service Commission in 1951, three years before McCarthy's hearing, and both had ignored the Bureau and the witness. In the Rothschild case, the FBI had made known to the GPO as early as 1943—ten years before McCarthy's hearings—that information on the Rothschilds' communist activities was available. In 1948 the Bureau offered a list of forty witnesses against Rothschild to the Loyalty Board of the GPO, but not one was called. In 1951 the FBI had provided more information on Rothschild, but the GPO, under new security rules formulated by the Eisenhower Administration, cleared him in 1953.[5] For all of the rhetoric about the "stringent" security rules established under Truman and Eisenhower, those who administered these rules were often either too indifferent or too incompetent—these are the most charitable interpretations—to avail themselves of reliable evidence on the presence of Communists and security risks in sensitive positions of the federal government.

The Moss and Rothschild cases are only two relatively clear instances in which McCarthy exposed the presence of Communists or subversives in government. His investigation of security risks in the defense establishment in 1954 led to the removal of more than thirty individuals from employment in defense plants as a result of their having been identified as Communists by witnesses before his subcommittee. When confronted with these accusations and provided opportunities to respond, these individuals had generally taken the Fifth Amendment—i.e., refused to state whether they had been or

4. See *Security—Government Printing Office,* Hearings before the Permanent Subcommittee on Investigations of the Committee on Government Operations, U.S. Senate, 83rd Congress, 1st Session, Part 1, August 17 and 18, 1953; Roy Cohn, *McCarthy* (New York: New American Library, 1968), 53; Reeves, *McCarthy,* 509–11.

5. Reeves, *McCarthy,* 548, 509–10.

were Communists and often whether they had committed espionage.[6] Perhaps they all were high-minded civil libertarians who merely took the Fifth on principle, but perhaps also there is no reason for persons who refuse to deny they are Communists or spies to work in defense plants.

The case of Owen Lattimore, first accused by McCarthy and later found by the Senate Internal Security Subcommittee to have been "a conscious articulate instrument of the Soviet conspiracy"—a judgment based on the testimony of ex-Soviet diplomatic and intelligence officers and of former Ambassador William Bullitt, as well as on analysis of Lattimore's own publications, the statements of ex-Communist witness Louis Budenz, and other evidence—is another complicated but reasonably conclusive instance of McCarthy's discovery of a Communist.[7] In addition, there are a number of cases first publicized by McCarthy in which the evidence is not conclusive but highly suggestive—patterns of association, membership in communist front organizations, political activities, and public statements—of communist or procommunist sympathies or of inability to make responsible judgments about communism.[8] The cliche that "McCarthy never discovered a single communist," repeated ad nauseam by the performing dogs of the academic branch of the elite, is simply untrue.

Nevertheless, it was not the minutiae of congressional investigations and the administration of federal laws and regulations that created McCarthy's following, nor did they significantly contribute to the hatred of him that the new elite exhibited. Had McCarthy announced, in Wheeling, West Virginia, on February 9, 1950, the discovery of Communists in labor unions rather than in the State Department, his speech would have attracted little notice. The State

6. Cohn, *McCarthy,* 55–56; see also *Subversion and Espionage in Defense Establishments and Industry,* Hearings before the Permanent Subcommittee on Investigations of the Committee on Government Operations, U.S. Senate, 83rd Congress, 1st and 2nd Sessions, 1953–1954.

7. *Institute of Pacific Relations,* Report of the Committee on the Judiciary, U.S. Senate, 82nd Congress, 2nd Session, July 2, 1952, 214–18, for summary of the evidence against Lattimore.

8. See William F. Buckley, Jr. and L. Brent Bozell, *McCarthy and His Enemies: The Record and Its Meaning,* 1954, reprint (New Rochelle, N.Y.: Arlington House, 1970), esp. chap. 7 and app. A, 343–51; and Cohn, *McCarthy.*

Department and the individuals whom McCarthy proceeded to identify by name were at the heart of the establishment and its agenda, and when McCarthy made bald assertions about their connections to communism, he was launching an attack upon the establishment that it could not ignore and which it could reciprocate only with hatred. Other criticisms of the elite from the Right—of its economic and foreign policies or of the constitutionality of its legal measures—did not challenge its fundamental legitimacy or its basic loyalty and integrity, nor did they generally suggest that the establishment was a distinct social and political, as well as an ideological, formation, implicitly and inherently alien and hostile to the mainstream of the nation. Hatred and destruction of McCarthy were the only possible responses to this kind of attack. Thomas Reeves says in his large biography of McCarthy that he is our King John. It may be more appropriate to say that he is the liberals' Trotsky, their Emmanuel Goldstein, their Jew. His very existence was a threat to their interests and power and was ultimately incompatible with their dominance in the United States.

It was McCarthy's accomplishment to infuse into the American Right the militancy of a counterrevolutionary movement, and the large following he attracted tends to confirm that there was indeed what Chambers called a "jagged fissure" between the elite and the "plain men and women of the nation"[9] on the issue of the relationship between the elite and communism. The militant anti-liberal and anticommunist movement that McCarthy was the first to instigate also underlay the Goldwater movement of the early 1960s, the Wallace following of the late 1960s and early 1970s, and the "New Right" of the last decade.

Every time these mass expressions of anti-liberalism have appeared, mainstream conservatives and the Republican party have hastened to take political advantage of them and use them to gain political office—as Eisenhower did in 1952, Nixon in 1968, and Reagan in 1980. Yet every time also, those who gained office have proceeded to ignore, to compromise, or actually to betray the constituency on which their officeholding was based. They have done

9. Chambers, *Witness,* 793.

so because they are themselves part of or closely connected to the elite against which this constituency is mobilized.

In recent years, particularly under the Reagan Administration, attempts have been made to formulate a more "responsible," a more "credible" and "respectable," version of conservatism that pays lip service to the anti-liberal and antiestablishment (populist, if you will) constituency but which in fact seeks to defuse its militancy and consolidate it into the apparatus of elite power. It is no accident that many of the older exponents of this "neoconservatism" were themselves among the foremost critics of McCarthyism in the 1950s and 1960s and that many of its younger exponents take the lead in urging the repudiation of McCarthyism and other symbols of militancy by "responsible conservatives."

To repudiate McCarthyism, however, would be to accept not only the establishment but also the premises and agenda on which it operates, for the complex of public and private bureaucracies that compose the establishment is inseparable from the environmentalist, utopian, and social engineering functions that the premises and agenda of liberalism express and rationalize. The American Right, then, if it is serious about wanting to preserve the nation and its social fabric and political culture in any recognizable form, must continue to embrace Joe McCarthy and the kind of militant, popular, anti-liberal, and antiestablishment movement that he was the first to express on a national scale.

There is, of course, such a thing as "liberal anticommunism," and there is no doubt that liberals such as Sidney Hook, John P. Roche, and the late Senator Thomas Dodd, among others, have long been uncompromising enemies of communism within and without the United States. In recent years, anticommunist liberals of the Kennedy-Johnson era have played an important role in trying to reshape right-wing anticommunism into molds more acceptable to the establishment. Anticommunist adherents of liberalism may bring a more cautious and skeptical assessment to their own ideological premises than is common with most of their colleagues and thus refuse to be swallowed up by the enthusiasm such premises more often generate. As a general rule, however, anticommunist liberals tend to reflect these premises in their opposition to communism. To them, communism is not, as Lenin always claimed it was, the result of an organized, highly disciplined, and ruthless apparatus, but is itself another deformation of the social and economic environment, like crime and war, a product of ignorance, poverty, oppression, and neglect. Hence, their idea of the proper means of fighting communism is not the use of force to suppress its apparatus but more reform, the removal of its "causes," with more foreign aid, more education, more development, and, most recently, more democracy—all of which "solutions" ignore the main cause of communism but accrue to the advantage of the educators, economists, social engineers, political technicians, and professional verbalists who undertake to administer the solution. "The seeds of totalitarian regimes," said Harry Truman in announcing his doctrine in 1947, "are nurtured by misery and want. They spread and grow in the evil soil of poverty and strife," and it was "primarily through economic and financial aid" that Truman proposed that the United States resist the expansion of communism. From Truman's day through Lyndon Johnson's "TVA on the Mekong" to the present efforts of aging social democrats and neoconservatives in the Reagan Administration to fight communism by undermining our best anticommunist allies— in the Philippines, South Africa, Chile—for the sake of "human rights" and "democracy projects," the incompetence of liberal anticommunism to defeat communism is clear. No one who seriously subscribes to the premises of liberalism can for long countenance the thought that the only way to deal with communism is through the timely and efficient use of force, nor can he support the idea that those who share the premises of communist doctrine constitute an alien and hostile presence that cannot be tolerated in a society determined to survive.

Anticommunist liberalism does not, then, contradict the McCarthyite perception of an inherent softness toward communism deriving from liberal premises. These premises manifest themselves even when those who share them are sincerely anticommunist, and they serve to undermine the effectiveness of their anticommunist measures. Yet, despite the existence of liberal opposition to communism, anticommunism has never been a dominant strain in the ideology of the liberal elite that emerged in the early part of the century. Anticommunist sensibilities were not prevalent in McCarthy's day, when the elite in both political parties did everything it could to resist, weaken, obstruct, and distract serious anticommunist efforts and was itself the source of the appeasements and retreats that we have long since consigned to oblivion.

And it is not the dominant strain in liberalism today. Private efforts by journalists and investigators have shown in recent years how campaigns such as the antinuclear movement, much of the opposition to American policy in Central America, the movement to weaken the CIA and FBI, and opposition to virtually every new weapons system proposed by the Defense Department have been led by persons and groups whose attitude toward communism and the Soviet Union is at best equivocal and who often show no hesitation at working with Soviet-controlled front groups and known Communists. Such campaigns are neither largely composed of nor led by card-carrying Communists, nor do they enjoy success because of communist assistance. On the contrary, their following and leadership consist precisely of persons who regard themselves as liberals or roughly equivalent persuasions, and they enjoy success because they are generally well funded by establishment foundations, well received by establishment media and political figures, and well organized and packaged by establishment intellectuals and verbalists. When such movements and their leaders and followers worry as much about Soviet military programs as they do about those of the United States and NATO, when they denounce "human rights violations" in Cuba and Angola with as much fervor as they do in El Salvador and South Africa, when they protest the Soviet invasion of Afghanistan as strongly as they do the U.S. liberation of Grenada, and when they speak with as much hatred and fear of the KGB as of the FBI and CIA, then I shall regard them as the "humanists," "pacifists," and "civil libertarians" that they profess to be. Until that time—and I do not hold my breath—I shall believe that Joe McCarthy tore a mask from the face of liberalism, and I shall regard the mainstream of its adherents under another label, which, even if not printed on a membership card, is more truthful and more terrible.

The Cult of Dr. King

The third annual observance of the birthday of Martin Luther King, Jr., passed happily enough in the nation's capital, with the local merchants unloading their assorted junk into the hands of an eager public. It is hardly surprising that "King Day," observed as a federal legal public holiday since 1986, has already become part of the cycle of mass indulgence through which the national economy annually revolves. Christmas itself, commemorating an event almost as important as the nativity of Dr. King, has long been notorious for its materialism and appetitive excesses, and a visit to any shopping mall will alert the consumer to the next festal occasion on the public calendar and instruct him in what ways and to what extent he is expected to turn out his pockets in its celebration. Since Dr. King, wherever he is now, has been promoted to full fellowship in the national pantheon, it is to be expected that he too must perform his office in keeping the wheels of American commerce well greased.

What is remarkable about the King holiday, however, is that, alone among the ten national holidays created by act of Congress, it is celebrated in other ways that are pretty much in keeping with its original purpose. While the other nine festivities are merely excuses for protracted buying and selling, three-day weekends with an attractive compadre, or orgies of eat-and-swill punctuated by football games, only the second Monday in January is the regular subject of solemn expatiations by the brahmins of the Republic as to what the day really means. Newspaper columnists, television commentators, and public school teachers, the nearest things we have to a priesthood, devote at least a week to discussing Dr. King's life and achievements and their place in our national consciousness. Certainly they do not explore the lives of Jesus, George Washington, or Christopher Columbus with such piety, nor do they usually dedicate much time to reflecting on the less anthropomorphized occasions that celebrate national independence, public thanksgiving, or remembrance of Americans fallen in war for the fatherland. Only Dr. King seems to elicit effusions from the guardians of the public tongue, and, as in the rituals of the heathen gods of eld, woe to the blasphemous wretch who fails to bend the knee or touch the brow.

The fate of Jimmy "the Greek" Snyder is a case in point, though not unique. Approached at table in Duke Zeibert's restaurant in Washington on the Friday before the official ceremonies, Mr. Snyder, a sports commentator created and employed by CBS, was asked by a local reporter for his views on the progress of blacks in professional athletics. Mr. Snyder perhaps had dined too well, and he was foolish enough to say what he really thought in response to the uninvited question. He praised the accomplishments and hard work of black athletes, made some insulting remarks about the laziness of white athletes, and suggested that the alleged athletic prowess of blacks was due to their having been bred for size and strength in antebellum days, specifically for their "big thighs, . . . they can jump higher and run faster because of their bigger thighs." It is not known if the Greek, a professional gambler, gave odds on how long he would keep his $750,000-a-year job after uttering his insights, but there was little time to place any bets, and probably few would have taken them. Within twenty-four hours Mr. Snyder was in the ranks of the unemployed, and the incident provided fodder for the capital's professional gumbeaters for the next week.

Mr. Snyder was not the first offering to the new deity, and the practice of ruining a white person once a year in honor of Dr. King is becoming a national tradition. Last year the victim was another sports figure, Los Angeles Dodgers official Al Campanis, who was asked on ABC-TV's "Nightline" about black athletic performance and wound up discoursing on the comparative buoyancy of the races when immersed in water. He too got his clock cleaned by his employers, and though the incident did not occur in connection with Dr. King's birthday, it did happen to fall during the week of the nineteenth anniversary of the civil rights leader's assassination in April 1968.

In 1986, when King Day was first celebrated after its enactment by Congress in 1983, the god was more merciful. In Montgomery County, Maryland, Mrs. Karen Collins, a part-time music teacher in a Silver Spring elementary school, made the mistake of giving her private opinion to a colleague that the country was making too much of Dr. King and that she had heard he had been a communist supporter and had communist friends. Her remarks were overheard by some students, who ran home to tell their parents, who alerted the local NAACP to the presence of un-American activities. Even before the NAACP invited itself to settle the matter, however, Mrs. Collins had received a reprimand from her principal, had been placed on administrative leave, transferred to another school, and required to enroll in a "human relations" course where she could learn something about the American Way before she trampled on it again by spouting off her opinions in private.

The NAACP was not at all satisfied with such lax discipline and demanded her dismissal. "Any person who says Dr. King was a communist is either maliciously racist or uninformed," said Roscoe Nix, president of the local chapter. Actually, it was never certain exactly what Mrs. Collins had said. She denied saying that King was a Communist, and after her disciplining, school superintendent Wilmer S. Cody acknowledged that "although her exact words are still in dispute, she did express some dissatisfaction about the school system's special program concerning Martin Luther King's birthday." Despite her crime of offering her views of the special program, Mrs. Collins appears to have kept her job, but the god whom she blasphemed had tasted blood.

If the reader thinks I exaggerate the metaphor of King as god, consider the demand in 1979 (and since) to add Dr. King's "Letter from the Birmingham Jail" to the Bible. At the third annual conference of the Black Theology Project in 1979, a proposal to add the letter as another epistle in the New Testament was approved by the convention of about forty black ministers, theologians, and lay people, and the Reverend Muhammed Kenyatta, instructor in sociology at Haverford College, held that "we believe God worked through Dr. Martin Luther King in that jail in Birmingham in 1963 to reveal His holy word." The pious sociologist also noted that "people generally do not realize that the process of deciding what is or is not Holy Scripture has been an ongoing one."

If the thirst of the new god were slaked only by the ritual slaughter of schoolteachers and sports commentators, Dr. King's apotheosis might actually represent a step forward for the country, but evidence mounts that more is being demanded. King Day in fact represents a revolution in our national mythology, a transformation that seeks to delegitimize the symbols of American history and national identity and to redefine the meaning of the American Republic—perhaps even the meaning of the Christian faith. This at least is the explicit understanding of the holiday that the dominant molders of public opinion articulate every year in their ceremonial ruminations. Thus, writing in the *New York Times* on January 18, 1988, Vincent Harding, Professor of Religion and Social Transformation at the Iliff School of Theology in Denver, rejected the notion that the King holiday commemorates merely "a kind, gentle and easily managed religious leader of a friendly crusade for racial integration." Such an understanding, he writes, would "demean and trivialize Dr. King's meaning," and the higher truth of King Day is made of sterner stuff. "The Martin Luther King of 1968," writes Mr. Harding,

> was calling for and leading civil disobedience campaigns against the unjust war in Vietnam. Courageously describing our nation as "the greatest purveyor of violence in the world today," he was urging us away from a dependence on military solutions. He was encouraging young men to refuse to serve in the military, challenging them not to support America's anti-Communist crusades, which were really destroying the hopes of poor nonwhite peoples everywhere.
>
> This Martin Luther King was calling for a radical redistribution of wealth and political power in American society as a way to provide food, clothing, shelter, medical care, jobs, education and hope for all of our country's people.

Roger Wilkins, civil rights activist and now a senior fellow at the far-Left Institute for Policy Studies in Washington, had some similar thoughts about the meaning of Dr. King's legacy in the *Washington Post,* and indeed similar interpretations of the man and the holiday could be reproduced from the major media of public opinion for every year since the holiday was created.

To be sure, the use of the King holiday to legitimize the Left's long march through American institutions is not the only meaning attributed to it. At the time of its enactment by Congress, various rationales were offered by liberals and conservatives alike: that the holiday was merely a celebration of the personal virtues of a man of courage and vision, that it honored the national rejection of racial bigotry, or that it was a holiday for American blacks, who, it was patronizingly said, "needed their own hero," much as children in a restaurant need their own menu. Yet these are not the presiding apologiae for the holiday, nor were they at the time it was adopted; and the radical interpretation of Dr. King and his legacy is both the dominant as well as the more accurate version.

The objective meaning of the King holiday—the actual meaning independent of what its sponsors thought they meant or what some of its celebrants think they mean now—has little to do with the renunciation of cross-burnings and lynch parties or even of less malevolent incarnations of Jim Crow such as segregated lunch counters. To be sure, a nation that honors Dr. King and his legacy renounces such manifestations of racial inequality, but it also must renounce all forms of inequality, racial or other, because if all men are indeed equal, then it is absurd to say that only some forms of inequality are evil. If, as Dr. King understood it, the Declaration of Independence is a "promissory note"—not merely declarative of national independence but also imperative of social reconstruction in accordance with an egalitarian commandment—then the delegitimization of the traditional symbols, values, and institutions of America is not only in order but also long overdue, and the radical reconstruction of American society is not only a legitimate goal but also the principal legitimate goal of our national endeavors.

Dr. King understood this well himself, expressing it in the millenarian imagery he loved and used so effectively—"I have a dream that one day every valley shall be exalted, every hill and mountain shall be made low, the rough places shall be made plains, and the crooked places shall be made straight, and the glory of the Lord shall be revealed, and all flesh shall see it together." Dr. King, of course, seldom troubled to ask for the sources of his dream, and today it occurs to no one to ask why *his* dreams should prevail over the less grandiose dreams of others. Like all charismatic prophets, he was the fount of his own authority, and his private visions were intended to become law for lesser men.

Among the several hills and mountains that await lowering by the new god and his gnostic bulldozers is the tradition, common among white southerners, of displaying the Confederate flag in places of honor. Some southern states, Alabama and South Carolina in particular, still fly the banner over their state capitols, while the official flags of several other southern states retain its St. Andrew's Cross design in one way or another. The NAACP has recently decided that the flag must go and has given the project priority in its current legislative agenda, and innumerable southern schools already have been obliged to give up using the flag as the symbol of their local football teams, along with playing "Dixie," calling the team "The Rebels," and other traditional usages distinctive of southern cultural identity.

In Alabama, State Representative Thomas Reed threatened to tear down the flag over the statehouse if it were not removed. It wasn't, and Governor Guy Hunt had the local head of the NAACP arrested when he clambered over the fence with his merry band of icon-smashers. Alabama Representative Alvin Holmes readily compares the Confederacy to Nazi Germany and instructs the people of his state, "They need to forget about the Confederacy." Earl Shinhoster, head of the southeastern division of the NAACP, says of the flags, "They're racist symbols. . . . These flags stand for racism, divisiveness and oppression," and also for "defiance and resistance to school desegregation."

Columnist Carl Rowan, who seldom declines to dance to the NAACP's tune, compares the flag to the Nazi swastika and writes, "Show me a guy who rides around with Confederate flags flying on his front fenders, and I'll show you someone who thinks the Civil War still goes on. I'll give you a racist who thinks that it is only a matter of time before this nation makes white supremacy its official policy and returns to slavery, with black people the God-designated hewers of wood and drawers of water." Mr. Rowan apparently has never had a dream of a day when men would not be judged by the color of their front fenders.

But the fact that many southerners (and some non-southerners) regard the Confederate flag as a symbol of things other than racism—southern cultural identity, sacrifice for a cause, an interpretation of the Constitution, or simply ancestral piety—does not really help. Mr. Shinhoster, Mr. Rowan, Mr. Reed, and Mr. Holmes all are correct that the Confederate flag symbolizes a cause that was defeated in 1865 and which is not compatible with the world-view symbolized by Dr. King's holiday. If, as a nation, we are going to adore Dr. King as an official hero, then we cannot also continue to honor the Confederate flag and the political and cultural identity that is the main content of its symbolism.

It is merely a matter of time before the Confederate flag is surrendered, along with local statues of Confederate veterans and heroes, "Dixie," and most other memorials of antebellum civilization. Their passing may not be a cause of mourning among many outside the South (or many within the South, for that matter), but the same logic that compels their abandonment reaches further. The three most prominent monuments in Washington, D.C., are those dedicated to George Washington, Thomas Jefferson, and Abraham Lincoln. Is there a schoolchild in the United States today who does not know that the first two were slaveowners? Is there any literate person in America who does not know that none of the three was a racial egalitarian, that every one of them uttered statements that make Jimmy the Greek sound like an ACLU lawyer? The same argument that drives Mr. Snyder from his low but honest trade and pulls down a banner commemorating the last stand of a desperate people will demolish the obelisk and temples that memorialize the major statesmen of the American nation.

Nor is it merely the physical symbols of the old America that are shattered by the new god we have chosen to worship. In May 1987, Supreme Court Justice Thurgood Marshall proclaimed in a public speech that he could not "find the wisdom, foresight and sense of justice exhibited by the framers" of the U.S. Constitution "particularly profound." Because they did not bow to the egalitarian and universalist idols in the shrines where Justice Marshall has worshipped all his life and because they failed to include blacks and women in the Constitution, the document they drafted was "defective from the start." No doubt it is astonishing that an associate justice of the Supreme Court could say that the fundamental law of the country, which it is his business and his duty to interpret, is inherently flawed, but the justice merely forces us up another rung on the ladder. We forfeited the right to revere the Constitution, the governmental principles and mechanisms it established, and the men who wrote it when we put Dr. King into the pantheon. The federalism, rule of law, states' rights, limits on majority rule, checks and balances, and separation of powers that characterize the Constitution all are incompatible with and constraints on the full blossoming of the egalitarian democracy that Dr. King envisioned and which is the completion of the radical reconstruction to which his holiday commits us.

Political symbols in the form of the Confederate flag, anthems such as "Dixie" and "Maryland, My Maryland," and the Constitution itself are not the only roots to be pulled up, however. Last year, the Reverend Jesse Jackson led a protest march at Stanford University in one of the more explicit demonstrations against the humanities curriculum of the school, giving the chant, "Hey, Hey, Ho, Ho, Western culture's got to go." This year the faculty senate of the university considered a proposal to abandon a required course on "Western Culture" and to replace it with one entitled "Cultures, Ideas and Values." The latter contained no core list of assigned readings, and the only requirement was that professors include in their assignments "works by women, minorities, and persons of color" and emphasize "the last six to eight centuries in particular." One alternative course, developed by Professor Clayborne Carson, director of the Martin Luther King, Jr., Papers Project, required such texts as *Black Elk Speaks,* "Ain't I a Woman," W. E. B. Du Bois's *The Souls of Black Folk,* Frantz Fanon, and those long-neglected Third World persons of color, Herbert Marcuse and Karl Marx. Whatever merits such writers might have over the ancient, medieval, and modern classics of the West, it should be clear that the alternative curriculum was intended as part of the radical reconstruction of the American mind and the extirpation of the philosophical roots of Western predominance. The demand for the change at Stanford, according to news reports, was led by black, Hispanic, and Asian students, who denounced the traditional curriculum as a "year-long class in racism."

The point, of course, is not that the establishment of the King holiday makes the extirpation of the traditional symbols of American and Western civilization inevitable—anti-American and anti-Western movements founded on militant egalitarian universalism are powerful forces and would make gains regardless of the holiday—but that, once the United States, through its national government, chose to adopt Dr. King as an official hero, neither the American people nor their leaders had any legitimate grounds to resist the logic and dynamic of such forces and the radical reconstruction of American society that is implicit in them. It is one thing to say that Dr. King was a great man and a great American, a man whose personal courage and vision, despite his human flaws, errors, and enthusiasms, challenged lesser men of both races and forced them to confront evils, falsehoods, and obsolete ways. It is quite another to say, as the U.S. government does say in creating a legal public holiday for him, that Martin Luther King, Jr., was the most important American who ever lived, at least the peer of George Washington, the Father of his Country, the only American in history to have his birthday made a national holiday, the man who is now first in the hearts of his countrymen. Conservatives, some of whom, like Representatives Jack Kemp and Newt Gingrich, voted for the King holiday in 1983, may devise whatever clever rationales for supporting it they can imagine, but the truth is that Mr. Harding's understanding of the meaning of King's career is far closer to the truth. In any case, aside from obligatory genuflections to King by neoconservatives, "cultural conservatives," and the adherents of Mr. Gingrich's "Conservative Opportunity Society," I know of not a single serious, sustained effort by those on the contemporary American Right to substantiate their endorsement of the holiday or of any serious argument why conservatives should honor Dr. King at all. If there are valid reasons why we should do so, we do not hear them. What we do hear are sermons from apostles such as Mr. Harding and company, most of whom can press a far more persuasive claim to King's legacy than conservatives of any description.

That legacy, as its keepers know, is profoundly at odds with the historic American order, and that is why they can have no rest until the symbols of that order are pulled up root and branch. To say that Dr. King and the cause he really represented are now part of the official American creed, indeed the defining and dominant symbol of that creed—which is what both houses of the United States Congress said in 1983 and what President Ronald Reagan signed into law shortly afterwards—is the inauguration of a new order of the ages in which the symbols of the old order and the things they symbolized can retain neither meaning nor respect, in which they are as mute and dark as the gods of Babylon and Tyre, and from whose cold ashes will rise a new god, leveling their rough places, straightening their crookedness, and exalting every valley until the whole earth is flattened beneath his feet and perceives the glory of the new lord.

Who's In Charge Here?

America, in case you haven't noticed, is lost in the throes of celebrating the writing of its Constitution, which is two centuries old this year. The somewhat labored efforts to fix public attention on the historic document are largely the work of former Chief Justice Warren Burger and his own private bureaucracy in the Commission on the Bicentennial of the U.S. Constitution, as well as the legal profession, the mass media, and the usual contingent of do-gooding schoolteachers, who have temporarily suspended their instruction in the intricacies of sexuality and collective guilt over what we did to Indians, blacks, women, and buffaloes and are now passionately handing out trivia quizzes on the color of James Madison's socks.

But the national rapture over our fundamental law does not match the fevers manufactured a few years ago when we observed the centennials of the War between the States and the American War for Independence. War, wrote Thomas Hardy, makes ripping good history, but it also makes for historic rip-offs every hundred years or so, when we pine for the return of bloodshed fraught with moral import. Somehow the sober deliberations of the Framers in the Philadelphia Convention just don't stir the glands like Gettysburg and Bunker Hill, and the attempts of public officials to instruct us in the minutiae of the Framers' debates come off rather like the efforts of earnest mothers who insist on reading their children old-fashioned fairy tales when the urchins would much prefer the Saturday morning cartoons.

Among the year's festivities have been some rather glum proceedings in the U.S. Congress having to do with the Constitution and its proper interpretation. The recently concluded necktie party that passed as the Senate Judiciary Committee's hearings on Judge Robert Bork dealt tangentially with this matter, but more expansively on the character and personality of the jurist who was unwise enough to allow his name to come under the purview of the committee. Although it did not appear in the hearing record, information revealed by one of the lesser lights of Washington journalism, the *City*

Paper, helped set the tone of the inquiry. Its reporters managed to procure a list of video films that Judge Bork had rented and proceeded to regale their readers with the titles. They seemed to be mainly Alfred Hitchcock films of the 1940s, and some disappointment was expressed that the nominee was not a fan of "Story of O" or "Ilse, She-Wolf of the S.S." The District of Columbia City Council quickly developed legislation to forbid video stores from releasing information on the films their patrons rent and, given the probable tastes of Mayor Marion Barry and the several members of his administration who have been jailed for corruption since he entered office, the legislation was probably wise.

The other main celebration of the Constitution by the Congress was the now largely forgotten Iran-Contra hearings, which raised to stardom Oliver North, Daniel Inouye, Fawn Hall, and other luminaries who today seem as distant as Halley's Comet, and which immersed itself in the metaphysics of something known as the Boland Amendments and the mystery of why Colonel North purchased his snow tires. The distinguished chairman of the joint committee, hailing from sun-drenched Hawaii, could not have been expected to understand the purpose of such paraphernalia, though one would have thought that living in the vicinity of Washington for some twenty-eight years would have served to inform him. My own guess as to the motives of the combat officer-turned-bagman—sadly disproved by subsequent events—was that he planned to necklace two members of the committee when he finally appeared before it.

Yet for all its irrelevance, the joint committee did broach a subject of some significance for the Republic. The attentive citizen could discern, well disguised by the protracted caterwauling emitted by the senators, congressmen, and their flying squadrons of counsels and investigators, the kernel of a constitutional crisis centering on the problem of who—the president or the Congress—is properly in charge of American foreign policy. The debate was duly joined in the national media, and if the hearings themselves were not very helpful in answering the question, a good deal was learned from those writers who offered their own views to public scrutiny.

In general, the ideological breakdown of those who expressed themselves on whether the Congress or the president should have authority over a foreign policy that seems to consist of the systematic violation or evasion of treaty commitments, the incremental massacre and abduction of U.S. citizens and soldiers, the abandonment of allies, the gradual surrender of power and territory, and the Higher Bribery known as foreign aid was that conservatives almost universally supported the claims of the presidency, while liberals equally unanimously upheld the rights of Congress. Defenders of Mr. Reagan and his Central American policies held that the Boland Amendments, which sought to restrict or curtail U.S. funding of the Nicaraguan anticommunist guerrillas, were unconstitutional invasions by the Congress of what they made out was a unilateral presidential prerogative of designing and implementing foreign policy. Liberals, on the other hand, firmly upheld the legality and propriety of the amendments as well as of other congressional measures, such as the War Powers Act of 1973, that constrain the ability of the president to carry out a policy without congressional permission. The most articulate of the progressive set murmured darkly about "another Vietnam" and drew grim pictures of a White House, National Security Council, and CIA once more out of control, stampeding about the world in intrigues with ayatollahs, shady arms merchants, professional assassins, and miscellaneous desperadoes of the international demimonde.

Given the partisan complexion of the Iran-Contra controversy, this breakdown was not surprising. Conservatives understandably defended the propriety of Mr. Reagan or his lieutenants seeking to preserve a semblance of freedom in Central America from a Congress that refuses to recognize the nature of a "people's democracy" guided by commissars imported from Havana and Moscow, while liberals, whatever ideals remain in their jaded hearts, understandably sought to weaken their most powerful and popular foe to occupy the White House in this century.

What is perhaps more surprising about this breakdown is that it represents a complete reversal of the positions assumed by liberals and conservatives on the issue of congressional-presidential powers in foreign policy in the 1950s and 1960s. When, in September 1983, the U.S. Senate debated the War Powers Act and its applicability to Mr. Reagan's deployment of U.S. Marines in Lebanon, Senator Barry Goldwater, defending the president's power to dispatch troops without congressional permission, was reduced to the ignominy of citing

Dean Acheson, Harry Truman, and Franklin Roosevelt as authorities for his view that "once the military forces are established and equipped, it is for the President alone to decide how to deploy and use those forces." Senator Goldwater, in the later parts of his career, never tired of excoriating the Reverend Jerry Falwell, Senator Jesse Helms and kindred souls among his colleagues in the Senate, and other figures of the "New Right" for their alleged deviations from conservative orthodoxy as defined by himself. In the principal statement of that orthodoxy in 1960, however, he had lamented that "The Achesons and Larsons have had their way. . . . Inside the federal government both the executive and judicial branches have roamed far outside their constitutional boundary lines," and he had correctly pointed out the intentions of the Framers in "dispersing public authority among several levels and branches of government in the hope that each seat of authority, jealous of its own prerogatives, would have a natural incentive to resist aggression by the others." As late as 1978, Senator Goldwater's name appeared as the author of a learned study published by the Heritage Foundation that argued against the legality of President Carter's claim to the right of abrogating the Mutual Defense Treaty with the Republic of China.

Yet it is not necessary to cite "Mr. Conservative" in his dotage to show that the American right seems to have experienced a conversion. Walter Berns, distinguished neoconservative philosopher and disciple of Leo Strauss, writing in the *Washington Times* on June 3, 1987, expressed the view that "the Framers . . . knew, what some members of Congress today seem unwilling to admit, that much as one might like to do everything by or by means of law, the conduct of foreign affairs especially cannot be subjected to the rules of law." He defended this proposition with reference to John Locke's precepts on the "power to act according to discretion for the public good, without the prescription of law and sometimes against it," and by citing Abraham Lincoln's multifarious wartime violations of law and Constitution, which show that "Somewhere in the interstices of the Constitution, apparently—the alternative is to regard Lincoln as some sort of usurper or dictator—the president is vested with a power that, in some circumstances, resembles or approximates Locke's prerogative." Dr. Berns made much of the ruling of Justice George Sutherland in *U.S. vs. Curtiss Wright Export Corpo-*

ration, a New Deal–era decision that recognized in the president the "sole organ of the federal government in the field of international relations" and which has become the classic Supreme Court case on the subject of presidential power in foreign policy.

Perhaps an even more aggressive statement of the doctrine of presidential supremacy in foreign affairs was offered by Dennis Teti, a staff member of the Iran-Contra committee itself, in the Fall 1987 issue of *Policy Review.* While acknowledging that "Congress has a genuine but subordinate role to play in the formulation of foreign policy," Mr. Teti argued,

> A close look at the Constitution shows that, while the executive branch does not possess the entirety of foreign policy power, it has most of it. Under Article II, "executive power" is lodged in the president. By definition the executive power comprehends the conduct of foreign policy. The Framers found it unnecessary to define the term, but the inclusion of foreign policy under executive power is discussed at length in John Locke's *Two Treatises of Government,* a fundamental source for the Founders.

Aside from the utility of such views in contemporary political disputes, however, there is little merit in them from the perspective of traditional constitutional theory. Contrary to Mr. Teti's assertion of the implicit powers of the executive branch in foreign policy, the text of the Constitution rather clearly grants to the Congress expansive powers in this area as well as in defense matters and only restricted responsibilities to the president. Article 1, section 8 states,

> The Congress shall have power to . . . provide for the common defense and general welfare of the United States . . . to borrow money on the credit of the United States . . . to regulate commerce with foreign nations . . . to define and punish piracies and felonies committed on the high seas, and offenses against the law of nations . . . to declare war, grant letters of marque and reprisal, and make rules concerning captures on land and water . . . to raise and support armies . . . to provide and maintain a navy . . . to make rules for the government and regulation of the land and naval forces . . . to provide for calling forth the militia to execute the laws of the Union, suppress insurrections and repel invasions . . . [and] to make all laws which shall be necessary and proper for carrying into execution the foregoing powers, and all other powers vested by this Constitution in the Government of the United States, or in any department or officer thereof.

The same article also forbids to the states any powers in foreign policy, and the next article governs the very limited foreign policy prerogatives granted to the president. These consist only of being the commander in chief of the army and navy, the power "by and with the advice and consent of the Senate, to make treaties, provided two-thirds of the Senators concur," and the power to "nominate, and by and with the advice and consent of the Senate . . . [to] appoint ambassadors, other public ministers and consuls." It may be noted that Alexander Hamilton in *Federalist* 69 considered the power of receiving ambassadors to be "more a matter of dignity than authority" and "without consequence in the administration of the government." The very carefully expressed congressional limitations on the foreign policy powers of the president and the specific authorization of extensive foreign policy powers for the Congress suggest almost conclusively that the Framers had no intention of permitting the executive branch to carry out a foreign policy that contravened the wishes of the Congress or at least of the Senate, and that they intended the Congress to take a major role in the conduct of international relations and national defense.

The argument that Locke's view of executive powers is in some way germane to the meaning of the Constitution is not only without merit but borders on absurdity. Whatever Locke may have thought about executive power or the conduct of foreign policy, it was not, according to constitutional historian Forrest McDonald, from his *Two Treatises of Government* that the Framers derived their view of executive power, but from Sir William Blackstone. "Experience," writes McDonald, "was not an adequate guide, for their experience with colonial and state governors was largely irrelevant to the task presently at hand. Hume was silent on the subject, Montesquieu muddled, Locke too general. That left Blackstone's description of the royal prerogative as the only readily available account of what had traditionally been regarded as the executive power in a mixed form of government." The English jurist did indeed acknowledge that the executive power, lodged under the British constitution in the crown, included the conduct of foreign relations and of war, including the right to declare war and make treaties without parliamentary consent. Obviously, the Framers did not provide the American presidency with such powers, nor with the absolute veto of the British king, which also belonged to the executive power in Blackstone's view.

Dr. Berns's belief that "the conduct of foreign affairs especially cannot be subjected to the rules of law" has merit, though it is not a constitutional argument and might give pause to other nations contemplating making treaties with the United States. Conservatives also might pause to consider the implications of foreign policy powers, lodged exclusively in the chief executive and exempt from the constraint of law, as they would be exercised by a President Jesse Jackson or Michael Dukakis. Nevertheless, the question does not really concern the application of legalism to foreign policy but rather the determination of which branch of government is legally responsible for the conduct of foreign relations. To deal with Nicaragua or Canada as though either were bound by the rights and obligations of U.S. law is indeed an absurdity, but to determine who in the U.S. government is ultimately responsible for defining U.S. policy toward Nicaragua and Canada is an essential question that must be settled by law in a state pretending to the title of a constitutional republic.

Nor is the appeal to Justice Sutherland's opinion in *U.S. vs. Curtiss Wright Export Corporation* a sound basis for the doctrine of executive supremacy. Raoul Berger, after a three-page scrutiny of the decision in his *Executive Privilege,* considers that "the mischievous and demonstrably wrong dicta of Justice Sutherland deserve no further credence," though he devotes another six pages to its pulverization. The late Alexander Bickel similarly held that Justice Sutherland's "grandiose conception never had any warrant in the Constitution, is wrong in theory and unworkable in practice."

Conservatives today may perhaps be excused for allowing their commitment to Mr. Reagan and his support for anticommunist forces in Central America to get the better of their constitutional judgment, but their abandonment of a strong, legitimate congressional role in foreign policy is of more than antiquarian interest. Conservative reversal on this issue in fact represents a major redefinition of the terms of public discourse in American political culture.

Historian George H. Nash noted, in the 1950s and 1960s, "the growing conservative tendency to rely on the one branch of government which had proved immune to radical assault: the Congress." Conservative political leaders like Robert Taft, Richard Nixon, Joseph McCarthy, and John W. Bricker all insisted that Congress had a right and a duty to contribute to, investigate, and oversee presidential conduct of foreign policy, and their practice found theoretical justification in the writings of Frank Meyer, Willmoore Kendall, James Burnham, and Russell Kirk, among others.

Aside from the constitutional merits of the position, the reason for the conservative defense of Congress lay, as Nash suggests, in the fact that the locally based Congress was in large part "immune" to the political influence of the forces that dominated the executive branch. The latter, increasingly controlled by a new managerial elite that used New Deal liberalism and progressivism as its ideological formula, sought to implement a globalist foreign policy that would complete the interdependence and integration of the United States in a transnational world order in which American national sovereignty and cultural distinctiveness would evaporate. The United Nations, large regional security pacts, international financial and legal institutions, and multilateral treaty regimes on matters ranging from genocide to the law of the sea to arms control provided the framework for this new global order, in which a technically skilled and cosmopolitan-minded elite would displace traditional, local, and national elites.

The transformation of conservative opinion from support for a congressional role in foreign policy to virtually unanimous endorsement of presidential supremacy or even monopoly in foreign affairs thus represents more than a partisan eagerness to defend Mr. Reagan's White House or resist communist power in Central America. The very ability of conservatives to win and hold the presidency for eight years indicates less their successful challenge to the established elite and its domestic and foreign agenda than their assimilation by the elite itself. Conservative willingness to use the rhetoric and ideas of progressivism in foreign policy—"human rights," the sponsorship of global democracy, defense of an "international economy"—matches the recent conservative reliance on the executive branch in international relations and helps to reconcile the new conservative program in foreign affairs to the interests and ideology of the dominant elite. Contemporary conservatism offers little serious resistance to further absorption of American sovereignty and civilizational integrity into what neoconservative Zbigniew Brzezinski calls the "technetronic age," and the number of conservatives who today defend classically nationalist policies such as protectionism and restrictions on immigration is microscopic.

Present-day conservative anticommunism increasingly resembles the ineffectual containment strategy of the elite of the 1950s and 1960s and is largely predicated on humanitarian and moral concerns over the lack of civil and political liberties in communist states rather than on an understanding of the strategic dangers to American national interests of a world-revolutionary ideology. Instead of calling openly for the overthrow of the Sandinistas and other communist gangs, it gingerly demands "free elections" and negotiated settlements, and the recent movement of Mr. Reagan's foreign policy toward acceptance of the Marxist state in Mozambique, the appointment of Armand Hammer's protégé C. William Verity as secretary of commerce, and the quest for arms control treaties with the Soviets are merely the logical extrapolations of the recent tendency of the American Right to accommodate itself to the goals of the incumbent elite. Exactly how the Right has been subsumed by its one-time rivals for political and social dominance is a complicated story, but what is now regarded as "mainstream conservatism" has been so enervated in its willingness to offer resistance to the dominant elite and its basic ideology and policies that the fact of its assimilation cannot be doubted.

The bicentennial of the U.S. Constitution deserves a bit more in the way of celebration than firecrackers, docudramas, and the banalities from Right and Left of the Iran-Contra hearings. What came out of the Great Convention two hundred years ago remains the principal political symbol of a unique and ancient civilization that managerial globalism and social engineering are trying to subvert, and it is doubtful that reliance on the instruments that our technocratic brahmins have devised can preserve either the Constitution or the cultural fabric that underlies it. If the new generation of conservatives is serious about wanting to defend either its civilizational inheritance or the political and legal mechanisms by which its civilization has been governed, it might begin by resisting the temptations of partisan convenience and the baubles of power and reputation that its enemies have dangled before it and try to reclaim a way of life and a method of ruling and being ruled that its predecessors once understood.

Imperial Conservatives?

American conservatives have come a long way since Ohio's Senator John Bricker introduced a constitutional amendment to restrict the treaty-making power in 1952. Perhaps they've come too far. Today few on the Right share Mr. Bricker's belief that Congress ought to have a significant role in shaping U.S. foreign policy. Nothing brings foam to the conservative mandible more easily than a favorable allusion to the Boland Amendments or the War Powers Act, and cries against "congressional micromanagement" and "535 secretaries of state" became watchwords among Washington conservatives under the Reagan presidency.

John Bricker certainly would never have endorsed either Boland or War Powers—both are stupid measures, the one as harmful in its effects on Central America as the other is frivolous and unenforceable—but he surely would have argued for the validity of their basic assumption of legislative supremacy. The idea that the legislative branch has a vital role to play in the conduct of U.S. foreign policy and the disposition of American troops, now anathema to most conservatives, was fundamental to the principles espoused by Bricker, Robert Taft, Barry Goldwater, and other spokesmen of the Right. Taft, in the words of Russell Kirk and James McClellan, asserted "the right and the necessity, in the American democratic republic, for Congress to participate with the Executive in the conduct of foreign affairs," and "Mr. Republican" himself wrote in *A Foreign Policy for Americans:* "If in the great field of foreign policy the President has the arbitrary and unlimited powers he now claims, then there is an end to freedom in the United States not only in the foreign field but in the great realm of domestic activity which necessarily follows any foreign commitments."

In a recent issue of *Policy Review,* Representative Mickey Edwards undertook to defend and articulate the Taft-Bricker view that the U.S. Congress possesses a strong and legitimate role in foreign policy. He did so with learning and eloquence, urging that the intent of the Framers, more recent scholarship, and the conservative principles that "the separation of powers and the balance of powers were the greatest protectors of our freedoms" all support his conclusion that "foreign policy is an arena in which the powers and responsibilities of the Congress and the executive share a poorly defined playing field, each with important roles to play." But Mr. Edwards's effort, valiant as it was, has generally been greeted ferociously by his conservative critics and colleagues.

Nevertheless, conservatives ought to pause and retrace the steps that have brought them close to being what Mr. Edwards calls "New Age monarchists." Constitutional arguments aside, there are plenty of sound, pragmatic reasons for conservatives to defend a strong congressional role in foreign policy. Even under Mr. Reagan, conservatives in the Senate and House were vital in resisting efforts to circumvent the Taiwan Relations Act and adhere to the unratified SALT II treaty, among other silly State Department ideas. The propensity of the executive branch to commit the United States to foreign involvements that the Senate has not approved and would not condone was precisely part of what the Bricker Amendment sought to challenge. Moreover, conservatives like New Hampshire's Senator Gordon Humphrey have been instrumental in pushing the administration into more support for the Afghan resistance. Moderate Democrats like Arizona's Dennis DeConcini have played similar roles with policies toward Angola and UNITA. Senators Steve Symms, Orrin Hatch, and the late John East, and former Senator Jeremiah Denton all at one time or another (and Senator Jesse Helms in some respects almost continuously) have opposed executive-branch policies and actions on arms control, trade with the Soviet Bloc, foreign aid, treaties, appointments and nominations, and diplomacy in Latin America, Southern Africa, and the Far East. If such congressional activities aren't "micromanagement," the term has little meaning. Long before Boland, the main symbol of "congressional micromanagement" was the Jackson-Vanik amendment of 1974, which forbids granting most-favored-nation status to communist states that restrict emigration, and it too won virtually unanimous support from congressional conservatives.

Most conservatives, even while denouncing micromanagement, have defended all these instances of it. Their view of who should run U.S. foreign policy seems to be approaching incoherence, and as Mr. Edwards warns, "Conservatives need to remember that the powers we would give to a Ronald Reagan or a George Bush will someday be used by a Walter Mondale or a Michael Dukakis." As recent history shows, however, these powers are already being used by a foreign policy bureaucracy uncontrolled by elections and often independent of Congress and president alike.

It's easy for conservatives today to defend virtually exclusive presidential powers in foreign affairs by pointing to the rightward-leaning Reagan and Bush administrations and by citing not only left-wing congressional partisanship in foreign policy but also clear instances of legislative irresponsibility: security leaks, junketeering that compromises official U.S. policy, and general dithering, appeasement, and catering to special interests. But the conservative shift in perspective on the Congress and the presidency transcends current policy disputes and partisan bickering. It implies, logically and eventually in practice, a decisive erosion of some of the fundamental premises of conservative thought on which a good many other conservative positions depend.

No conservative theorist has articulated these premises and their connection with congressional authority more clearly than the late James Burnham in his 1959 *Congress and the American Tradition.* Long before Arthur Schlesinger discovered the "imperial presidency" (after serving and salivating over it for most of his life), Burnham, as William F. Buckley wrote in 1973, carefully charted "the usurpations of power by the Executive over a generation, done needless to say to the elated applause of liberal intellectuals."

Congress and the American Tradition is a work that must be read on two levels. On one level, it is an exposition of the historical and theoretical role of the Congress in the design of the American Republic and of the eventual capture of that role by the executive branch. On another level, however, the book is a study of why the survival of congressional authority is essential for the survival of political freedom.

Burnham saw the rise of the presidency as an integral part of the world-historical transformation that in 1940 he labeled "the managerial revolution," the displacement by massive, bureaucratically controlled organizations, often transnational in scope, of small-scale entrepreneurial, private capitalism; locally based, constitutionalist, parliamentary government; and the independent and sovereign nation-state. A new elite, the managerial class, was emerging into economic, political, and cultural dominance, in the United States using the liberal formulas of the New Deal to delegitimize the old elite and its institutions and legitimize its own power. The supposed need for centralized social and economic management, lodged in the federal bureaucracy and circumventing local and congressional resistance through direct appeals to the mass electorate, was the main rationale that the new class and its intellectual apologists articulated. "These tendencies," wrote Burnham, "—democratist, plebiscitary, bureaucratic, centralist, Caesarean—are the political phase of the general historical transformation of our era that in 1940 I named 'the managerial revolution.'"

The threat represented by this "political phase" was the curtailment of the social basis of political freedom in intermediary institutions, through which the deliberate and refracted will of the national community is expressed and in the conflict and opposition of which freedom resides. "Within the United States today," wrote Burnham, "Congress is in existing fact the prime intermediary institution, the chief political organ of the people as distinguished from the masses, the one body to which the citizenry can now appeal for redress not merely from individual despotic acts . . . but from large-scale despotic innovations, trends and principles."

Although Burnham himself was a strong advocate of a vigorous international role for the United States, he saw the erosion of the treaty-making and war powers of Congress and their effective transfer to the presidency (in reality, to the executive branch bureaucracy that is part of or sibling to the managerial class) as a threat to both freedom and national sovereignty. Presidents, untrammeled by congressional restraints in foreign affairs, could make executive agreements and treaties that substantially changed U.S. and state laws. They could commit American troops to foreign conflicts without adequate national consensus or even pro forma congressional consent and (as Truman tried to do in seizing the steel mills) threaten individual liberties by invoking "national emergency." The tendency of the managerial revolution to consolidate independent national states into integrated, supra-national blocs and thereby to supersede national sovereignty was manifest in the U.N. treaty, regional or global security pacts, and collective treaties that overrode the legal and institutional arrangements of particular nations and cultures.

It is precisely because of such tendencies, executed in the name of "world peace," the "global economy," and "transnational issues" and generally emanating from the executive branch, that congressional conservatives today resist monopolization of foreign policy by the executive as they resisted it in the days of Bricker and Taft. Despite the institutional corruption of Congress by its own absorption into the "administrative state" (another label for the "managerial state" applied by the contributors to the Heritage Foundation's recent volume on *The Imperial Congress*), at least some states and congressional districts and their representatives retain sufficient autonomy to offer an effective brake on some executive branch policies that in effect would jeopardize not only national interests abroad but also the integrity of freedom and sovereignty at home.

Conservatives may well support presidents like Ronald Reagan who seek to restore strength abroad in opposition to partisan and ideological distraction in Congress; but to leap from such practical measures to a philosophic defense of a presidential monopoly in foreign policy could lead alarmingly close to future compromises of traditional conservative commitments to limited government and national independence.

The original idea of postwar American conservatism and of the "Reagan Revolution" was not simply to take over the American megastate but to begin dismantling it; not for conservatives to lodge themselves in the institutional woodwork of the federal bureaucracy but to start reducing its size, its costs, its personnel, and its powers. That goal involved deregulation of the economy and restoration of authority and independence to states and localities, but also a diminution of the powers of the presidency and the augmentation of the powers of the Congress as the representative of local and state communities, the expression of the deliberate sense of the American people. Not only has that goal not been achieved, but now appears a body of ideas that supports a shift in the goal itself, the beginnings of a theoretical justification on ostensibly conservative grounds of the mega-state and of the centralized power of the presidency as its core. In recapitulating the liberal defense of the "imperial presidency," conservatives may soon find themselves metamorphosing into something they never wanted to be.

Inhospitable Neos
A Reply to Ernest Van den Haag

Ernest Van den Haag has been an active and valuable voice in American conservatism for over thirty years, and no one on the American Right would seem to be better qualified to survey the battlefields of "the war between Paleos and Neos" and to reconcile the opposing sides. Yet his account of the conflict is that of a partisan, not an even-handed elder statesman. His characterization of the Old Right or "paleoconservatives" is subtly inaccurate and misleading, and his conclusion—that the paleos are to blame for the war and had better give up before they jeopardize the larger crusade against the Left—casts the Old Right as the agents of a "petty and counterproductive" resentment and seeks to legitimize neoconservatism as the authentic American Right.[1]

Nowhere in his article does Mr. Van den Haag refer to the long series of slights, slanders, and backhanded power-plays that some neoconservatives, in the view of many paleos, have directed at the Old Right. The smear campaign against M. E. Bradford in 1981 over the appointment to the National Endowment for the Humanities chairmanship is perhaps the best known such incident, but almost every Old Rightist can detail others of a similar character. Such tactics were generally unknown to intraconservative disputes before the last decade, and, more than any "sectarian" purism on the part of Old Right ideologues, they help to account for the paleo-neo war and for the continuing suspicion in which many paleos hold their neo cousins.

Mr. Van den Haag tends to minimize ideological distinctions among neos and paleos and to emphasize what he calls "sociological" differences between them. Yet his "sociology" is really a polemical

---

1. This article is in response to Ernest Van den Haag, "The War between Paleos and Neos," *National Review* (February 24, 1989). Professor Van den Haag replied to my response in the same issue of *National Review* as the one in which this article was published, April 7, 1989.

weapon. By depicting paleos as a breed of Babbitts and Dan Quayles of liberal folklore, who inherited their ideology along with their golf clubs, he tries to dismiss them intellectually. By contrast, "the Neos became anti-Communists and finally conservatives not by inheritance, but by conversion," and "some of the Neos have thought more deeply and systematically about their new beliefs than most of those who absorbed them at their father's knee."

But the conflict between paleos and neos has largely been one among intellectuals, and the Old Right intelligentsia certainly did not inherit its ideas (or indeed much wealth) from its forebears. The biographies of James Burnham, Frank Meyer, Willmoore Kendall, Whittaker Chambers, and Richard Weaver, among others, should testify to this fact. All were Old Right intellectuals whom contemporary paleo intellectuals respect, and most passed through the crucible of communism or far-Left ideology before they forged their anticommunism and their various formulations of conservatism.

I am not aware of too many neos who were as seriously involved with the hard Left as many of the older paleos were, nor, despite the maturation of the "Second Thoughts" generation, do I know of too many who agonized over their intellectual and spiritual break with the Left as those of the Old Right did. The most representative neos, it seems, emerged from the liberal Left, a persuasion that, because of its deep permeation of the dominant American culture, is often more difficult to extirpate from the mind than outright Marxism. Philosophically, the main Old Right charge against the neos has been that they have not entirely broken with that persuasion; that, consciously or unconsciously, they retain what James Burnham called the "emotional gestalt of liberalism," despite their overt rupture with its formal doctrines and policies.

When Mr. Van den Haag gets to the paleos' "intellectual leaders," it is only to relegate them to the old curiosity shop. They "trace the legitimacy of their beliefs to the past. Not uncommonly they are *laudatores temporis acti*. Some are romantic medievalists, others Aristotelians, or followers of Thomas Aquinas, Edmund Burke, and Samuel Johnson. Nothing wrong with these mentors; but, perhaps, they are a little too distant from industrial society to have the answers to current problems." Perhaps they are—if, as the liberal Left believes, the nature of man and society changes in accordance with economic and social structures. That is one of the presuppositions that Old Right intellectuals exorcised from their minds. Perhaps the neos haven't.

Mr. Van den Haag is in error when he says Edmund Burke "unhelpfully described capitalism as the age of 'sophisters, economists, and calculators.' " Russell Kirk has generally emphasized the agreement of Burke and Adam Smith on economic matters, and F. A. Hayek has generally been sympathetic to Burke. In fact, Burke was describing the attack on Marie Antoinette by a revolutionary mob, and his phrase refers to the brutal misapplication of economic and utilitarian standards to social, political, moral, and aesthetic institutions. Unlike the liberal Left, Burke did not subscribe to a materialistic reductionism, and that too is one of the premises that the Old Right has been careful to uproot from its thought.

Mr. Van den Haag also seems to equate "conservatism" with "democracy and capitalism," though neither term is defined, and the neos' adherence to them is taken as proof of the legitimacy of their conservatism. Yet paleoconservatives (and most conservatives throughout history) have been skeptical of "democracy." If Mr. Van den Haag and the neos mean by the term the kind of constitutional republic the Framers established, there is no disagreement. But it should be noted that (a) James Madison specifically distinguished between a republic and a democracy in *The Federalist* and (b) it is not clear that the United States today retains the form of government the Framers intended. If "democracy" means what it generally has meant—the unrestricted rule of the majority—then the Old Right dissents. If it means the kind of "social democracy" that Sidney Hook and Andrei Sakharov endorse, then there must be a lot more discussion about what kind of conservatives the neos are.

The Old Right has generally supported the rule of law and the rights of property rather than any specific political and economic system. Hence, paleoconservatives have generally opposed the civil rights movement because it sought the legislative creation of rights derived from a fallible conscience rather than from a historic consensus ratified through deliberate constitutional processes. They also opposed the welfare state because it violated historically recognized property rights for the goals of "economic justice" and collective affluence. Neoconservative economic thought has tended to replace both Old Right and libertarian concerns with property and freedom with a preoccupation with economic growth and national prosperity. Perhaps the sophisters and calculators remain amongst us.

Mr. Van den Haag also makes much of the different priorities of neos and paleos, contrasting the secularism of the former with the "transcendent moral order" emphasized by the latter. The distinction is generally valid, though some paleos are not religious at all. But Mr. Van den Haag misses the point of the distinction. No one denies that regimes acknowledging a transcendent moral order can be and sometimes have been cruel and oppressive or that purely secular states can be benevolent. The Old Right point is that the recognition of a transcendent moral order at least allows for an ethical criticism and eventual change of the flaws of the secular regime, while the denial of such an order removes the ground of such a critique. The state that denies there is anything higher than its will is likely to be an unpleasant one sooner or later, given the well-known proclivities of human nature. Certainly it is true that "a regime influenced by the secular Andrei Sakharov, or by the religious Aleksandr Solzhenitsyn, would be an immense improvement over any Communist one." So would a regime run by Olof Palme or Harold Wilson, but no real conservative would be satisfied with it, and the secularist social democratic state that Mr. Van den Haag seems to prefer would be unable to recognize any higher restraint on the manipulation of its citizens.

Virtually all Old Rightists would agree with the neos that "religion" is "necessary" and would acknowledge its "social functions." Eating also is necessary and serves a social function, but that doesn't tell you what or how much to eat. If the neos have nothing more to say about the role of religion in society than this, their contributions are thin gruel indeed.

Mr. Van den Haag ends his account with an appeal for unity among conservatives that is really an invitation to the paleos to fold their flags. It is quite true that neos and paleos agree on many policy (and even philosophical) issues, but there remain significant differences among them. There should be no reason why the two cannot bloody each other in debate but learn from each other and continue to cooperate politically. The conservative movement has long welcomed internal disagreement—among libertarians and traditionalists, historicists and apostles of the natural law, Bradfordites and Jaffaites, even among free marketeers and a Keynesian conservative. But the neos themselves do not seem to welcome this kind of exchange or understand how to conduct it.

The neos seem to be no less uncomfortable with the paleos than the paleos are with the neos, and however "inclusive and latitudinarian" the neos may be toward each other, paleos have not found them particularly hospitable. Neoconservative influence is dominant at various philanthropic foundations, but paleoconservatives' grant proposals have often been refused. Such institutions frequently have endowed lucrative academic chairs for neoconservative scholars while lifelong paleoconservative intellectuals must scrape and hoe to sustain themselves in the twilight of their careers. Neoconservatives sponsor many academic and think-tank seminars but paleoconservatives are seldom invited.

One of the few efforts to bring neos and paleos together to air their differences occurred at the meeting of The Philadelphia Society in 1986. It was organized by paleos, and ended with neo accusations (generally whispered in private after the event) of racism, anti-Semitism, and extremism. In short, the mind-set of the neos toward the paleos is pretty much the same as that of liberals and the Left toward conservatives. The neos seem to think the paleos are "the stupid party," if not actually dangerous.

Yet neoconservatism is itself something of a danger to the conservative coalition because, through their replication of liberal-Left premises in contemporary policy debates, the neos may undermine the intellectual opposition to a dominant liberalism. Coalitions and elections will come and go, but only if a coherent and genuinely anti-liberal conservatism persists can the Right hope to preserve the basis for future coalitions and electoral victories. The neos ought to examine their own presuppositions more deeply than they seem to have done and show themselves a bit more willing to learn from a school that has been around rather longer than some of them.

As We Go Marching

Gregory A. Fossedal,
The Democratic Imperative:
Exporting the American Revolution

"When a term has become so universally sanctified as 'democracy' now is," wrote T. S. Eliot in 1939, "I begin to wonder whether it means anything, in meaning too many things: it has arrived perhaps at the position of a Merovingian Emperor, and wherever it is invoked, one begins to look for the Major of the Palace. . . . If anybody ever attacked democracy, I might discover what the word meant."

If Eliot could read Gregory A. Fossedal's *The Democratic Imperative,* he would remain as mystified today as he was fifty years ago. Mr. Fossedal certainly does not attack democracy, and his response to the classical criticism of it is cursory. He dismisses this criticism in two pages, quoting no less an authority than H. G. Wells to show that "Aristotle would have enjoyed the electoral methods of our modern democracies keenly." But if Mr. Fossedal does not reveal the meaning of democracy by attacking it, neither does he clarify it by any precise definition. Not until the end of the second chapter does it occur to him that some clarification of what he has been and will be talking about throughout his book might be called for. Although he is content to relegate his definition to a long footnote, the passage merits quotation at length and consideration in depth.

> In this book, the term ["democracy"] refers to a political system run by leaders chosen in periodic elections open to general participation and free debate. These leaders serve a government of limited powers, with certain rights such as free speech, a fair trial to those accused of serious crimes, and so on, the denial of which is beyond the state's reach. It is assumed that with those rights intact, voters will be able to choose the optimal arrangements for, say, economic freedom.

The crucial footnote continues for most of the page with further distinctions and elaborations, but neither there nor elsewhere does

Mr. Fossedal tell us what certain key elements of his definition mean. How "general" does participation have to be before a nondemocratic system becomes democratic? What are "free debate," "free speech," and a "fair trial"? What is "and so on"? The content and meaning of such terms are so variously interpreted in the United States and other countries that reliance on them for defining a word such as "democracy" is not helpful. Moreover, it is odd that Mr. Fossedal nowhere specifically includes in his understanding of democracy the element of opposition, though the right or power of opposition to an incumbent set of rulers is essential to most Western ideas of freedom.

In the second paragraph of the Great Footnote, Mr. Fossedal tells us, "For the purposes of this book, where an advance of economic or civil freedom occurs, even without the function of a representative body, it will be equated with an advance of 'democracy.'" But in the next paragraph, he says he "will not be offended if readers mentally scribble in the word 'representative' before the word 'democracy' wherever it appears throughout most of the book." Thus, we are to assume that Mr. Fossedal's democracy is representative, even when there is no representation.

To clarify further what he means, Mr. Fossedal has appended to his book three world maps for the years 1875, 1935, and 1988, to show the ebb and flow of democracy across the globe, rather like the advertisements for Sherwin-Williams paint. The first map shows Panama and Yugoslavia as nondemocracies, though neither state existed in 1875. It also shows the whole of the continental United States in 1875 as simply "democratic," but the U.S. territory of Alaska is only "partly democratic," though much of the western part of the country then enjoyed precisely the same legal and political status as Alaska. Great Britain also is shown as completely democratic in 1875, though its electorate was still strictly limited according to economic class and excluded about 80 percent of the adult males and all women; and its landed aristocracy, established church, and hereditary monarchy and House of Lords were then far more powerful than they are today. In the U.S. "democracy" of 1875, universal suffrage for white males existed in all states, though it was not mandated by the Constitution, and women, blacks, and Indians were not guaranteed the vote. States determined for themselves who voted; senators were not popularly elected, and direct primaries were virtually unknown. Few reactionaries today would be unhappy with this degree of democracy.

The map for 1988 tells us that Taiwan and Mainland China belong in the same category of "partly democratic," which is a step ahead of South Africa, Communist Ethiopia, Angola, and Mozambique, all of which are "undemocratic." Zimbabwe also is classed as "undemocratic," though on page 203 Mr. Fossedal refers to it as a "one-party democracy." Japan and India are democracies according to the map, while Mexico is only partly so. In all three countries, however, universal suffrage, more-or-less free debate, and regular elections pertain, though single parties have dominated their governments for so long that formal rights of opposition are somewhat academic. The reader will be happy to learn that Alaska, still only "partly democratic" even in 1935, has by 1988 mastered whatever examinations Mr. Fossedal put to it and taken its degree as a full democracy.

Whatever democracy is and wherever it might be, Mr. Fossedal's book is devoted to the thesis that its development everywhere in the world should be the main (perhaps the only) goal of American foreign policy. The bulk of his volume expounds how this goal may be pursued—through propaganda by the broadcasting facilities of the U.S. government and education by the National Endowment for Democracy, through support for guerrilla forces, and through international economic policies. Mr. Fossedal begins his book with a salute to the Abraham Lincoln Brigade as "an active American attempt to extend democracy beyond its own shores." Unfortunately, as he acknowledges, the naifs of the brigade soon met the majors of the palace in the shape of the Comintern agents who ran the brigade and used it to try to subvert Spain on behalf of Joseph Stalin. More fortunately, freedom in Spain was saved by the very undemocratic General Franco, who knew political fraudulence when he saw it. The support of communist fronts does not seem to perturb Mr. Fossedal, however, since he later writes that "the United States should have considered support for the African National Congress as early as 1983," despite the control of the ANC and its terrorism by the Soviet Union and the South African Communist party. Even if all the members of the ANC were devoted readers of *Human Events,* however, to support an armed insurgency in another country is an act of war. It does not occur to Mr. Fossedal that what he is contemplating is unprovoked aggression against a state that has never threatened the United States and in fact has been its loyal supporter since World War II.

Instead of spending his energies in the study of how the United States could export democracy, Mr. Fossedal might have been better advised to have concentrated on pondering three fundamental questions, affirmative answers to which appear to be largely unexamined presuppositions of his book.

First, he might have asked whether democracy is an intrinsically good form of government. If the contemporary United States is the model of democracy, the answer is not self-evident. The expansion of the franchise in the United States has occurred in tandem with the enlargement and centralization of the state, with reliance on socialist economic policies, and with the systematic use of concentrated power to uproot social institutions and classes, cultural patterns, and local and regional pluralism. Despite the vast technological and economic resources of the United States, American democracy is only marginally able to protect its citizens and interests abroad and seems utterly incompetent to enforce minimal standards of order at home. The criminal corruption of officeholders—in Congress, the executive branch, and in many urban and state governments—is commonplace, but corruption in the broader sense of the use of public power for private ends, ideological or material, is so routine that it has become an acknowledged part of our government.

These disadvantages might be bearable if democratization were accompanied by an enlarged control of governmental power at the popular level, but this does not seem to be the case. Despite universal suffrage, increased openness in government, and more active participation in some public forums, American democracy is governed largely by a permanent and only partially visible elite of bureaucrats, managers, advisers, staff aides, technicians, and clerks whose role in decision making is seldom disclosed, whose power is never subjected to popular judgment, and whose ability to subvert, co-opt, or deflect even the most intrepid reformers of the Right or Left seems virtually invincible. Even in popular elections, the dependence of candidates and parties on massive amounts of money and the arts of political manipulation serves not to enhance popular control but to avoid it, leading to what liberal journalist Sidney Blumenthal has called "the engineering of consent with a vengeance."

It may be that there is no necessary connection between the forms and processes of American democracy and these obvious flaws of the current political order, though their historical conjunction suggests that there may well be a connection. In any case, Mr. Fossedal does not consider the question.

Secondly, Mr. Fossedal might have asked, assuming that democracy is a good or desirable form of government, whether it is possible in various non-Western or nonmodern states and societies. His assumption, again, is affirmative, based in large part on a wave of democratic movements of the 1980s in such societies as the Philippines, South Korea, and several Latin American states. Yet he conducts no serious analysis of this trend, its causes, its capacities for success, or its possible consequences. While Mr. Fossedal recognizes the connections between economic strength and a stable liberal democracy, he tends to neglect other preconditions, such as a high degree of literacy, a stable infrastructure of governmental control, a national consensus shared by all parts of the population, and, perhaps most important, a cultural tradition that includes the many presuppositions about power and its uses characteristic of Western society. Mr. Fossedal does not sufficiently reflect upon the fact that Western democracy is less the product of "natural rights" than of several centuries of evolution within a particular civilization that recognizes and rewards individuality and opposition to a far greater degree than Oriental, African, and Islamic cultures do. Such concepts as a "loyal opposition," a public rather than a dynastic or patrimonial idea of political office, a distinction between secular and religious authority, the legitimacy of political involvement by subordinate social groups, the effectiveness of voting, a national rather than a tribal, feudal, or sectarian identity, and the willingness of those who control the instruments of force to abide by noncoercive political decisions all are basic to Western ideas of modern democracy but may not pertain in many non-Western or pre-modern societies and may not be exportable in the same way that Coca Cola is.

Mr. Fossedal does not consider the argument that Latin America seems to undergo cycles of democracy and dictatorship at intervals of every thirty years. He never mentions the classic case of the Weimar Republic, in which a society utterly unprepared for democracy voted itself into dictatorship. He never discusses the concept of "totalitarian democracy," in which mass participation is manipulated to represent the General Will, the *Volk,* the proletariat, the People, or other abstractions useful to modern tyrants. Nor does he deal with the argument that democratic movements in many Third World societies may be the expressions of relatively new, modernized elites of intellectuals and technocrats alienated from traditional ruling classes composed of clergy, landowners, and military and who may seek to use democracy as a means of displacing the older elites and seizing power for themselves. Such new classes in Third World states, as political scientist Barry Rubin has argued, can easily form the social base of modern dictatorships rather than democracy. It may be that democracy is indeed on the march across the globe, but Mr. Fossedal does not consider the alternatives sufficiently to persuade us.

Thirdly, Mr. Fossedal does not deal at all adequately with the question of whether the export or development of democracy is compatible with American national interests. Given the way in which he defines "national interest," however, he manages to give a quick and easy affirmative answer to this question as well.

"The purpose of American foreign policy, then," he writes, "cannot be explained without first answering a prior question: What is the purpose of the American government? To know what we are for in the world, we must know what we are for at home. . . . The goal, as our framers put it, is to secure the rights of mankind." Mr. Fossedal goes so far as to suggest that anyone who doubts that the purpose of U.S. foreign policy is to promote the "rights of man" is un-American—"To argue against a foreign policy to promote the rights of man, then, is to argue against the rights themselves, and thus against our own institutions"— and he relies on the equality clause of the Declaration of Independence to justify his interpretation of America's purpose.

We have been through all this before, but let us rehearse it briefly once again. The Declaration says nothing about the "purpose" of the U.S. or any other government. It is not even a charter of government but a proclamation of national independence and a catalogue of the abuses of power that justified the act of separation. The real purposes or goals of the U.S. government are quite clearly spelled out in the Preamble of the Constitution, and they say nothing about equality, human rights, or even foreign policy. The Constitution did not establish the political equality of individual citizens, and its toleration of slavery, the nonenfranchisement of blacks in most non-slave states, the diversity of state political practices and the indirect election of senators and the president would seem to contradict the Straussian-Jaffa-Charles Kesler interpretation of the American political tradition that Mr. Fossedal endorses.

From the false premise that the "rights of man" are the goal of the U.S. government, Mr. Fossedal draws the non sequitur that the same goal and purpose must animate our foreign policy. It is at this point that his book ceases to be merely frivolous and becomes dangerous. Other possible goals of foreign policy—national independence, territorial security, economic prosperity, and the physical protection of our own citizens and their property, rights, and interests at home and abroad—simply are not encompassed within Mr. Fossedal's goals. Indeed, it is possible that a good many of our legitimate national interests would be transgressed by Mr. Fossedal's foreign policy. Treaties with nondemocratic governments, private business contracts enforced by them, and geopolitically necessary alliances with them might all be jeopardized by the democratically elected regimes that replaced them. The genuine democratization of the Soviet Union and Eastern Europe, for example, would almost certainly transform world power relationships and perhaps lead to the disintegration of the USSR and even to protracted warfare in Europe, Western Asia, and the Far East. "Majority rule" in South Africa almost certainly would result in an anti-Western (and probably brutally racist) government oriented toward the Soviet Union and commanding the sea routes and vast mineral resources of the southern African subcontinent. The democratization of Saudi Arabia or other Persian Gulf states could lead to radical Islamic and anti-Western regimes that could jeopardize oil flows to the West. The democratization of Greece has already led to the most anti-American government in Europe, and the democratization of Spain has already endangered our military bases there. The democratization of the Philippines has led to the doubling of the communist insurgency there, to increased political corruption and anti-Americanism, and also to endangerment of our bases.

Mr. Fossedal's division of the world into "democracies" and non-democracies proceeds from an abstraction that bears no relationship to concrete U.S. interests or to what the United States must do to protect those interests. It lumps pro-American but nondemocratic governments such as those of South Africa and Chile in the same pot with nondemocratic enemies like Cuba and the Soviet Union. It puts democratic close allies such as Great Britain in the same camp as democratic uncooperative governments like India. It places irrelevant democratic states such as Botswana on the same level as states like democratic Japan. The fact is that democracy/nondemocracy is simply not a useful standard by which to govern our foreign policy. It obscures or ignores too many other significant variables to offer a reliable guide for evaluating our interests or knowing how to pursue them.

One of the persistent flaws of Mr. Fossedal's book is his confusion of democracy with liberal government, though F. A. Hayek in *The Constitution of Liberty* long ago clearly distinguished them: "Liberalism is a doctrine about what the law ought to be, democracy a doctrine about the manner of determining what will be the law." As Hayek (and many others) noted, there is no necessary connection between liberalism and democracy, and in fact liberal government was secured in England and the United States in the eighteenth and nineteenth centuries well before the advent of democracy. The growth of democracy, as noted above, is historically associated with the diminution of liberal government.

Yet one of the characteristic beliefs of the modern democratic Left has been that democracy is essential for the protection of liberal government. Mr. Fossedal adheres to this belief and states it explicitly: "It may be possible that other forms of government would satisfy the rights of man, but practical human experience suggests that certain institutions are needed for government to respect those rights consistently." Among these institutions, he suggests, are elections, constitutions, and divisions of powers, though the latter two are properly liberal rather than democratic institutions. In any case, his statement is simply erroneous.

It is a fallacy of both the liberal and the democratic mind that a set of formal procedures, by itself, will protect freedom. A more realistic view has long recognized that while certain procedures can help protect freedom under some circumstances, in other circumstances they only endanger it. This is why the case of the Weimar Republic, which enjoyed the formal procedures of liberalism and democracy, is classic. The procedures and forms of liberalism, democracy, or any other constitutional type must reflect a balance of power among significant social forces—e.g., rural vs. urban, business vs. labor, religion vs. secular authority, class vs. class, region vs. region—if they are to institutionalize real freedom and social diversity and enhance the level of civilization. The existence of this kind of balance may be formalized through legal and political procedures, but it can exist independently of them as well, and while clear and stable procedures are helpful in institutionalizing the balance of social forces, it is the substance and not the form that is important. Statesmen should design the forms to reflect the substance, as *The Federalist* recognized, and not try to engineer the substance to fit forms derived from "natural rights" or other abstractions. Like the man who believes that milk comes from supermarkets rather than from the careful cultivation of cows, liberals and democrats believe that freedom comes from the procedures themselves, and they ignore or take for granted the underlying and largely invisible social and cultural substratum that allows procedural liberalism and democracy to flourish. Unlike Hayek, they fail to recognize that "freedom is not a state of nature but an artifact of civilization."

Moreover, if the pluralism offered by the balance of social and political forces is not to degenerate into an anarchical factionalism, it must be limited by common acceptance of a social myth that at least implicitly defines the ends of the public order and the legitimate means by which they may be pursued. Mr. Fossedal's "natural" or "human" rights provide one such myth that has proved useful to certain groups aspiring to power throughout modern history, but the universalism of this myth tends to ignore or even undermine the particular cultural framework and social balances necessary for the preservation of concrete freedoms. In any case, whether the distinctly post-Christian, Western myth of "human rights" exerts any enduring appeal to non-Western cultures is a question Mr. Fossedal never explores seriously.

Mr. Fossedal's prolonged ode to global democracy is characteristic of the neoconservative-social democrat-Straussian-"progressive conservative" school of political thought that now seems to prevail on the mainstream American Right. Both his text and his acknowledgements are filled with quotations from the exponents of this movement and expressions of gratitude to them. The chief goal of this movement seems to be not a serious exploration of and challenge to the presuppositions of the dominant American political culture but rather the pursuit of its own political and cultural power. Hence, it is content to adapt prevailing liberal humanist presuppositions to its own purposes and avoids expressing any thought (or tolerating expressions by anyone else) that might offend, threaten, or frighten our own Majors of the Palace who guard the public discourse. To challenge the dominant presuppositions would mean isolation from the mainstream of political debate that these presuppositions define and would make the quest for power far more difficult. The result has been the intellectual impoverishment of the American Right, the emasculation of a genuinely radical conservatism, and its replacement by bubble-talk and sophomoric cant more suitable for the Boy Scout Jamboree than for consideration by grown men and women concerned with the prospects of their civic culture. Mr. Fossedal's contribution to the body of thought and scholarship produced by this movement is no doubt destined to find a place as one of its classic expressions.

Rouge on a Corpse's Lips

Whittaker Chambers,
Ghosts on the Roof:
Selected Journalism of Whittaker Chambers,
1931–1959

Two ironies attend the life and career of Whittaker Chambers. The first is that the one-time communist spy, foreign editor of *Time,* and witness against Soviet espionage became notable during his life and afterwards only because of the Hiss case, which brought him such notoriety that his career as a professional journalist came to a quick end. The second is that the Hiss case itself was a distraction from Chambers's larger legacy as a thinker and writer to a world he believed was dying, even though his reputation issued from the Hiss case and from what he had to tell that world about the meaning of the case. Unable to continue the profession he followed after leaving the Soviet underground, Chambers evolved into a prophetic figure, an almost Dostoevskian character, whose brooding vision of a decadent West engaged in a desperate death struggle with communism and with its own poisons has haunted those few Westerners who have perceived the unfulfilled greatness of the man.

Terry Teachout's collection of Chambers's miscellaneous writings, from the Marxist fiction of his early days to his last mordant syllables in *National Review,* is in part intended to correct the view we have had of Chambers as either (on the Left) a "messianic anticommunist" or (to much of the Right) a bottomless pit of often lachrymose horror stories about the god that failed and its worshippers. It is no fault of Mr. Teachout's that his anthology does not entirely succeed in this effort. What Chambers wrote for *Time* and *Life* during the period he called in *Witness* "The Tranquil Years" conspicuously lacks the power that *Witness* itself, the posthumous *Cold Friday,* and his letters to William F. Buckley, Jr., possess. That is not entirely Chambers's fault either; the pieces for *Time* and *Life* contain most of the flaws those magazines have inflicted on the

191

192 Beautiful Losers

reading public throughout their history. Usually, when Chambers's own glimpses of some of the major minds of his era—Albert Einstein, Arnold J. Toynbee, Reinhold Niebuhr, James Joyce—were allowed to be seen, they were quickly dimmed by editorially necessary trivia about personalities and the glib oversimplifications in which American mass journalism likes to swaddle itself.

Nor, probably, was Chambers yet capable of that power. Only when the ordeal of the Hiss case had brought him to that "last path of the earth, in the Scythian country, in the untrodden solitude" of which he wrote in *Cold Friday,* when his mind had been stripped and concentrated on the meaning of his life and its meaning for the West, did he become privy to his country's fate and able to foretell and analyze it in his final testimony.

Yet the glimpses are there, and to those who recognize in Whittaker Chambers not only a man who altered the course of history but also one of the most compelling American writers of this century, Mr. Teachout's anthology is indispensable. It includes four short stories Chambers wrote for the *New Masses* while he was still a fledgling apparatchik. It continues with all the major essays and reviews he wrote for *Time* and *Life* in the 1940s, when his mind had been cleared of Marxism and was beginning to see more distinctly the lines his age was etching in the dust of history, down through his contributions to the *American Mercury* and *National Review,* when he had become the prophet for a cause. But even in the early short stories, despite their rigid adherence to the party line, the embryo of the mature Chambers is visible.

The major value of Mr. Teachout's collection consists not so much in the intrinsic worth of what Chambers was writing in his early postcommunist period as in what these pieces show about the development of Chambers's mind and world-view. By examining what he had to say in the Tranquil Years, before the Hiss case forced him for the rest of his life to defend his own integrity and to play a role that merely distracted him and his readers from his essential message, we now can see more plainly not only what Chambers had to tell the West about its enemies in Moscow and their agents in Washington but also what he wanted to tell the West about itself. That message, whatever happens to communism and the West in the future, is likely to prove more enduring than the facts about the Woodstock typewriter, the prothonotary warbler, and the vapid young traitor whose perjury made Chambers famous.

"The social symbol of our age," Chambers wrote in the *American Mercury* in 1944, "is autolysis, a medical term for the process whereby the stomach, for example, by a subtle derangement of its normal functions, destroys itself by devouring its own tissues." He could not, before the Hiss case, fully substantiate his belief, implicit in this passage, that the West was dying by suicide. To have done so would have involved telling what he later would tell the House Committee on Un-American Activities about his own descent into the Marxist Avernus, and Chambers was not yet ready to tell, nor was the world yet prepared to listen. Throughout these popular pieces there runs the theme of the world-historical meaning of current events and the suggestion that the West, even as it was crowing with glee in its triumph over the Axis and its grand illusion of global peace and progress, is of the same flesh with Nineveh and Tyre, yet finds its own mortality altogether inconceivable. But the experiences that had brought Chambers to this bleak vision remained known only to him, and his effort to convince his readers of his belief, never quite fully stated in these pieces, relied on symbolism and suggestion rather than the police blotter factuality of *Witness* and the hearing room. "The rouge applied by an undertaker to the lips of a 20th Century corpse," he wrote in *Time* in 1947, "is one measure of 20th Century civilization. But modern man's effort to deny or minimize death is part of a much more important necessity—the need to deny or minimize God."

To Chambers, the most complete organization of that need was communism itself, "the world's second oldest faith," as he calls it in *Witness,* whose "promise was whispered in the first days of the new Creation under the Tree of Knowledge of Good and Evil: 'Ye shall be as gods.'" But communism was not the only manifestation of that need, which permeated the West and, in what became Chambers's view of history, modernity itself. From Toynbee's *A Study of History,* Chambers came to believe that "one hopeful meaning stands out: not materialist but psychic factors are the decisive forces of history." His seven-part series for *Life* on "The History of Western Culture" extrapolates the "psychic factors" that had brought the West to the brink of its dissolution.

The Enlightenment, he wrote, was the "one great source of modern culture." It "revised the fundamental idea of man's destiny and purpose which civilization had developed over more than 1,000 years" and was "the intellectual chemistry whose gradual precipitate was the modern mind—secular, practical and utilitarian." The denouement of the Enlightenment he saw in the Edwardian era, which was

> the fulfillment of the 18th Century's Enlightenment, and the Enlightenment's basic intuition was the idea of progress—the belief that man, by the aid of science, can achieve a perfection of living limited only by the imaginative powers of the mind. Implicitly the Enlightenment denied faith in the name of science and the Kingdom of God in the name of the kingdom of this world. It whetted that knife-edge, dividing the world's greatest focuses of force—the power of religion and the power of science—along which the thoughtful man has teetered ever since.

The Edwardians—not merely the British in the decade after Queen Victoria's death but also the Americans and Europeans—wrapped themselves in the exuberant confidence of the Enlightenment's legacy. "A new tempo was entering life with the abridgement of time and distance by speed and the multiplication of power by the generation of energy. . . . the Edwardian era was one of those rare interludes of history where everybody who could possibly do so had a wonderful time."

Of course, it was all an illusion, had been illusory ever since the Enlightenment, and would be dashed in World War I and the Russian Revolution, the political, economic, and intellectual wreckage of the twentieth century, and the chaos that ensued. It was neither Voltaire nor the Edwardians who understood what would happen when the illusion broke but a squat little gentleman unknown to and unimagined by their cherubic innocence. "When the train of history makes a sharp turn," said Lenin, "the passengers who do not have a good grip on their seats are thrown off."

The shallowness of the Enlightenment and its legacy in the liberal, democratic, and industrialized West in Chambers's view had weakened the grip of Western men on their seats and had failed to prepare them to survive the sharp turn history was about to take. That Chambers saw the weakness of Western liberalism in the face of the challenge is clear enough. That is why he can never be a hero to contemporary anti-Soviet social democrats and neoconservatives who pride themselves on their pragmatic humanism and their own adherence to the values of the liberal, modern West. Only by ignoring Chambers's dark vision of human unreason and sin and his belief that liberalism was a close cousin to communism or by twisting him into a Third Generation yuppie chirping about the Strategic Defense Initiative, tax cuts, and Jonas Savimbi can today's "Right" honestly regard Chambers as an icon. "For, of course," he wrote in *Life* in 1953,

> there is a strong family resemblance between the Communist state and the welfare state. The ends each has in view have much in common. But the methods proposed for reaching them radically differ. Each is, in fact, in direct competition with the other, since each offers itself as an alternative solution for the crisis of the 20th Century; and Fabian Britain has at last supplanted Soviet Russia in the eyes of political liberals when they look abroad. Nevertheless, that family resemblance is nerve-wearing, since all the minds that note it are not equally discriminating, especially in a nation that has only just become conscious of Communism and still rejects socialism. So, at every move against Communism, liberal views come unglued, and liberal voices go shrill, fearing that, by design or error, the move may be against themselves.

Yet if Chambers rejected twentieth-century liberalism, he was not much more sympathetic to the conservatives of the 1950s. He declined to attach himself in any way to Joe McCarthy, less perhaps from dislike of the man than a belief that McCarthy would eventually taint his witness. He was not comfortable at *National Review* and found preposterous the quaint dogmas of classical liberalism dressed up as conservatism. In a letter to Buckley in 1957, he called the free-market economist Ludwig von Mises "a goose," and Frank Meyer's self-appointment as the ideological gatekeeper of the American Right seems first to have amused, then bored, him. The ideas of Meyer and Russell Kirk struck Chambers as "chiefly an irrelevant buzz." Of Kirk's *The Conservative Mind* he asked, "if you were a marine in a landing boat, would you wade up the seabeach at Tarawa for *that* conservative position? And neither would I!" Only with Buckley himself and James Burnham did he seem to share anything like a common outlook, and at last he resigned from *National Re-*

view, acknowledging to Buckley and himself that he was not a conservative in any serious sense but "a man of the Right."

What exactly Chambers meant by this term is far from clear, but he contrasted it with "conservatism" and seems to have identified it with a defense of capitalism. "I am a man of the Right because I mean to uphold capitalism in its American version. But I claim that capitalism is not, and by its essential nature cannot conceivably be, conservative." Yet despite his identification with capitalism, almost nowhere did Chambers offer an explicit defense of it, and in both his letters to Buckley and in a *National Review* piece of 1958 on federal farm policy, he was perfectly conscious of the contradiction between capitalism and conservatism and the link between capitalism and the advance of socialism. Like most conservatives and like his neighbors in rural Maryland, Chambers saw the freedom and independence of farmers threatened by federal regulation of agriculture. But he also believed such controls were "inescapeable."

> The problem of farm surpluses is, of course, a symptom of a crisis of abundance. It is the gift of science and technology—improved machines, fertilizers, sprays, antibiotic drugs, and a general rising efficiency of know-how. The big farm, constantly swallowing its smaller neighbors, is a logical resultant of those factors. . . . If farmers really meant to resist these trends, to be conservative, to conserve 'a way of life' (as they often say), they would smash their tractors with sledges, and go back to the horse-drawn plow. Of course, they have no intention of doing anything so prankish. . . . Controls of one kind or another are here to stay so long as science and technology are with us.

Chambers's belief, expressed as early as 1944, that "the land-owning farmer, big and little, is the conservative base of every healthy society, no matter how many miles of factories may be required to keep the average city dweller in a state of civilized neurosis" reflects an apparent sympathy for agrarianism and the American South. But his recognition of the self-destructive dynamic of modern capitalism, relying on science, sponsoring continuous enlargement and social innovation, and eventually spawning socialism, brings him close to Burnham and Joseph Schumpeter.

Nowhere in all his writing does Chambers more clearly show the weaknesses of unrestrained capitalism and its kinship with communism than in his devastation of Ayn Rand's *Atlas Shrugged* in *Na-*

tional Review in 1957. "Randian Man," he wrote, "like Marxian man, is made the center of a godless world. . . . If Man's 'heroism' . . . no longer derives from God, or is not a function of that godless integrity which was a root of Nietzsche's anguish, then Man becomes merely the most consuming of animals, with glut as the condition of his happiness and its replenishment his foremost activity." Like the materialism of "godless communism," the hedonism of godless capitalism winds up as the tool of a political despotism that manages the pursuit of happiness as pleasure.

> In the name of free enterprise, therefore, she plumps for a technocratic elite (I find no more inclusive word than technocratic to bracket the industrial-financial-engineering caste she seems to have in mind). When she calls "productive achievement" man's "noblest activity," she means, almost exclusively, technological achievement, supervised by such a managerial political bureau.

The significance of Chambers's witness, then, is considerably diminished if it is mistaken as merely an account of Soviet communism and its Western stooges. His point throughout his writings in the 1940s and 1950s was that the roots of communism lie in the West itself and that they flourish because the modern age has chosen to credit the serpent's promise. That promise and its lethal consequences for the West were as palpable to him in the United States of Truman and Eisenhower as they had been under the Edwardians and as they were in the Soviet Union under Lenin and Stalin. Only when the West had awakened to the falsehood of the promise could it bear what he called "that more terrible witness" by which it would destroy its external enemy and begin to purge itself of its internal toxins. But he had no expectation that the West would do so, and no suggestions on how to do it.

For all the authority Chambers commanded in *Witness,* in the last decade of his life he seemed uncertain about many things and had no clear answers for the political crises of his age. "There are a lot of things I am becoming less and less sure about," he wrote Buckley in 1957. He was not at bottom a political thinker but a Christian existentialist who shunned politics by enveloping himself in suffering and dwelling on the hopelessness of man's fate without God. Christianity and the tragic vision of history became for him an intellectual crutch with which history's walking wounded could limp away from a battle they could not win. Like Burnham, as Chambers himself wrote to Buckley, he sought "to understand what the reality of the desperate forces is, and what is their relationship in violent flux," and he had what he called "the direct glance that measures what it leaves without fear and without regret." But despite his grasp of the main forces of the twentieth century, Chambers was unable to communicate the realities he saw in a form that would allow a secular resolution of the challenges they presented. Hence, his response was one of other-worldly withdrawal—from journalism and *National Review* to his farm and family, to a furtively private pietism, to an autobiographical justification of his vision, to a handful of occasional essays for the conservative press, to an intensely emotional (often maudlin) prose published mainly in posthumous fragments and filled with introspection, grotesque anecdotes, bizarre characters, and metaphors of death, lunacy, and decay. Chambers relentlessly smashed his readers' faces against the window panes of history and forced them to look at scenes few of them wanted to see. But having shown them the worst that human beings in this century could do, he had little to offer them except to burrow deeper within a storm cellar of intense devotionalism. His oeuvre, for all its merits of style and truth and all that it has to tell the West about why it is dying, is not what a Marine wading up the seabeach at Tarawa would carry in his knapsack.

The Secret of the Twentieth Century

Kevin Phillips,
The Politics of Rich and Poor:
Wealth and the American Electorate
in the Reagan Aftermath

When Kevin Phillips's *The Politics of Rich and Poor* hit the best-seller list last summer, the Gipperites began to squeal like a worn-out fan belt in a used Toyota. "Anti-Reagan sophistry," sneered David Brock of the Heritage Foundation in the *Wall Street Journal.* "A book-length tantrum," wept Warren Brookes in the *Washington Times.* "Garbage," pronounced Republican wheeler-dealer Eddie Mahe. "I refuse to read that fraud's book," declared GOP consultant John Buckley in what must have been one of the more honest comments on Mr. Phillips's most recent contribution to scholarship.

Such, of course, is the predictable reception of a book proposing ideas and advancing arguments that cannot be comfortably hammered into existing ideological and partisan holes, and such especially is it the kind of reception to be expected from the lowing herd of pseudoconservatives who in the past decade have succeeded in hornswoggling themselves into the courtyards (but not the corridors) of national power. When Mr. Phillips in his youth was designing the "populist" theories and strategies by which conservative Republicans could gain the votes of rank-and-file Democrats and challenge the political hegemony of a liberal elite, these same courtiers pranced for joy. Then they were happy to hear of his cyclical theory of American politics, how at approximately thirty-year intervals, one political elite is displaced by another when the incumbents have become a stale establishment. Then they were pleased to clamber into the cockpit his theory seemed to assign them as the pilots of the "emerging Republican majority" that would hijack the country away from the New Deal coalition.

But it might have occurred to them, as it evidently did not, that if Mr. Phillips had a shred of intellectual integrity, which he evidently has, then sooner or later the cycle he claimed to have discovered would swing about, and some other rough beast would slouch toward a political Bethlehem to be born. It is Mr. Phillips's thesis in his present book that that hour has come round at last, and here he is to pluck his lyre in honor of the animal's arrival.

In other words, Mr. Phillips's belief that the Reagan era saw the entrenchment of a new political establishment that is about to be challenged by a wave of populist revolt is merely the logical extension of the interpretation of American politics that he first advanced (and which most conservatives embraced) in 1969 and has adapted and amended in a series of later books ever since. Remaining faithful to and consistent with his own theory does not make him, as conservative chuckleheads claim, a "liberal"; then again, it doesn't make him right either.

What really makes the Gipperites gasp, however, is not just Mr. Phillips's prediction that Reaganism is scheduled to fail politically but also that Good Old Dutch and his "revolution" were in large part fraudulent—that, far from helping the middle-income strata of the electorate who enabled Reagan to win and hold the White House, the economic, fiscal, and regulatory policies of the 1980s gave these very groups a fat lip, while allowing the corporate rich, a cadre of felonious financial wizards, and a select band of well-fed "conservative populists" to become opulent. Mr. Phillips buttresses this argument with the same kind of statistical megatonnage that has made his other books so formidable, and he has framed it in a breezy style laced with anecdotes that lend life to his numbers.

Here the reader nostalgic for the 1980s may trip down memory's lane to such triumphs of "populism" as Malcolm Forbes's birthday party in 1989, complete with Moroccan horsemen. Here he may revisit such glowing symbols of Mr. Reagan's Augustan age as the teeth of Ivan Boesky, the modest couture of Nancy, and the cultural renaissance spawned by the baby-boomers. Here too the reader may glimpse through the glory of the Reaganite dawn such misty vestiges of the old America as family farms now repossessed by banks and sold to corporations in New York and Japan, mines and factories now idle, and endless tracts of American land and buildings once actually owned by Americans themselves.

But to be quite fair, Mr. Phillips rather exaggerates the economic damage done to the American middle class in the Reagan era. He acknowledges that the real losers in those years were largely confined to certain categories—"manufacturing employees, farmers, people in the oil industry, young householders and the working poor"—while others held steady or made small gains. The latter, however, were able to do so largely because their wives left home and went to work and because they simply worked harder to keep afloat. From 1973 to 1987, Mr. Phillips points out, Americans' leisure time actually fell by 37 percent, from 26.2 hours a week to 16.6 hours, while the real average weekly wage of all workers (white collar and blue collar) declined from $191.41 a week in 1972 to $171.07 in 1986 in terms of constant 1977 dollars.

> Many families found themselves emptying savings accounts and going into debt, often to meet the soaring price of home-ownership or to put a child through college. . . . Homeownership had reached a record 65 percent of U.S. households in 1980, after climbing steadily from 1940, when 43.6 percent of households owned their own residences. After 1980, however, the homeownership rate would drop year by year, falling to 63.8 percent in 1986 and leveling off. Young people, in particular, found that home buying was next to impossible.
>
> For much of Middle America, then, the Reagan years were troubling and ambiguous as the contrast intensified between proliferating billionaires and the tens of millions of others who were gradually sinking.

Mr. Phillips frames much of this economic analysis and what he calls "plutography"—a neologism that seems destined to enter the language as easily as his earlier coinage "Sunbelt"—in terms of his historical theory of American politics. Hence, there is much analogizing between the Reagan era and those of William McKinley and the 1920s. "Each Republican coalition," he writes, "began by emphasizing national themes and unity symbols while subordinating commercial and financial interests. Lincoln's struggle to maintain the union is famous, but lesser efforts by McKinley in 1896 and Nixon in 1968 go little noticed." But the phase of appealing to "national unity" usually doesn't last long once the GOP sets up shop in the White House. "Beyond its emphasis on the politics of national unity, dynamic capitalism, market economics and the concentration of wealth are what the Republican party is all about. When Republicans are in power long enough, that is what America gets, by the traditional

Republican methods of disinflation, limited government, less regulation of business, reduced taxation and high interest rates."

Mr. Phillips may or may not be on firm ground in his analogical theory. Like most historical interpretations, it is one that can never be proved and must be tested by its ability to explain known facts. Moreover, even if it is true, it may reveal the outer mechanics of American political history, but it doesn't really grasp the world-historical drift of what is happening in the United States and the world in the last part of the twentieth century.

What Mr. Phillips is really talking about, though he may not know it, is not just the ebb and flow of political parties in White House and Congress, but rather the continuing civilizational crisis, in its economic and political phases, of what James Burnham called "the managerial revolution." The liquidation of the middle class and its bourgeois cultural order are essential parts of that revolution, which does not consist only in the material dimension of the rolling up of comparatively small owner-operated business enterprises and farming units by colossal corporate organizations and the replacement of local, legislative, and constitutionalist government by centralized, executive, bureaucratic regimes. It also consists, in its cultural dimensions, in the delegitimization and eventual extirpation of bourgeois culture—first on the grounds that that culture is the product of a selfish "capitalist" oligarchy, and later, in our own times, that it is the institutional framework by which a "white, male, heterosexual, Christian" ruling class maintains cultural hegemony. The technically skilled managerial elites that hold power in corporations, unions, universities, mass media, foundations, and government cannot secure and enhance their dominance without also undermining the cultural basis of bourgeois power, which acts as a constraint on the power of the new elite.

While Mr. Phillips sees American history in terms of a never-ending conflict between "elite" and "populist" forces, it is perhaps more accurate to see it in terms of a conflict of one elite against another. The Progressive Movement and the New Deal represent the emergence of a managerial elite that holds power through its expertise in the technical and administrative skills that enable it to operate and control overgrown organizations in the state, economy, and culture and which makes use of what has come to be known as liberalism to justify its challenge to an older bourgeois elite that seized national power in the Civil War and its aftermath. Having entrenched themselves in political, economic, and cultural power by the end of World War II, managerial forces were resisted only by the remnants of the bourgeois elite and by newly formed social strata that found managerial liberalism a profound source of resentment and frustration. Until the 1980s, what was known as "conservatism" generally represented this bourgeois and postbourgeois political and cultural resistance to the managerial apparatus of power and its agenda—heavy regulation of the economy by the state in the interests of big corporations, unions, and governmental bureaucracies but at the expense of small businessmen; social reconstruction in the interests of the underclass and the managerial theoreticians who designed, planned, and implemented it, but against the interests and values of those who had to pay for it and suffer its consequences; and a globalist foreign policy that vaguely recognized a communist threat to the country but was steadfast in its refusal to deal with the menace effectively and adamant in its preference for transnational diplomacy and global social engineering over any sustained use of force.

The high point of the bourgeois conservative resistance to the now dominant managerial regime was the presidential campaign of Barry Goldwater in 1964, but under Richard Nixon and Ronald Reagan, "conservatism" began to change its colors. While Nixon tended toward the abandonment of the pure milk of bourgeois economic dogma—as Mr. Phillips points out, as early as the Checkers speech, "Nixon had no interest in unbridled capitalism"—he sought to build what he called the "New American Majority" based precisely on those social groups that resented and feared liberal-managerial dominance and found it a frustration of their own interests and aspirations. As Mr. Phillips has also suggested elsewhere, it may be no accident that it was principally the managerial bureaucracy of the executive branch in alliance with the managerial intelligentsia that largely did Nixon in through systematic leakages to the press during Watergate. But while Nixon seems to have contemplated a simple abandonment of bourgeois ideology and institutions in favor of a more centralized and authoritarian managerial regime, Reagan cooked up something more complicated.

It was Reagan's achievement to formulate an ideology and a political style that could accommodate both postbourgeois resentments and frustrations through an appeal to "social issues," patriotism, and "traditional morality"—what Phillips calls the symbols of "national unity"—as well as managerial interests in preserving the scale and scope of the mass organizations the elite controlled—the corporations and the federal state. It was not, of course, Mr. Reagan himself who was the author of this formula, though as a former liberal Democrat he was a perfect expression of the centrist imagery that the new formula used. The formula itself was the work of what came to be called neoconservatism, which distinguished itself from Old Right bourgeois conservatism by its willingness to accept the New Deal and the progressivist tradition. The goal of neoconservatives was never to reverse or move beyond the New Deal legacy but simply to make it work more efficiently than it did in the 1960s and 1970s. That goal, though usually masked by the neoconservatives themselves, was obvious to many of the more percipient exponents of Old Right ideology, but only after Reagan had departed the political scene was the mask thrown off and "Big Government Conservatism" unveiled in all its splendors.

"Reaganism," then, was neither a continuation of the bourgeois conservatism of the Old Right nor one more installment of an eternally recurring William McKinley nor the culmination of a cycle in American politics by which one elite ousted another and then itself succumbed to corruption. It was rather an effort to wed or fuse those destabilizing movements, fed by resentment, fear, and frustration, which gelled in the New Right and the candidacy of George Wallace, with still-dominant managerial elements in the state, economy, and cultural apparatus. Those elements saw their institutional apparatus of power and the "consensus" that rationalized it jeopardized by an insurgency from the right as well as from the left in the 1960s and 1970s and by the whole unraveling of American society that their own efforts at social reconstruction had helped cause. So far from challenging or displacing an old elite, Reaganism simply allowed the leadership of the insurgent forces to crawl into bed with the managerial establishment and sample its favors, thereby effectively decapitating (or, to extend the sexual metaphor, emasculating) the insurgency.

The formula worked as long as the Teflon President was there, and it has worked for his successor since Good Old Dutch was strapped to his pony and hauled back to his ranch. But it may not work much longer if recession and the economic woes Mr. Phillips discusses pop out of the political woodwork as they seem to be doing.

What is surprising in Mr. Phillips's analysis is not his conclusion that Reaganism actually endangered middle-class aspirations but his neglect of the continuing power of the cultural and social frustrations he has so admirably penetrated elsewhere. In his 1982 book, *Post-Conservative America,* he predicted that what historian Fritz Stern called "the politics of cultural despair"—racial, national, and social hostilities and dislocations—would coalesce with economic frustrations to yield a chauvinist, authoritarian, and perhaps overtly racialist political movement on the order of what occurred in Weimar Germany. In his present book, there is virtually no reference to that thesis despite its continuing relevance.

Instead, he suggests that a new "populist" movement led by liberal Democrats in the image of Michael Dukakis, Richard Gephardt, or Jesse Jackson could successfully challenge the Reaganite Republican establishment through a "New Nationalist" program that recalls the similar slogans adopted by Theodore Roosevelt and Herbert Croly in the early twentieth century. Such a program, as Mr. Phillips envisions it, would evidently be little more than a revival of the redistributionist politics and policies of the progressivist, New Deal, and Great Society eras. What he does not seem to recognize is that the kind of electoral coalition necessary for this kind of movement is today not possible.

Mr. Phillips's model presupposes that a crippled middle class could be brought into the same political tent with an underclass that, he argues, also suffered from the policies of the Reaganite corporate establishment. The fact is that in the 1990s the dominant noneconomic issue that is emerging is that of race and group identity—manifested in the rise of black demagogues such as Jackson, Louis Farrakhan, Marion Barry, Al Sharpton, and a host of lesser fry, as well as in white counterparts like David Duke and those who will soon be emulating him. The Reaganite formula did not really close the fissures that were causing what Mr. Phillips earlier called the

"Balkanization of America" but only covered them up with a generous serving of political applesauce, and the emergence of overt racialism is one species of the decomposition and fragmentation that has been occurring in the United States ever since the unifying bourgeois fabric was shredded. But since purely racialist movements can appeal only to members of a given ethnic group, which by itself is a minority, no such movement, black or white, can take power in the United States merely by relying on racial rhetoric and ideology. If, however, such a movement can synthesize its appeal to group identity (racial or national) through an imagery of "us against them" with a demand for the redress of perceived economic grievances (the burden of poverty or of taxation or of the loss of a material lifestyle), then it might take wing and fly. Such a synthesis, the combination of nationalism and socialism that has been the dominant theme of twentieth-century democratic politics, not only in Weimar but also in the United States, would broaden the racial and national appeal beyond biology to non-racial social and political aspirations.

Mr. Phillips is surely aware of the opportunities offered by such a nationalist-socialist program and of the power of such issues as immigration, civil rights laws and litigation, and the emergence of a Sorelian myth of racial consciousness among American blacks, though he does not address these opportunities in this book. He does, however, quote liberal economist Robert Kuttner on the failure of Michael Dukakis to exploit the nationalist-socialist synthesis effectively in 1988. Dukakis, in Kuttner's view, "had violated one of his party's basic historical verities: that 'Democrats do best when they develop broad, embracing, expansive visions combining national purpose with economic advancement, and rally masses of non-rich voters.' "

That is simply a more elegant way of stating a secret understood by successful politicians from Adolf Hitler and Franklin Roosevelt to Lyndon Johnson and also by historian John Lukacs, who writes that nationalism and socialism and their relationship are "the principal political phenomena of this century." The political masses are motivated largely by slogans, programs, and policies that revolve around the sentiments of "us against them" and "something for nothing." As long as the Democrats understood this secret, they flourished. When they forgot it and went in for Viet Cong flags, paroling rapists, homosexual rights, national guilt trips, ACLU membership cards, and especially for the interests of non-whites at the expense of their traditional white working-class constituency, they flopped. Mr. Reagan successfully exploited the Democrats' neglect of the nationalist sibling of the nationalist-socialist Siamese twin while seeming to offer what Mr. Phillips (and the Democrats) argue is an illusory economic security that defused economic issues in politics. Those who have followed Mr. Reagan are far less aware of the secret power of group identity and far less skilled in exploiting it, nor will emerging economic dislocations allow them to rely exclusively on national-cultural-racial themes to gain and keep power.

If there is to be a successful "new nationalism" in the next decade, its leaders will have to understand the secret of the twentieth century and how to use it, whether the "nation" is that of Jesse Jackson or George Wallace. *The Politics of Rich and Poor* is a good place for them to begin to understand the economic aspects of that secret, though it is unfortunate that Mr. Phillips, whose chillingly cold-blooded analyses of politics and power have proved so fruitful in the past, has neglected any clear discussion of the secret in his present book. But he is undoubtedly right that one thing is clear: the emerging economic dislocations that the Reagan era bequeathed to the United States will bring an early death to the apparent social and political equilibrium that characterized the 1980s.

Equality as a Political Weapon

For many years, a staple theme in traditionalist conservative political theory has been the critique of egalitarianism. Indeed, some Old Right theorists have gone so far as Willmoore Kendall and George Carey to argue that "the common denominator of the liberal positions . . . the principles or beliefs common to all of them" is the principle of equality itself.[1] The conservative critique of egalitarianism has in large part been a formal critique—that is, one that takes egalitarian expressions at more or less their face value and then proceeds to criticize the logic of these expressions or the degree to which they correspond, or fail to correspond, to the realities of human nature and human society. Kendall and Carey themselves initiated a critique of egalitarianism on both philosophical and historical grounds, arguing that the doctrine of equality as currently understood by its champions on the Left has little intrinsic merit and has played a mischievous rather than a wholesome role in American political thought and history. The historical and political critique of egalitarianism among Old Rightists has been ably continued by M. E. Bradford in his continuing polemics with Harry Jaffa, and more recently in the work of Thomas Fleming and Steven Goldberg, among others, the critique has made good use of sociobiology and anthropology.

The formal critique of egalitarianism by the Right has thus been a rewarding one, touching on and illuminating political theory, philosophy, history, and science. But I have to say—and indeed I will say, perhaps more than anyone wants to hear—that I think much of the Old Right formal critique of egalitarianism has been somewhat misdirected. In a sense, I believe that it has been beating a dead horse—or, more strictly, a dead unicorn, a beast that exists only in legend. The flaw, I believe, in the conservative formal critique of

---

1. Willmoore Kendall and George W. Carey, eds., *Liberalism Versus Conservatism: The Continuing Debate in American Government* (Princeton, N. J.: D. Van Nostrand Company, 1966), 66.

egalitarianism is that the formal doctrine of equality is itself nonexistent or at least unimportant.

The doctrine of equality is unimportant because no one, save perhaps Pol Pot and Ben Wattenberg, really believes in it, and no one, least of all those who profess it most loudly, is seriously motivated by it. This is a truth expressed by the Italian social theorist Vilfredo Pareto in his *Treatise of General Sociology*.

> The sentiment that is very inappropriately named equality is fresh, strong, alert, precisely because it is not, in fact, a sentiment of equality and is not related to any abstraction, as a few naive "intellectuals" still believe; but because it is related to the direct interests of individuals who are bent on escaping certain inequalities not in their favour, and setting up new inequalities that will be in their favour, this latter being their chief concern.[2]

The real meaning of the "doctrine of equality," in other words, cannot be grasped, and its real power as a social and ideological force cannot be countered, merely by a purely formal critique such as that traditionally mounted by the Old Right. The real meaning of the doctrine of equality is that it serves as a political weapon, to be unsheathed whenever it is useful for cutting down barriers, human or institutional, to the power of those groups that wear it on their belts; but, because equality, if nothing else, is a two-edged weapon, it is a sword to be kept well away from the hands of those who merely want to fondle it.

It was precisely this understanding of equality as a political weapon that is enshrined in George Orwell's famous but belated insight in *Animal Farm*—that all animals are equal, but some are more equal than others. Yet the irony of that slogan is perhaps too rich to be realistic. Orwell's porcine totalitarians evidently possessed enough intellectual integrity at least to try to reconcile two contradictory claims and to juxtapose them in a public display. In the real world of egalitarian tyranny, as opposed to that of Orwell's fictional satire, even that degree of intellectual honesty is absent. Even the Communists, despite their own egalitarian dogmas, soon rediscovered the

2. Vilfredo Pareto, *The Mind and Society [Trattato di Sociologia generale]*, ed. Arthur Livingston, trans. Andrew Bongiorno, Arthur Livingston, and James Harvey Rogers, 4 vols. (New York: Harcourt, Brace and Company, 1935), 2:735–36, § 1227.

elementary facts of human inequality and the elementary principle of the division of labor and social function, which necessarily involves economic and social hierarchy. But it is doubtful that any Communist, however skilled a dialectician, would ever acknowledge that the existence of a *Nomenklatura* or entrenched elite in the Soviet Union in any way needed to be reconciled with Marxist egalitarian utopianism.

Yet the use of equality as a political weapon was known long before Orwell, or the Communists, or the radical Enlightenment, discovered it. At least three authors of classical antiquity recount a story illustrative of the nature of the weapon and of its valuable applications.

Periander, the tyrant of Corinth, learned that there were certain nobles in his city who were conspiring against him, but he was unable to discover exactly who they were. So he sent an envoy to his fellow tyrant, Thrasybulus of Miletus, to ask his advice. As the Greek historian Herodotus described it,

> Thrasybulus invited the man to walk with him from the city to a field where corn was growing. As he passed through this cornfield, continually asking questions about why the messenger had come to him from Corinth, he kept cutting off all the tallest ears of wheat which he could see, and throwing them away, until the finest and best-grown part of the crop was ruined. In this way he went right through the field, and then sent the messenger away without a word. On his return to Corinth, Periander was eager to hear what advice Thrasybulus had given, and the man replied that he had not given any at all, adding that he was surprised at being sent to visit such a person, who was evidently mad and a wanton destroyer of his own property—and then described what he had seen Thrasybulus do. Periander seized the point at once; it was perfectly plain to him that Thrasybulus recommended the murder of all the people in the city who were outstanding in influence or ability. Moreover, he took the advice, and from that time forward there was no crime against the Corinthians that he did not commit.[3]

No one would argue that tyrants such as Thrasybulus and Periander were egalitarians or that they really believed in or were motivated by any doctrine of equality founded in Natural Rights or other

---

3. Herodotus, 5.92, trans. Aubrey de Selincourt, 376–77; see also Aristotle, *Politics,* 3.13, trans. Ernest Barker, 135; and Livy, *History of Rome,* 1.54, trans. Aubrey de Selincourt, 94, who tells the same story of Tarquinius Superbus and his son, Sextus.

pseudosciences, yet their use of equality as a weapon to commit the crime of what Stefan Possony and Nathaniel Weyl have called "aristocracide,"[4] the mass murder of the best elements in a society, and to cut down the social constraints and potential threats to their power is not significantly different from the use made of it by modern tyrants, whether they are self-proclaimed totalitarians or global democratists. Indeed, the use of equality as a weapon by the ancient tyrants, like so much else in classical history and literature, is paradigmatic, and in the modern bureaucratic states and managerial regimes, the same application of egalitarianism is made for the same reason, though not always as dramatically as in the days of Periander and Thrasybulus. The irony—not to say the hypocrisy—of modern egalitarianism is that it is used not, as its proponents claim, to restrain or reduce the power of all but to get rid of the power of some while at the same time perpetuating or augmenting the power of others. It is my view that once this real, as opposed to formal, meaning of egalitarianism is grasped, the apparent contradiction between egalitarian preaching and egalitarian practice resolves itself, and the invocation of equality, even in sophisticated ideological forms, is seen clearly to be not mere hypocrisy or a logical contradiction but the strategic deployment of a weapon for the seizure of power.

In the twentieth century, egalitarianism has been used principally as the political formula or ideological rationalization by which one, emerging elite has sought to displace from political, economic, and cultural power another elite, and in not only rationalizing but also disguising the dominance of the new elite. In the late nineteenth and early twentieth centuries, the development of new physical technologies and a new kind of social organization in the form of bureaucracy served to create within the bosom of traditional aristocratic and bourgeois elites a new class of functionaries that gained economic, political, and social rewards from their ability to operate the new technologies and organizations. In the economy, corporations allowed for the bureaucratization of functions, removing the operation and control of corporate business from the hands of stock-

4. Nathaniel Weyl and Stefan T. Possony, *The Geography of Intellect* (Chicago: Henry Regnery Company, 1963), xi.

holders and owner-operators and delivering them increasingly into
the control of professional, technically trained managers. An analogous transformation occurred in the state as political institutions
began to carry out social and economic functions that involved spe-
cialized knowledge and skills that were quite beyond the capacities
of elected or hereditary officeholders to perform. In cultural institutions also, educational institutions and later the media of mass
communication expanded dramatically in scale and in the number
and complexity of the functions they performed through their adap-
tation of new technological processes and their transformation into
bureaucratic structures. In all of these social organizations in the
economy, the state, and the culture, there developed an at least latent
conflict of interest between, on the one hand, those trained in the
technical and managerial functions that enlarged organizational
scale demanded and, on the other, those who were not so trained
but who occupied positions of traditional leadership due to their
social status or their own personal talents and qualities of leadership. Members of the former group, the emerging elite, increasingly perceived their own interests as lying in the further enlargement and further complexity of organization, while the latter, the
old or incumbent elites, increasingly saw their own power, economic resources, social status, and social codes as jeopardized by
the organizational and managerial revolutions and the rise of the
new class that benefited the most from these revolutions.

Yet the material forces that drove these revolutions in the forms of
new technologies and new kinds of bureaucratic organizations were
not sufficient in themselves to carry the emerging elites to social
dominance. Their emergence engendered resistance from older
elites that retained vested interests in older forms of organization—
in small-scale business firms owned and operated by the same individuals in the form of family firms and partnerships; in parliamentary or congressional institutions and in local and state governments
that lacked the legal jurisdiction, fiscal resources, or physical scope
for enlargement on the same scale as the centralized, executive-
dominated state favored by the new elite; and in compact, locally
oriented schools, colleges, churches, newspapers, and other cultural institutions that served compact, largely homogeneous com-

munities of similar class, ethnic, and cultural backgrounds. The persistence of such small, local, and personalized institutions served not only to preserve the power of older elites but also represented a barrier to the power of the newer elites lodged in large, bureaucratically organized, and technologically expansive organizations.

The conflict between these two elites thus tended to assume an ideological and political form as the newer elites sought the direct aid of the state to dislodge their rivals and to displace them from power, and the doctrine of egalitarianism was an essential component of their ideological struggle. It is hardly an accident that the Progressive Movement flourished at the same time that the organizational and managerial revolutions were occurring, for progressivism served as the main ideological vehicle by which the new elite spawned by these revolutions rode to power and challenged the power of the incumbent elites. It was the inculcation of progressivist premises and doctrines into American culture through the new bureaucracies the emerging elites controlled that remains today the main ideological support of the new elite's power, and its hegemony cannot be challenged until its ideological base is discredited and broken up.

Egalitarianism played a central role in the progressivist ideological challenge, and the main form it assumed in the early twentieth century was that of "environmentalism"—not in the contemporary sense of concern for ecology but in the sense that human beings are perceived as the products of their social and historical environment rather than of their innate mental and physical natures. Egalitarianism was implicit in environmentalist ideology. If the natural or inborn traits of human beings are minimal or nonexistent and if the differentiation among human beings according to class, race, sexuality, nationality, culture, etc. is rooted in social environments rather than in nature, then human beings are conceptually reduced to a set of identical reflexes and may be said to be "equal." Taking Rousseau's famous sentence in *The Social Contract,* "Men are born free but everywhere are in chains," the environmentalist egalitarianism of the Progressivists identified "freedom" as release from the "chains" and a restoration of what they regarded as the natural equality that existed before the chains were clapped on, and they identified the "chains" themselves as the institutional, intellectual, and moral fabric of bourgeois society as it was perceived in the late nineteenth and early twentieth centuries.

Surveying what they took as the impending social and economic chaos of the late nineteenth century—urban poverty, crime, disease, racial conflict, and the dominance and exploitation of industrial wealth through monopoly—progressivist reformers articulated a social and political theory that centered on environmentalist explanations of and solutions for these problems. "An environment that had been made by human beings and could be changed by human beings," wrote Eric Goldman in an account of the ideas of socialist Henry George, who exerted a profound influence on progressivism in the United States, "determined all men, institutions, and ideas. . . . Legislating a better environment, particularly a better economic environment, could bring about a better world."[5]

Environmentalist ideology was thus especially useful for progressivist reformers and their allies and sponsors in the emerging elites in state and economy. On the one hand, environmentalism challenged the institutions, ideas, and values of the older elites, arguing that they were not "natural," "normative," or "necessary," but merely adaptations to specific historical circumstances and masks for the continued preeminence of these elites. Laissez-faire economic theory, constitutionalism, doctrines of individual responsibility, the bourgeois ethic of work, thrift, providence, and deferral of gratification, and the institutions and codes that enshrined these beliefs, especially in the family, local community, and religion of traditional society, in the environmentalist critique were not absolutes but relative and could be overcome by those who understood them scientifically and had the administrative and political power to challenge them. Progressivism, through its ideology of environmentalist egalitarianism, rejected, called into question and, in Marxist parlance, "demystified" and "delegitimized" not only the "excesses" of the age—e.g., corruption and exploitation—but also the very foundations of the bourgeois order: its ethics, its religion, its law, and its concept of government and sociopolitical relationships.

5. Eric F. Goldman, *Rendezvous with Destiny: A History of Modern American Reform,* rev. ed. (New York: Random House, 1966), 78.

Secondly, while environmentalism challenged the institutional and ideological fabric of incumbent elites, it also offered a highly convenient justification for the power of the rising elite. It was the members of this new elite, skilled in the social and physical sciences and their applications to the social and physical environment and in the functions of bureaucratic organizations and administration, who understood how to manipulate the environment for progressivist ends. Granted the premises of environmentalist ideology, it was logical that the emerging elites should be empowered to work their will on social injustice and that older elites and the institutions and ideas they favored should get out of their way.

Logically also, environmentalism as it was developed in progressivist thought was closely related to egalitarianism. The environmentalist argument is that there are no men, no sexes, no classes, no races, and no social institutions that are inherently or by nature any better than any other. Indeed, the whole thrust of environmentalism is toward relativism, the denial of moral absolutes, and behaviorism, the denial of an inherent human nature apart from minimal physiological response mechanisms triggered by the external stimuli of the environment, a position basic to Marxist social science as well as to that of B. F. Skinner. And progressivist ideologues were quick to draw these conclusions, at least when and where it suited their ulterior purposes. They are found throughout the work of Franz Boas and his studies of racial differences and in the similar work of his disciples Ruth Benedict and Margaret Mead, and in the latter case at least have been shown to be entirely fraudulent. (And in all cases unsupported by later, more serious scientific research). Since apparent racial differences, in the doctrine of the Boas school, are due to environmental rather than genetic or biological factors, it followed that such differences can be removed by managing the environment. In Boas's view, "no group of human beings was more or less advanced than the others. Their developments, coming about in different environments, represented specializations in different directions. . . . Culture was a cumulative evolutionary product, not a function of racial heredity."[6]

6. Ibid., 97.

Environmentalist egalitarianism also informed the progressivist critique of criminal law and penology, and its best known exponent on the popular level was the famous shyster Clarence Darrow, who was deeply influenced by Henry George and who devoted his life to wrecking both the American criminal justice system and Aristotelian logic. Environmentalism was fundamental to Darrow's lachrymose defense of the child-murderers Nathan Leopold and Richard Loeb in 1924, when he argued that a combination of the killers' endocrine systems and their environment, not the killers themselves, were responsible for the murder of Bobby Franks. Darrow argued it would be cruel for the judge to sentence them to death, though it does not seem to have occurred to him that their executioners could equally claim to be merely the victims of their own environments. In 1902, Darrow was somehow permitted to address the inmates at Chicago's Cook County Jail, telling the throng of felons that "there is no such thing as crime as the word is generally understood. . . . If every man, woman, and child in the world had a chance to make a decent, fair, honest living, there would be no jails and no lawyers and no courts." Again, it never seemed to occur to Darrow that his later clients, "Babe" Leopold and "Dicky" Loeb, were both the sons of millionaires. After hearing his speech to the inmates, the warden of the jail must have been in a quandary whether to throw Darrow out or to lock him up. He clearly was too dangerous to be allowed to run about loose, but equally he was perhaps too dangerous to lock up with known criminals, and exposing the convicts to an endless barrage of Darrow's drivel, even in the 1900s, would surely have been cruel and unusual punishment.

On the formal level, the logical hop-scotch and forged research of progressivist ideologues like Margaret Mead and Clarence Darrow turn their environmentalist dogmas into clam chowder. But of course their goal was not to discover truth but to wield power. Enveloping their pseudoscience in a syrupy utopianism, the Progressives appealed to moral sentiments, guilt, hope, fear, envy, and resentment in delegitimizing traditional ideas and institutions and those whose own power and status were connected to them, and in such episodes as the administrations of Woodrow Wilson and Franklin Roosevelt, they and their heirs managed to get their hands on national political power. Nor were environmentalist egalitarian ideas confined to criminology and anthropology. They also informed the progressivist views of economics, law in general, education, psychology, and sociology and thus formed the basis of progressivist and liberal social policy for the bulk of the twentieth century. "It is important to see," wrote sociologist E. Digby Baltzell, "that the New Deal's efforts to change the economic and cultural environment, largely through legislating greater equality of conditions between classes of men, were a reflection of the whole intellectual climate of opinion at the time. In almost every area of intellectual endeavor— in the theories of crime, in law, in religion, and in the arts—there was general agreement as to the sickness of bourgeois society and the need for environmental reform."[7]

Indeed, the ideological function of progressivism in delegitimizing bourgeois society was accomplished by its identification of the society itself as the "environment" to be altered through social management. Crime, as Darrow's remarks imply, was a result of poverty and dirty neighborhoods, which in turn were the products of economic inequality and could be rectified through redistribution of wealth and the abandonment of classical economic theory in favor of deliberate manipulation of the economy by the state to accomplish social goals. Rights of property, traditionally grounded in customary and natural law, were delegitimized by the "sociological jurisprudence" and "legal realism" of Oliver Wendell Holmes, Roscoe Pound, and Louis Brandeis, among others, who portrayed law as merely the codification of the interests of the bourgeois elite. "Laws, institutions and systems of government," wrote progressivist political scientist J. Allen Smith in *The Spirit of American Government* in 1907, "are in a sense artificial creations, and must be judged in relation to the ends which they have in view. They are good or bad according as they are well or poorly adapted to social needs."[8] In itself, this sentiment is largely unobjectionable, but the context in which it and similar such bromides were trumpeted forth by Smith and his progressivist colleagues was to wield it against the legitimacy of the Constitution and the traditional forms of American

---

7. E. Digby Baltzell, *The Protestant Establishment: Aristocracy and Caste in America* (New York: Random House, 1964), 271.
8. Quoted in Goldman, *Rendezvous with Destiny*, 113.

government and law. Charles Beard's *Economic Interpretation of the Constitution* (1913) similarly depicted the Constitution itself as the product of the economic interests of the Framers, and Frederick Jackson Turner's "frontier thesis" offered an environmentalist explanation for American history. Federalism, the dispersion of political power through the balance of local and central authority, was regarded by the Progressives as a device by which a bourgeois elite controlled and limited centralized government and prevented the state from intruding on their private and local power centers. The family, a special target of behaviorist psychologist John B. Watson, was depicted as the source of neurosis, social conflict, and maladjustment, and behaviorism became an important ideological instrument by which managerial corporations disciplined their workers and the consumers of their products. Edward Bernays, a nephew of Sigmund Freud, also helped develop behaviorist psychological techniques for the managed economy in the science of "public relations," which he helped found. "Treating all people as mechanically identical," writes historian Stuart Ewen, Bernays "called for the implementation of a 'mass psychology' by which public opinion might be controlled."[9] Environmentalist egalitarianism became imbedded in the very structure through which the elite exercised power. The new technologies and organizational forms that the new elite controlled allowed for the envelopment of larger and larger numbers of people by governments, corporations, and mass media, but only if the unequal differentiations among people were broken down and homogenized. The reliance on egalitarianism by the modern bureaucratic state is relatively clear. Universal suffrage and equality of rights are created and rigorously enforced by the state, and the mass electorate becomes a perpetual horn of plenty from which the bureaucratic elite of the state can continuously accumulate new power. The enlargement of the central state reduces the diversified authority of state and local jurisdictions, and through judicial expansion of the "equal protection" clause of the Fourteenth Amendment, the agents of enhanced federal power have used the Constitution

---

9. Stuart Ewen, *Captains of Consciousness: Advertising and the Social Roots of the Consumer Culture* (New York: McGraw-Hill Book Company, 1976), 83.

itself as a hammer by which private, social, and local impediments to equality can be broken down.

But equality is no less useful for large corporations, which require a nationally homogenized market of consumers that can be manipulated into buying their products and which find abhorrent and dysfunctional the persistence of local variations in their markets caused by smaller, localized competitors or class, ethnic, and regional diversities of taste and demand. Only if such variations and diversities are broken up and homogenized by the inculcation of an egalitarian ethic of universal consumption, immediate gratification through credit, and upward social and economic mobility and a uniform range of wants can large corporate enterprises operate on a national (and now a global) scale. It is thus basic to the interests of the large corporation to erode social and cultural diversity and promote egalitarian uniformity, as well as to cooperate with and support political egalitarianism, the costs of which in increased unionization, protection of the labor force, regulation, civil rights legislation, and ecological environmentalism, are ruinous to the smaller competitors of the corporations but much less harmful to those larger economies that can absorb such costs and pass them on to consumers. Similarly, the mass media organizations that dominate culture cannot effectively communicate with and propagandize a mass audience unless the ideas and tastes of the audience are homogeneous, and the homogenization of ideas and taste must be paralleled by the homogenization and levelling of the social institutions that breed inequality and diversity. The contemporary power structure of late twentieth-century America, therefore, in government, economy, and culture is in large part based on an egalitarian ethic, one that starts from the premises that human beings are fundamentally identical, that variations and inequalities among them are due to an artificial environment, and that that environment can be molded, manipulated, and reconstructed to make of men what you will.

If the progressivism of the nineteenth and early twentieth centuries had been merely the maunderings of malcontents like Clarence Darrow and frauds like Margaret Mead or even if it had simply been the ideology of convenience for a few politicians like Wilson and Roosevelt and their cronies, its legacy would have long since passed. But the historical significance of progressivism and its doctrine of environmentalist egalitarianism is, as I have argued, that it represented an ideological blunt instrument by which an emerging elite battered its way to cultural as well as economic and political power, an elite that was specially equipped to apply scientific (and pseudoscientific) ideas and techniques to social, economic, and political arrangements and to do so through its control of the bureaucracies of the state, corporations, labor unions, universities, foundations, and mass media. As an elite, it was able to straddle and transcend specific political parties, administrations, and personalities and to infect almost the whole of American culture with its revolutionary ideological norm of environmentalist egalitarianism. That norm did not triumph or flourish because of its intrinsic merits or because most Americans were rationally persuaded of it or because the intellectuals and politicians who preached it really believed it, let alone really practiced it in their own lives, but because it offered opportunities for some to gain power at the expense of others, because it was able to serve as a convenient political weapon.

Today, in such movements as "multiculturalism" and "Afrocentrism" in schools and universities and in reliance on "therapy" curricula in the form of "sensitivity training" and "human relations" courses, we are witnessing what many consider the *reductio ad absurdum* of progressivist egalitarianism. Yet it is not really a reduction to absurdity but merely another twist of the egalitarian dagger. Progressives such as Boas and Darrow never heard of the Italian Communist Antonio Gramsci, but what they argued about the "environment" of bourgeois society in nineteenth-century America is not fundamentally different from Gramsci's argument about "cultural hegemony"—that elites rule through their dominance of culture more than through their control of the means of production and that revolutionaries who seek to overthrow an elite must first make a long march through the institutions of culture before trying to wield political or economic power. It is Gramsci's doctrine that is being put into practice today. From the chant "Western culture's got to go" at Stanford a few years ago to the tax-funded perversions of Robert Mapplethorpe to the claims that Beethoven and Cleopatra were really Africans, the argument is that "Western," heterosexual, and Caucasian institutions and beliefs are corruptive, repressive, and exploitative encrustations of a hegemonic environment that, when scraped away by egalitarian social (and now psychic) engineering, will yield the same kind of egalitarian utopia the Progressives envisioned. Only the specific targets have changed, and indeed the targets have always changed throughout the history of the Left, as each new utopia turns out to be fake. In the Enlightenment and in much of classical liberalism, the target was the state—the established churches, aristocracies, guilds, and dynasties of the eighteenth century. When liberation from these political "chains" failed to bring about the promised land, the target became the economy—private property, classical economics, and the distribution of wealth—and it was mainly an economic target that the Progressives had in their sights. In the twentieth century, the target shifted yet again to social and cultural environment—the family, the school, religion, social class, and race as a social phenomenon. Eventually, we can predict, egalitarians will discover—and indeed now are discovering—that nature itself is the source of inequality, at which point they will have come full circle and find themselves in agreement with Dr. Fleming and Dr. Goldberg.

But it won't make any difference. Whether egalitarians, recognizing at last that inequality is ultimately rooted in man's nature, accept that lesson, or whether, through genetic engineering and state-funded lobotomies, they launch yet another revolt against inequality and against nature itself will depend less on who and how many really believe in the egalitarian lie than on who stands to gain from wielding the egalitarian sword.

Beautiful Losers
The Failure of American Conservatism

When T. S. Eliot said that there are no lost causes because there are
no won causes, he probably was not thinking of American conservatism. Nearly sixty years after the New Deal, the American Right is
no closer to challenging its fundamental premises and machinery
than when Old Rubberlegs first started priming the pump and schem-
ing to take the United States into a war that turned out to be a social
and political revolution. American conservatism, in other words, is
a failure, and all the think tanks, magazines, direct-mail barons,
inaugural balls, and campaign buttons cannot disguise or alter it.
Virtually every cause to which conservatives have attached themselves for the past three generations has been lost, and the tide of
political and cultural battle is not likely to turn anytime soon.

Not only has the American Right lost on such fundamental issues
as the fusion of state and economy, the size and scope of government, the globalist course of American foreign policy, the transformation of the Constitution into a meaningless document that serves
the special interests of whatever faction can grab it for a while, and
the replacement of what is generally called "traditional morality"
by a dominant ethic of instant gratification, but also the mainstream
of those who today are pleased to call themselves conservatives has
come to accept at least the premises and often the full-blown agenda
of the Left. The movement that came to be known in the 1970s as
neoconservatism, largely northeastern, urban, and academic in its
orientation, is now the defining core of the "permissible" Right—
that is, what a dominant Left-liberal cultural and political elite recognizes and accepts as the Right boundary of public discourse. It
remains legally possible (barely) to express sentiments and ideas
that are further to the Right, but if an elite enjoys cultural hegemony, as the Left does, it has no real reason to outlaw its opponents.
Indeed, encouraging their participation in the debate fosters the
illusion of "pluralism" and serves to legitimize the main Leftward
trend of the debate. Those outside the permissible boundaries of

discourse are simply "derationalized" and ignored—as anti-Semites, racists, authoritarians, crackpots, crooks, or simply as "nostalgic," and other kinds of illicit and irrational fringe elements not in harmonic convergence with the Zeitgeist and therefore on the wrong side of history. That is where the de facto alliance of Left and neoconservative Right has succeeded in relegating those who dissent from their common core of shared premises such as journalist Patrick J. Buchanan and anyone else who seriously and repeatedly challenges their hegemony.

"Neoconservatism" today is usually called simply "conservatism," though it is sometimes known under other labels as well: Fred Barnes's "Big Government conservatism"; HUD Secretary Jack Kemp's "progressive conservatism"; Representative Newt Gingrich's "opportunity conservatism"; Paul Weyrich's "cultural conservatism"; or, most recently, "The New Paradigm," in the phrase coined by White House aide James Pinkerton. Despite the variations among these formulas, all of them envision a far larger and more active central state than the "Old Republicanism" embraced by most conservatives prior to the 1970s, a state that makes it its business to envision a particular arrangement of institutions and beliefs and to design governmental machinery to create them. In the case of "neoconservatism," the principal goal is the enhancement of economic opportunity through one kind or another of social engineering (enterprise zones, for example) and the establishment of an ethic that regards equality (usually disguised as "equality of opportunity"), economic mobility, affluence, and material gratification as the central meaning of what their exponents often call "the American experiment."

Such goals are not conceptually distinct from those of the progressivism and liberalism athwart which the American Right at one time promised to stand, though the tactics and procedures by which they are to be achieved are somewhat (but not very) different. Indeed, much of what neoconservatives are concerned with is merely process—strategy, tactics, how to win elections, how to broaden the base of the GOP, how to make the government run more effectively, how to achieve "credibility" and exert an "impact"—and not with the ultimate goals themselves, about which there is little debate with those parts of the Left that also lie within the permissible range of "pluralistic" dialogue. Given the persistent cultural dominance of the Left, a conservatism that limits itself merely to procedural problems tacitly concedes the goals of public action to its enemies and quietly comes to share the premises on which the goals of the Left rest. Eventually, having silently and unconsciously accepted the premises and goals, it will also come to accept even the means by which the Left has secured its dominance, and the very distinction between "Right" and "Left" will disappear.

It was this kind of silent acquiescence in the premises of the Left that James Burnham identified as a salient characteristic of neoconservatism when it first began to appear in the early 1970s. In an exchange with neoconservative Peter Berger in *National Review* (May 12, 1972), Burnham noted that though neoconservatives had broken with "liberal doctrine," finding it "both intellectually bankrupt and, by and large, pragmatically sterile," they retained "what might be called the emotional gestalt of liberalism, the liberal sensitivity and temperament," the ideoneurological reflexes and knee-jerks of the Left. Since that time, those reflexes have not only not been recircuited but have been reinforced, so that today the neoconservative "Right" almost explicitly accepts and defends the New Deal and its legacy, seeking only to spruce them up and administer them more effectively and more honestly, but not to reverse them or transcend them—Old Right goals routinely dismissed by the neoconservative Right as "impractical."

But Burnham also remarked that "much of conservative doctrine . . . also is, if not quite bankrupt, more and more obsolescent," and the failure of conservatism and its eventual displacement by neoconservative formulas is closely related to its bankruptcy. The survivors of the Old Right today spend a good deal of their time complaining about their dethronement by pseudoconservatives, but those Old Rightists who survive are only the hardiest of the species, ever vigilant for camouflaged predators who slip into their herds. For the most part, their predecessors in the conservative movement of the 1950s and 1960s were not so careful, and indeed many of them failed to understand the ideological dynamics of liberalism, how the liberal regime functioned, or how to distinguish and insulate their own beliefs and organizations against the Left. That error was perhaps at least part of what Burnham meant by the "obsolescence" of conservatism. It was an error that was the principal weakness of conservatism and permitted the eventual triumph of neo-conservative forces and the assimilation of the Right within the dominant cultural apparatus that serves the Left's interests.

The Old Right, composed mainly of the organized conservative resistance formed in the mid–1950s and centered around *National Review,* failed to understand that the revolution had already occurred. Conventional Old Right doctrines revolved around the ideas of a constitutionally limited central government, largely independent local and state government, an entrepreneurial economy of privately owned and operated firms, and a moral and social code of restrained or "ascetic" individualism in politics, economy, art, religion, and ethics. These doctrines reflected the institutions and beliefs of the bourgeois elite that had gained political power in the Civil War and prevailed until the dislocations of twentieth-century technological and organizational expansion brought forth a new managerial elite that seized power in the reforms of the Progressive Era and the New Deal. These reforms constituted the revolution, not only in the political power of Roosevelt, Harry Truman, and the Democratic party but also in the construction of an entire architecture of economic and cultural power, based on bureaucratized corporations and unions, increasingly bureaucratized universities, foundations, churches, and mass media, and fused, directly or indirectly, with a centralized bureaucratic state. Since the revolution occurred legally and peacefully and assimilated traditional institutions and symbols to its use, it was not immediately apparent that it had taken place at all, that the dominant minority in the United States had circulated, that the bourgeois elite no longer called the shots, or that those who continued to adhere to Old Right doctrines were no longer in a position to "conserve" much of anything. But while the Old Right of the 1950s was in principle aware and critical of the new power structure, it continued to regard itself as essentially "conservative" of an established or traditional order rather than frankly acknowledging that it had been dethroned and that a counterrevolutionary mission, not "conserving," was its mission, its proper strategy.

Hence, the entire strategy of the Old Right of the 1950s was to seek accommodation with the new managerial-bureaucratic establishment rather than to challenge it. George H. Nash writes that William F. Buckley, Jr.,

forcefully rejected what he called "the popular and cliché-ridden appeal to
the grass-roots" and strove instead to establish a journal which would reach
intellectuals. Not all conservatives agreed with this approach, but the young
editor-to-be was firm. It was the intellectuals, after all, "who have midwived
and implemented the revolution. We have got to have allies among the intellectuals, and we propose to renovate conservatism and see if we can't win
some of them around."

Yet while Buckley seemed cognizant of the "revolution" that had
transpired and was, in fact, successful in attracting a number of intellectuals, he failed to see that the new intellectual class as a whole,
which had indeed "midwived and implemented the revolution,"
could not become conservative. It could not do so because its principal interest, social function, and occupational calling in the new
order was to delegitimize the ideas and institutions of conservatism and provide legitimization for the new regime, and its power
and rewards as a class depended upon the very bureaucratized cultural organizations that conservatives attacked. Only if conservatism were "renovated" to the point that it no longer rejected the
cultural apparatus of the revolution could intellectuals be expected
to sign up.

Moreover, by focusing its efforts in Manhattan, Washington, and
the major centers of the intelligentsia and other sectors of the new
elite, Buckley and his conservative colleagues isolated themselves
from their natural allies in the "grass roots." While there was clearly
a need for intellectual sophistication on the Right, the result of Buckley's tactic was to generate a schism between Old Right intellectual
cadres and the body of conservative supporters outside its northeastern urban and academic headquarters. Among these supporters
in the 1950s and 1960s there flourished an increasingly bizarre and
deracinated wilderness of extremist, conspiratorialist, racialist, and
even occultist ideologues who loudly rejected both the Old Right
mainstream and the Old Right's new friends in the intellectual and
cultural elite, but who failed to attract any but the most marginal
and pathological elements in the country and exerted no cultural or
political influence at all. At various times in its history, *National
Review* has found it necessary to "purge" itself of such adherents,
and each catharsis, no matter how prudent, has rendered its "renovated" conservatism less and less palatable to ordinary Americans

and more and more acceptable to the Manhattanite intelligentsia it has always sought to attract.

In any case, the Old Right intellectuals for the most part had few links with the "grass roots," the popular, middle-class, and WASP nucleus of traditional American culture. *National Review* itself was not only Manhattanite but also Ivy League and Roman Catholic in its orientation, as well as ex-communist and ethnic in its editorial composition, and not a few of its brightest stars in the 1950s were personally eccentric, if not outright neurotic. Moreover, few of them reflected the "Protestant Establishment" that, by the end of World War II, had largely made its peace with the new regime and was scurrying to secure its own future within the managerial state, economy, and culture. Of the twenty-five conservative intellectuals whose photographs appeared on the dust jacket of George H. Nash's *The Conservative Intellectual Movement in America since 1945,* published in 1976, four are Roman Catholic, seven are Jewish, another seven (including three Jews) are foreign-born, two are southern or western in origin, and only five are in any respect representative of the historically dominant Anglo-Saxon (or at least Anglo-Celtic) Protestant strain in American history and culture (three of the five later converted to Roman Catholicism). Theological meditation competed with free-market economic theory as the main interest of many Old Right intellectuals to a far larger degree than had been the case with such pre–World War II skeptics of progressivism as Albert Jay Nock, H. L. Mencken, or the "America First" opponents of foreign intervention.

The religious, ideological, and ethnic differentiation of the Old Right from the country's Protestant Establishment may have helped push its leaders in a more radical direction than they were inclined to go, but it probably also served to cut them off from both the Establishment's declining leadership and from the rank and file of Americans outside it. The Old Right could not help but remain an isolated circle of intellectuals and journalists, absorbed in rather esoteric theory, despised by the intellectual elite they hoped to impress and convert, and ignored by most Americans and their political leaders.

The Old Right's political aspirations were no less grotesque than its desire to win acceptance among the intellectuals and followed much the same strategy. Although the remnants of the bourgeois elite retained an important political base in congressional districts remote from the centers of the new regime, they could serve only as a brake on the regime's power and were unable to control either Congress or the presidency. Their inability to do so was directly related to conservatives' lack of cultural power, their lack of contact with and their not-infrequent contempt for Americans outside the circles of the national elite. Even when Old Right forces were able to capture the Republican party in 1964, the disastrous result of Barry Goldwater's candidacy was in large part due to his supporters' lack of access to the national organs of culture and opinion. Subsequent Old Right political efforts concentrated on attempts to gain influence within the political domain of the elite by means of endless searches for suitable presidential candidates who could seize national power at a single blow and through a kind of Fabian tactic of permeating the federal bureaucracy. As a result, there has now emerged an entire generation of what might be called "Court Conservatives" who devote their careers to place-seeking in the federal government and favor-currying with whatever president or satrap is able to hire them and who have long since abandoned any serious intention of challenging the bureaucratic organism they have infected with their presence.

In the absence of a significant cultural base, such political efforts not only were bound to fail but also had the effect of drawing the Right further into the institutional and conceptual framework of the liberal regime. Political maneuver by its nature is a process of bargaining, and the more conservatives have engaged in political action, the more they have found themselves bargaining and compromising with their opponents, who often do not need to bargain at all. Since their opponents on the Left, in Congress or the executive branch, have ready access to and sympathy with the mass media, they are able to discredit the men and measures of the Right that will not bend to their manipulation. Moreover, the Right's preoccupation with the presidency also forces it to seek acceptance by the national media and the dominant culture of the Left and focuses its efforts on an institution that is far less susceptible to grass roots influence than Congress. The modern presidency, as the lesson of the hapless Reagan Administration shows, is less the master of the bureaucratic elite than its servant, and while a powerful president could subdue and circumvent his own bureaucracy, he could do so consistently only if he were able and willing to mobilize mass support against it from outside the elite.

The political weakness of the Old Right and its failure to understand that it really represented a subordinate and displaced elite rather than a dominant incumbent one were instrumental in its gradual assimilation by the liberal regime. The crucial episode in the assimilation occurred during the Vietnam War, which the Old Right in general supported on the grounds of anticommunism. The war itself was a result of misconceived liberal policies and was effectively lost by liberal mismanagement, and there was no good reason for the Right (even the anticommunist Right) to support it. Yet, as the New Left mounted an attack on the war and broadened the attack to include the bureaucratized university and parts of the leviathan state, the Right's response was to defend not only the war and sometimes even the liberal policies that were losing it, but also the liberal power centers themselves. The Old Right critique of containment, mounted by anti-interventionists such as Robert Taft and John T. Flynn and by anticommunist interventionists such as Burnham, was forgotten, as was much of the Old Right cultural critique of the domestic liberal regime, which mirrored its globalist regime. It was at this point that the Old Right began to join forces with emerging neoconservative elements, whose concern was entirely with defending the liberal managerial system, foreign and domestic, and which never had the slightest interest in dismantling it. The result of the coalition between Old Right and neoconservatism has been the adoption by the Right of Wilsonian-Rooseveltian globalism and its universalist premises, the diffusion of those premises within the Right in defense of what are actually the institutions and goals of the Left, and the gradual abandonment of the Old Right goals of reducing the size and scope of centralized power. By swallowing the premises of the Left's globalist and messianic foreign policy, the Right has wound up regurgitating those same premises domestically. If it is our mission to build democracy and protect human rights in Afghanistan, then why should we not also enforce civil rights in Mississippi and break down the barriers to equality of opportunity everywhere through the sledgehammer of federal power? Conservatives do not yet advocate sending the Special Forces into Bensonhurst and Howard Beach, but the story is not over yet.

To say that the conservatism of the Old Right failed is not to dismiss the important contributions its exponents made to a critical analysis of liberal ideology or all of its work in political theory, international relations, economic and social policy, and religious, philosophical, and cultural thought. The Old Right intelligentsia as a whole was a far more exciting group of thinkers and writers than the post–World War II Left produced. Nor does pointing to its failure mean that a serious Right was not or is not possible. It is merely to say that the Old Right fundamentally misperceived its own position in and relationship to the emerging managerial regime and that this misperception led it into a mistaken strategy of seeking consensus rather than conflict with the dominant elite of the regime.

It remains possible today to rectify that error by a radical alteration of the Right's strategy. Abandoning the illusion that it represents an establishment to be "conserved," a new American Right must recognize that its values and goals lie outside and against the establishment and that its natural allies are not in Manhattan, Yale, and Washington but in the increasingly alienated and threatened strata of Middle America. The strategy of the Right should be to enhance the polarization of Middle Americans from the incumbent regime, not to build coalitions with the regime's defenders and beneficiaries. Moreover, since "Middle America" consists of workers, farmers, suburbanites and other non- or postbourgeois groups, as well as small businessmen, it is unlikely that a new Right will make much progress in mobilizing them if it simply repeats the ideological formulas of a now long-defunct bourgeois elite and its order. The more salient concerns of postbourgeois Middle Americans that a new Right can express are those of crime, educational collapse, the erosion of their economic status, and the calculated subversion of their social, cultural, and national identity by forces that serve the interests of the elite above them and the underclass below them, but at the expense of the middle class. A new Right, positioning itself in opposition to the elite and the elite's underclass ally, can assert its leadership of alienated Middle Americans and mobilize them in radical opposition to the regime.

A new, radical Middle American Right need not abandon political efforts, but, consistent with its recognition that it is laying siege to a hostile establishment, it ought to realize that political action in a cultural power vacuum will be largely futile. The main focus of a Middle American Right should be the reclamation of cultural power, the patient elaboration of an alternative culture within but against the regime—within the belly of the beast but indigestible by it. Instead of the uselessness of a Diogenes' search for an honest presidential candidate or a Fabian quest for a career in the bureaucracy, a Middle American Right should begin working in and with schools, churches, clubs, women's groups, youth organizations, civic and professional associations, local government, the military and police forces, and even in the much-dreaded labor unions to create a radicalized Middle American consciousness that can perceive the ways in which exploitation of the middle classes is institutionalized and understand how it can be resisted. Only when this kind of infrastructure of cultural hegemony is developed can a Middle American Right seek meaningful political power without coalitions with the Left and bargaining with the regime.

Eliot may have been right that no cause is really lost because none is really won, but victory and defeat in the struggle for social dominance have little to do with whether the cause is right or wrong. Some ideas have more consequences than others, and those that attach themselves to declining social and political forces have the least consequences of all. By allowing itself to be assimilated by the regime of the Left, American conservatism became part of a social and political force that, if not on the decline, is at least confronted by a rising force that seeks to displace it, even as the regime of the Left displaced its predecessor. If the American Right can disengage from the Left and its regime, it can assume leadership of a cause that could be right as well as victorious. But it can do so only if it has the wit and the will to disabuse itself of the illusions that have distracted it almost since its birth.

Index

About the Author

Samuel Francis, who completed his doctoral studies in history at the University of North Carolina–Chapel Hill, is a nationally syndicated columnist with the *Washington Times*. He is the author of *Power and History: The Political Thought of James Burnham* and *The Soviet Strategy of Terror*.